The Illustrated History of

CHESTER

The Illustrated History of

CHESTER

PHILIP JONES

First published in Great Britain in 2009 by
The Breedon Books Publishing Company Limited
Breedon House, 3 The Parker Centre,
Derby, DE21 4SZ.

ISBN 978-1-85983-684-2

Printed and bound by TJ International Ltd, Padstow, Cornwall.

CONTENTS

Chapter 1

A Sandstone Outcrop

Today, the city of Chester in the north-west of England is generally regarded as little more than one of a large number of relatively small county towns that are scattered throughout Great Britain and which are perhaps better known as retail or administrative centres, rather than a site of any national or regional historical importance. However, unlike some of its more modern counterparts, Chester is able to boast a history and heritage that stretches back thousands of years and has seen the city host some of the most notable characters in England's long and colourful history.

To fully understand the historical importance of the city and its almost inevitable later decline into the regional obscurity that faces it today, it is necessary to look at the history of the site prior to the arrival of the Roman legions who first brought the area to national significance, and to examine each subsequent period of settlement which has made Chester into the city it is today.

Around twelve thousand years before the birth of Christ, the last great ice age was slowly coming to an end and the vast glaciers and ice sheets that had scoured and shaped Britain for millennia, slowly began to recede northward. As they did so, they exposed the countless features that had been created by their very presence – the valleys, lakes and the plateaus that are part of our own modern day landscapes.

The rich red sandstone layers, a common geological feature of north-west England, were easily moulded by the glacial erosion caused by these vast ice sheets and the subsequent flow of tidal watercourses. This was probably the case for the sandstone outcrop on which our modern city stands. This extensive ridge of sandstone, stretching from Handbridge in the south through to Upton in the north, was no doubt first breached by the massive fingers of ice which stretched inland from the Irish Sea. Following the end of the ice age and the northerly retreat of the glaciers, the newly formed river most likely added to the feature, by further deepening the chasm which the ice had first created.

Historically, Cheshire's flat expanse of green pasture land was made up of both Glacial and Triassic clays and as a result had relatively poor drainage. This resulted in the heavy growth of trees and thick undergrowth, as well as the development of numerous marshes and bogs which would have prevented the widespread settlement in the region by its early indigenous people. Easy access through these lands would have been extremely slow and arduous, with extensive forests covering the Wirral Peninsula to the north and boggy marshland inhibiting easy access to the east of the county.

At Upton, just outside of the city, pollen analysis of samples taken on the site in 1997 revealed that at the same time that a Roman marching camp had been built there, the area was partially made up of woodland which was dominated by oak, alder, hazel and heather.

The extensive forests of self-seeding ash, oak and birch trees would have offered good cover for the many deer, wild boar and wolves that roamed throughout the region at the time and the local meres and ponds would have been filled with a wide variety of fish and their attendant waterfowl. Prior to the later arrival of the more technically advanced Roman engineers and their ability to build both military and civilian road networks, it has been speculated that travelling for the native peoples of Cheshire would almost certainly have been limited to their using ancient and well-established paths and tracks, as well as employing local watercourses.

The native settlement which may have pre-dated the Roman garrison at Chester was probably sited on or near the same river-cut sandstone outcrop as does the present-day city. It was in a highly defensible position, giving easy access to the river which ran through the gorge below. Although the site itself does not appear to have been of any regional or national significance, it has been suggested by some historians that Roman military bases were often built on or near sites that were extremely important to the local population. Assuming that such an approach was common, it seems entirely plausible to suggest that some sort of religious or cultural centre existed close to the site of the later Roman military camp, but evidence of its presence has long since been lost over time.

Whether or not the first people to settle in the site were simply native hunter-gatherers, Iron Age farmers or some other foreign sea-borne traders is not entirely clear, but there is evidence that all such peoples existed during the period. Throughout the lower reaches of the Dee Valley, evidence of cultivation and shards of Iron Age pottery indicating pre-Roman activity and settlement have been recovered. It is therefore not inconceivable to suggest that a large number of small farming and fishing communities existed along the banks of the River Dee at the time and that trading or bartering with local and foreign merchants formed part of their everyday lives. Both seed-corn and domestic animals are thought to have arrived in Britain sometime around 4000 BC and their introduction is said to mark the real beginning of widespread settlement, land management and crop cultivation.

A small number of sites in Cheshire have produced tangible evidence which supports the existence of hunter-gatherer groups living within the area well before the Roman Empire was even established. When the ancient Bache Pool was finally drained in the middle of the 19th century a number of Mesolithic flint microliths were found in its residual layers. The site, which is located just a couple of miles outside of the present city centre, was thought to be one such place which these groups regularly visited in order to hunt and gather fish.

At Carden, which is approximately 10 miles from Chester, a large number of flints dating from around 6000 BC have been recovered and are similar to those found at Poulton, Aldford and Tarvin. These flints were thought to have been used for a variety of daily tasks including fishing and scraping animal hides. At Poulton a ring-ditch provisionally dated to the late Bronze Age/early Iron Age has been discovered recently and findings from the site are said to have included a horse's skull, shards of coarse pottery and associated fragments of cremated human bone.

In 1966 evidence of pre-Roman ploughing was found during excavations in the Frodsham Street area of Chester. Similar striations were later found in the sandstone bedrock at Abbey Green in the centre of the city and pottery fragments which were found in the remains of the city's defensive ramparts have also since been identified as being from this Iron Age period. Given these finds, it does not seem

Nowadays Abbey Green is a simple central green space, that overlies 2,000-year-old Roman defences and even earlier evidence of prehistoric settlement and land use.

Manchester bank building on Frodsham Street by Francis Jones *c.*1921.

to be too fanciful to suggest that a British Iron Age settlement had indeed existed on the site before a legionary even set foot there, and that they were simply displaced or destroyed by the later Roman presence.

One possible reason for the lack of intensive archaeological evidence which would clearly identify Chester's earliest inhabitants is that these people almost certainly lived in temporary timber-built dwellings, which were eventually obscured or completely obliterated by later Roman and mediaeval development. Evidence of Iron Age hill forts in the wider region do still exist to the present day, including those at Eddisbury Hill, Beeston Castle, Oakmere, Peckforton Mere, Kelsborrow Castle, Helsby Hill, Woodhouses and Maiden Castle. The suggested similarities between some of these sites and others found in the Welsh Marshes have led some experts to speculate that these sites may have all been constructed by a native tribe called the Cornovii, who lived in the area of what is now modern-day Shropshire. The first examples of hill forts were thought to have been constructed around 1200 BC and been modified and adapted throughout the subsequent centuries. Some 200 years later horses were known to be commonplace in Britain and were being employed as both personal transport and pack animals. Around the same time carts were being manufactured to transport goods and the formidable English war chariot was in the process of being developed.

Eddisbury Hill Fort is a double bank and ditch enclosure which lies on the eastern flank of the mid Cheshire Ridge and close to the ancient Delamere Forest. It has been clearly identified as being of Iron Age construction and during the early 19th century a number of human cremations and five stone axes were discovered on or near the site. All of these finds have been dated from the late Neolithic to early Bronze Age periods and seem to indicate continuous use of the site for the best part of 2,500 years.

Given the relatively inhospitable nature of the immediate area around the site which was later to become the city of Chester, the native population would have been extremely sparse and was likely to consist of different itinerant groups from the surrounding tribal homelands. It is not hard to imagine the idea of individual hunter-gatherer groups wandering in and out of the general area to trap and hunt the wildlife that existed there and then returning to their homes at the end of each hunting trip, laden down with meat and fish for their families. Assuming that this is the case, it is entirely possible that at least one of these travelling bands inevitably made the life-changing decision to settle in the area and make it their permanent home.

Many notable historians believe that the first British settlers were Celts who had migrated from the continent, via a land bridge which had existed in the far distant past. Around 6000 BC, however, a general rise in sea levels caused this link to disappear and isolated the British people from their European forebears forever. Although these land-based migrations probably represented the first influx of settlers to Britain, later sea-based travellers would almost certainly have supplemented and added to the general population. Recent studies undertaken by historians and archaeologists seem to indicate that Britain has been subject to several inundations of immigrants during its history, often being reflected in an east/west division of the country. Migrants from northern Europe have often settled in the eastern counties of Britain, while those from southern Europe have settled in the west. In addition to this, migrants or refugees coming from northern France have typically chosen to settle in the southern counties of England before dissipating throughout the rest of the country.

By 4000 BC Stone Age agricultural settlements were known to have existed and a number of the native British tribes were reported to be erecting large stone monuments to mark significant times of the year or in deference to their ancient gods.

The Bronze Age, which lasted from around 2200 BC through to the later Iron Age, saw the advent of the barrow or burial mound, especially in the regions of north-east Wales and south-west Cheshire, although many of these early constructions have been subsequently destroyed by ploughing and rural development. These barrows were rarely established in isolation, but generally formed part of a cemetery complex that was closely associated with a nearby civilian settlement. Cheshire archaeologists have speculated that there are numerous undiscovered barrows within the county which have since been obliterated or hidden by later periods of development and still remain to be detected.

By around 700 BC the Iron Age in Britain was well underway and would continue largely unabated through to the arrival of the Roman legions some 800 years later. During these intervening years the whole country was said to have remained largely a collection of small farms, villages and protected settlements which were ruled over by an assortment of tribal warlords and consisted of numerous independent kingdoms. Few historical records exist to easily define the lives of these ancient Britons, but it has been suggested that the population was extremely diverse, with various dialects and traditions in everyday use.

It was around this same time that the city of Rome was said to have first been established in Italy, although the people who constructed the city were thought to have arrived in the area some 300 years earlier. Historians suggest that about 1000 BC the Prisci Latini people had migrated to the area of the later city and had established a number of small settlements there. There are indications that these early foreign settlers were generally rural homesteaders who, in common with their European counterparts, kept a range of domesticated livestock including pigs, sheep, goats and cattle. In later centuries these early settlements began to attract both Greeks and Etruscan migrants who brought with them their education and experience as sea-going traders, helping to develop these Latini settlements into the modern and vibrant city of Rome.

History suggests that the first people responsible for actually recording the lives and traditions of the early British tribes were the Druids, a pagan religious order that existed in both Britain and France and which had its roots in more ancient times. No written records are known to exist regarding the day-to-day lives of Iron Age Britons, which may in itself suggest that such historic records were often passed on by word of mouth rather than in a written form. The later annihilation of the Druidic religion by the armies of Rome may well have caused these extensive tribal histories to have been lost forever, always assuming of course that they ever existed in the first place.

Modern day excavations of Iron Age settlements and individual burial sites have done much to help enlighten and educate historians about our early ancestors and how they lived their lives. It has become apparent, for instance, that their lives were extremely hard and relatively short, with an average life expectancy of between 30 and 40 years of age.

Infant mortality among these early tribes seems to have been particularly high and might well indicate regular periods of malnutrition caused either by crop failures or just general poor diets.

Given the limited availability of cures and remedies, as well as the regular outbreaks of communicable diseases, it seems entirely likely that an individual's survival was as much a matter of luck than any sort of prevention or treatment. Common health problems such as colds, flu or even toothache would have more readily incapacitated a person and perhaps been more prevalent given the relatively poor quality housing, clothing and diet which existed at that particular time.

Most of Britain's Iron Age population seems to have lived in fairly small agricultural communities or on individual farmsteads. Their homes appear to have been fairly basic constructions, made up of timber-built round houses with thatched roofs which often housed their livestock as well as the family members. Most people did not own any items of great value and their personal possessions tended to be functional rather than ornamental. Much of what was worn by these early people was taken from their livestock and would have consisted mainly of leather and wool. Occasionally, people would possess one or more animal furs which could be used for warmth or as part of their bedding. Where valuable personal possessions did exist they were more likely to be made of bronze, or possibly there may have been a shale bracelet, an animal fur or a comb made out of deer antler or animal bone. Items made from precious metals or minerals were almost entirely owned by the wealthier classes or by royalty and were rarely possessed by the average Iron Age person.

Thought to originate from around 450 BC, La Tene, an early Celtic art form, was an abstract pattern which primarily employed curves into the design and was generally associated with the southern regions of Britain and specific areas of continental Europe. Typically this design feature was used on high status and high value items such as torcs, scabbards and mirrors, which were made of silver or gold and commonly owned or gifted to kings, tribal chiefs or noted warriors.

Later archaeological finds have indicated that there was a militaristic aspect to Iron Age life, but to what extent is not entirely clear. The weaponry that has been found thus far has tended to be of a high quality and it has been suggested that such items were generally owned by high ranking individuals who had great status within their own particular communities. Given the avaricious nature of the human race it also seems likely that regular regional confrontations took place, as the individual tribes vied with one another for the ownership of land, livestock or mineral deposits. It is also possible that by the time of the Roman invasion of Britain, the actual number of individual tribal homelands and independent kingdoms had been seriously reduced both by regional takeovers and the consolidation of certain areas of the country by the larger and more militaristic tribes that existed during the period.

In north-west Britain at that time there were at least four indigenous tribes known to have inhabited the region, any one of which may have held control of the Iron Age settlement at Chester. In what is now modern-day Shropshire the Cornovii tribe were thought to have led a mainly pastoral lifestyle and appear to have had little in the way of centralised government. Although evidence suggests they had many hill forts, it is thought that the majority of the people lived in timber-built dwellings which left little or no evidence of their actual existence. It also appears that they had little in the way of coinage and ceramics, which suggests that payment and tribute were generally made through a basic bartering system.

In the mountains of North Wales lived the Ordovices tribe, who were primarily farmers and shepherds but who appear to have had a very strong military tradition. They lived in or around heavily defended hill forts and were thought to have built a range of fortresses around the North Wales coastline. Said to be one of the few Celtic tribes that

Abbey Square is filled with terraces of Georgian buildings raised by local builders to house the well-to-do and those employed by the cathedral in a lay capacity. These buildings sit above earlier Roman and mediaeval remains from the city's past.

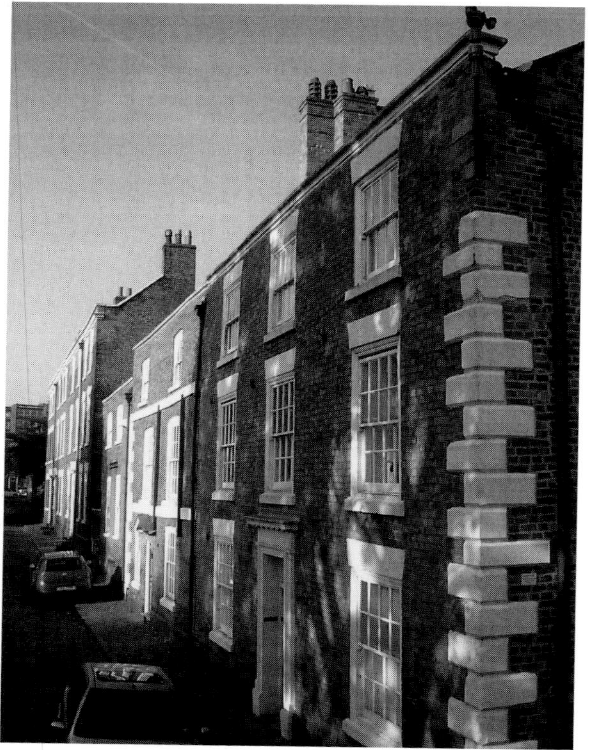

physically opposed the later Roman invasion of Britain, it was within their lands that the rebel British chieftain Caractacus carried on his fight against Rome. Their continued opposition to the rule of the Emperors and ongoing support for the rebel warlord was said to have eventually led to their near total destruction by the Roman General Julius Agricola in around AD 78.

The Deceangli people occupied what is now modern-day Flintshire and lived in a chain of hill fort settlements along the Clwydian mountain range. Unlike the Cornovii, the Deceangli did have a tribal capital which was located at Canovium but, like their neighbours, they seem to have had little in the way of a centralised structure and it is probable that their tribal leadership operated at a more local level.

To the north of the River Mersey lived the Brigantes who it was thought were an amalgam of a number of much smaller local tribes who had joined together for their mutual benefit and security. They were said to be an extremely war-like tribe that did not flinch from the prospect of military engagements against any enemy, regardless of their potential threat. As with the Ordovices, the Brigantes continued to fight against the Roman army for years after the initial invasion and may have been involved in at least one major uprising against the legions of Rome following the occupation of Britain. Their tribal name is believed to translate to the 'Hill People' and has led to speculation that they generally occupied a series of well-defended hill forts throughout their homeland region, the capital of which was Stanwick Hill in modern-day Yorkshire.

As yet no definitive archaeological evidence exists to suggest whether any or all of these tribes actually held direct control over the site that would later house the city of Chester. It may well be that the site was actually inhabited by an as yet unknown group who came from outside of the region. It does seem sensible to conclude that the area was indeed inhabited by at least one of a small number of disparate groups that were very well established by the time the first Roman soldiers arrived in Britain.

Typically, such peoples would have lived in circular huts built of timber and straw, or possibly of wattle and daub. Within these accommodations there would have been a central hearth where the occupants warmed themselves and cooked their meals. The floor of their homes would have been covered with animal skins or dried grasses that helped to retain the warmth which was generated by the fire. Their usual diet would have depended on their land and surroundings, but given the easy access to the River Dee it is likely that fish would have formed a good part of their everyday meals. Unlike the richer soils of southern England, it has been suggested that the lands of north-west Britain generally supported coarser grain crops, such as wheat and barley, implying that the bulk of the local people's diet consisted mainly of meat and milk, both of which could be easily provided by their own livestock. Typically, the average farmer of the time may well have owned a minimum number of domestic animals: possibly a cow, a female pig, maybe a goat or even a small flock of sheep. Either way, these animals would have provided the family with the very basics of life, from the clothes on their backs to the food in their stomachs.

These early settlements or homesteads would often have been surrounded by a rudimentary ditch topped with a wooden palisade within which their homes and valuable animals would have been protected from harm. Also within this same enclosure would have been the forges, kilns and ovens which helped to produce and support the local blacksmith and pottery industries, which were thought to have existed in most small rural communities. Gold, copper, bronze and iron were reported to have been used to produce the settlement's tools, jewellery, weapons and the more mundane everyday objects such as handles and pots.

With a readily available supply of animal skins, bones and fleeces, it is likely that weaving, spinning and leather crafts would have dominated the local economy, producing goods which could be used by themselves or traded in exchange for those that they could not produce from travellers and merchants that regularly visited the settlement.

When judged against our own modern standards, the lives of our Bronze Age and Iron Age ancestors would appear to be fairly primitive and yet they would have been typical of the time, given the processes and technologies that existed throughout most of Europe. Although the tribes of Britain had not yet received the road networks, sanitation systems and centralised government which would come with Roman occupation, it would be wrong to suggest that the Celtic world was in any way backward or uncivilised. Ample archaeological evidence has been uncovered to suggest that in certain areas of Europe new methods of construction and other technological advances were in fact being discovered and employed by these pre-Roman societies.

It has long been suggested that many of the early Celtic achievements were deliberately overlooked and omitted by Roman historians and recorders who, keen to justify their own military invasion and occupation of foreign lands, pointed out the uncivilized and savage nature of the indigenous tribes and the desperate need for Roman control which brought about these interventions. In truth, this Roman altruism was mostly little more than a speculative 'land grab', often driven by individual Emperors who were keen to enhance their position within the fledgling Empire and to further enlarge the sphere of Roman influence throughout the European continent.

As the Roman Empire slowly exerted its military control over much of continental Europe and brutally suppressed its native peoples, Britain inevitably became a sanctuary for the thousands of refugees that crossed the channel in a desperate bid to escape Roman rule. They brought with them stories about the new military threat that was facing

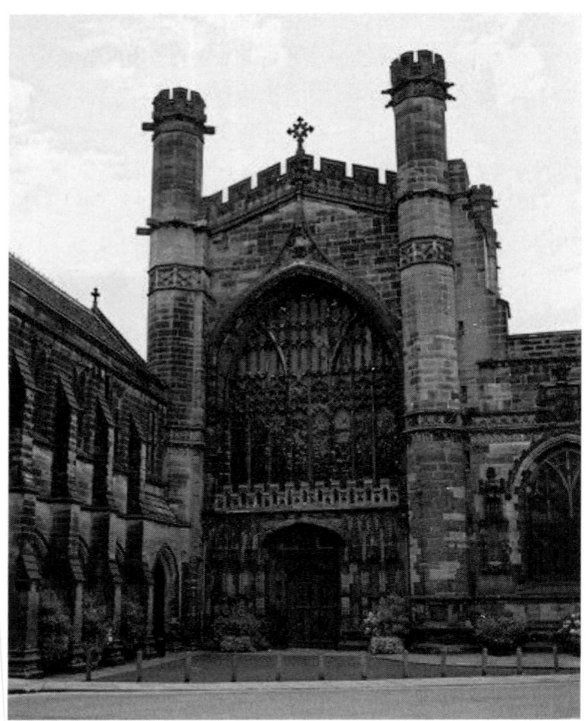

Chester's cathedral is thought to stand on the same site as a much earlier Roman temple dedicated to their deity 'Apollo'.

An alternative entrance to Chester's mediaeval abbey, the little abbey gateway dates from around the 13/14th century, is in a fairly ruinous condition and often overlooked.

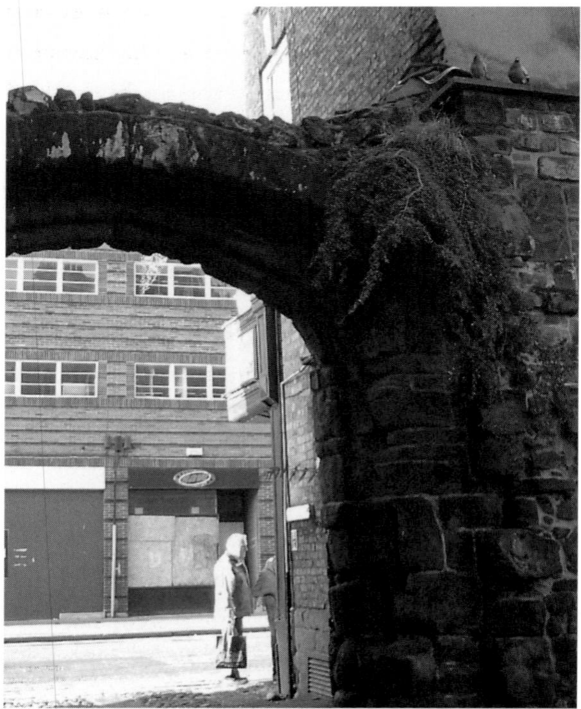

northern Europe and suggestions to British tribal leaders that they too should begin to prepare to face a similar invasion of their own lands.

In the north-west of Britain a local tale relates the story of a legendary king of the Britons, Marius, who was said to have built an Iron Age fortress at Chester in order to defend the region from the Roman invaders. The story continues that these native defences were fairly rudimentary affairs and provided little challenge to the highly professional legionaries who easily overcame them to defeat their British defenders and to subsequently build their own military fortress on or close to the very same site.

Another legend attributed to the same period tells of a Druidic temple that may have stood at the British Iron Age settlement on the River Dee during the time of King Marius and which was located close to a local sacred spring. The Romans, having seized the settlement, were then thought to have built a temple to their deity Apollo on the site, located on the very same spot as the later Anglo-Saxon abbey which later became the city's cathedral.

Whether or not these stories are true is impossible to say. What is certain, however, is that it was during this period that this relatively wild and inaccessible area of north-west England began its long and turbulent transformation into the city that stands on the Dee today. Driven by greed, a growing demand for essential metals and a fear for their northern frontiers, the Roman Empire – the military superpower of the age – finally turned its face towards Britain and began to covet its lands, its peoples and the rich mineral deposits that it possessed.

Chapter 2
The Long March to Chester

Trade between the British Isles and Rome is likely to have been the first contact between the two continental neighbours and it is believed that this had gone on for hundreds of years prior to any dispute arising between them. With the rapid development and growth of its nation state Rome was a leading trader within Europe and Britain was said to have surpluses of grain and metal ores which this new southern Empire was keen to acquire to fuel its growing economy and feed its burgeoning population.

The first of two early military reconnaissance expeditions to Britain had been led by the Roman General Julius Caesar in 55 BC. However, the mission had been beset by logistical problems and poor planning from the very beginning and consequently resulted in a total inability to secure a decisive victory over the local tribes. Caesar's second campaign against the British in 54 BC was much better planned and despite the unforeseen adverse weather conditions which had affected his fleet of ships he managed to successfully land his force on the English coastline. Facing Caesar's legionary army was a large force of native British tribesmen who had watched the arrival of the invading armada and were well prepared to meet them. Despite this, the highly experienced legionary force easily overcame the native warriors and within a day or so Caesar was able to begin consolidating his territorial gains and move further inland. Once again, though, the British weather proved to be his greatest adversary and a severe storm resulted in substantial damage to his ships which required a major reassignment of his legionary manpower. In order to protect his beachhead and the remainder of his fleet, Caesar found it necessary to construct a protective enclosure around his landing area, thereby diverting valuable military resources from his planned advance into the country. These unforeseen delays hindered the progress of Caesar's invasion forces and offered substantial benefits to his opponents. With a common enemy to unite against, the native British tribes put aside their regional differences and joined together to oppose the Roman invaders. Under the command of the British warlord Cassivellaunus the native warriors carried out a constant guerrilla campaign against Caesar's forces and continually threatened to disrupt his supply lines. The indigenous forces were also said to have adopted a scorched earth policy, removing people and livestock from the path of the advancing Romans and destroying crops or food stores that might have been of use to them.

Despite such tactics being employed against him and his soldiers, Caesar continued to progress towards his ultimate target, which was the tribal capital of the Trinovantes. Threatened by the forces of the warlord Cassivellaunus, the Trinovantes people had requested that Caesar offer their prince, Mandubracius, protection from his enemies and guarantee his safe return back from the European continent where he had fled following the death of his father. Following the restoration of Mandubracius to his tribe, Caesar was said to have simply retraced his path back to his landing area where his restored fleet was waiting to carry him back to the continent.

The intended purpose of these early forays into Britain appears to have been three-fold. Firstly, Caesar had managed to reconnoitre the British coast and determine the locations of possible landing points as well as the level of military forces required to achieve a successful invasion. Secondly, he had now met and measured the likely native opposition and studied the tactics that they were likely to employ against any future legionary force. Thirdly, and perhaps most importantly, Rome now had some influence and communication with a native British tribe, the Trinovantes, and through these relationships could gain influence within the British islands. Although it would be nearly a hundred years before the Romans once again set their forces against Britain, Caesar's own experiences, his recording of the events and the trade agreements that he signed would be instrumental in Rome's later decision to incorporate these islands into their vast western Empire.

Born in 10 BC, the Roman Emperor Claudius was the youngest son of Drusus, the brother of Tiberius, and Antonia, who was herself the daughter of the famous Roman General Marc Anthony. From childhood, Claudius had suffered from regular ill-health and persistently twitched and stammered when he was put under any sort of pressure. He was an old man by the standards of the day when his nephew, the Emperor Caligula, was assassinated in AD 41 and Claudius, at 51 years of age, was nominated as emperor by the Praetorian guards who discovered him cowering within the royal palace. No doubt considering him to be highly 'controllable', these army officers were said to have forced the senate to accept their choice for emperor and the fathers of Rome, no doubt in fear for their own lives, agreed to the succession of the faltering Claudius.

Throughout his reign he was generally distrusted by members of the senate who believed him to be incapable of fulfilling the role that was required of him. For his part, Claudius seemed to thrive after becoming emperor and the onerous responsibility of his new office seemed to improve his earlier, sickly nature. He was always extremely cautious about his own personal protection and employed stringent security measures to ensure his continued safety. It was fortunate that he chose to do so as he was thought to have survived at least six or seven attempts on his life by the time he died in AD 54 and even then it was suggested that he had been poisoned.

It was not long before Claudius chose to resurrect an earlier plan to invade the island of Britain. His predecessor, Caligula, had planned to invade the island during his own reign but a refusal by a large number of legionaries to cross beyond the known limits of the Empire and the belief that Britain was inhabited by demons and spirits had prevented the plans from going ahead. Britain and her people were regarded as a direct threat to Rome's northern borders and the known deposits of tin, gold and lead which existed there would in part pay for the cost of this new military venture. This decision was also influenced by the fact that Claudius had been asked for help by the ousted ruler of the British Attrebates tribe, Verica – part of whose homelands had earlier been seized by a rival tribal leader called Caractacus.

In AD 43 four Roman legions under the command of Aulus Plautius and supported by an equally large auxiliary force landed unopposed at Richborough and began their final and decisive invasion of Britain. The British tribes that were aware of the impending invasion threat held widely differing views as to how such an event would actually affect them, if at all. The Iceni and Coritani peoples seem to have initially adopted a fairly neutral stance to the invasion, choosing to believe that the arrival of a large number of Roman troops would have little direct effect upon them or indeed their regional standing.

The Trinovantes and the Catuvellauni tribes, on the other hand, believed that the arrival of any such force represented a direct military threat to them and their plans for further expansion within their home regions and chose to oppose Rome's legions at all costs. Others tribes, such as the Dobunni, were prepared to help resist the invasion, but only for as long as it suited their own purposes. The Attrebates, whose leader Verica had helped to persuade Claudius as to the merits of such an invasion, believed that the arrival of the Roman forces would ultimately help him to secure his tribal lands and future prosperity within mainland Britain and sought to offer unconditional support to the continental invaders.

The Roman expeditionary force that landed at Richborough was thought to have consisted of some

50,000 men including cavalry and auxiliary units. It landed at the Kent site in three separate waves, thus avoiding the possibility of individual units being caught in any sort of backlog which might make them vulnerable to attack. The native tribes that had earlier assembled to meet the invaders had since been informed of another potential mutiny among the ranks of the legionaries based in Gaul and had returned to their tribal settlements, only to find themselves unable to the meet the invasion when it finally did arrive.

Therefore, unexpectedly, Plautius found himself facing only a relatively small number of native British tribesmen once his men had come ashore. When the native Britons did finally manage to muster their armies to meet Plautius, they were subsequently routed by the highly professional and experienced legionnaires, both at Rochester and later on the banks of the River Thames.

It was here that the Roman legions were deliberately held by Plautius to await the arrival of Claudius from Rome, thereby allowing him the honour of leading his victorious troops into the enemy capital in what is now modern-day Colchester. The new emperor spent just over two weeks in Britain and then returned home to receive homage from the people of Rome. The senate, having heard of his successful conquest, ordered a series of celebrations and conferred on Claudius the title Britannicus. Now secure within the empire, he was able to use the remainder of his reign to modify and improve the lives of his people and the military that served them so well. Sadly for Claudius, his judgement seems to have failed him in later years when he took a second wife and formally adopted her son Nero, who would go down in history as the Emperor who fiddled while Rome burnt (although this particular legend has now been largely debunked).

Initially the Roman invasion force seems to have been content to limit their area of occupation and control and by about AD 47 had secured an area stretching from Gloucester in the South West to Lincoln in the North East. Legionary bases were established at both locations and it is thought a third was built somewhere in the Midlands. These three major military garrisons were probably protected along their lines of communications by a series of smaller forts and eventually developed into what we know today as the Foss Way. Although the Romans had achieved many of their initial objectives, the obvious delay caused by their having to wait for the arrival of the Emperor Claudius from Rome had allowed the native tribal leader Caractacus to evade capture, something which would prove to be a costly mistake for them in the future years.

Wherever possible and appropriate the Romans were known to have entered into political agreements with the native Celtic tribes who were willing to do so. However, some tribes, including the Silures from South Wales and the Ordovices in North Wales, were far more hostile to the invaders and took every opportunity to harass and attack the incoming Roman forces.

In response to these regular incursions against their bases, the Romans began a series of campaigns against their Welsh adversaries which resulted in the construction of additional bases and fortresses to support each subsequent military campaign. These included the legionary fortress which was constructed at Wroxeter near modern-day Shrewsbury. It was perhaps during these early forays against the tribes of North Wales that the native settlement on the River Dee was first identified as a potential military site from which to launch campaigns against the enemy forces.

The later arrival of Suetonius Paulinus as military governor in around AD 58 marked a sea change in the Romans' approach to the Welsh tribes' ongoing hostility with the new military commander immediately mounting a highly vigorous campaign against the island of Anglesey, which was thought to be the heart of the native opposition. As part of this major campaign, it was reported that a new supply base was located at Chester in order to provide stores for the campaigning Roman forces and was thought to have been protected by a small fort constructed nearby. Archaeological evidence from within the later fortress supports the idea of a Roman presence at Chester around this time and also suggests that this earlier fort was not sited on the same spot as the much later development. A Roman burial urn which was found within the precincts of the later fortress area has been dated to around AD 60, just two years following the arrival of Paulinus in Britain. However, Roman burials within a fort were strictly forbidden and would almost certainly have taken place outside of the immediate defensive ramparts. The discovery of these urns could be explained by the decision to build a more substantial fortress at a later date and which was of such a great size and area that it inadvertently incorporated the burial area within its defensive walls. Fragments of an early rampart were discovered during recent excavations at Abbey Green in the city. These finds have suggested the possibility of a pre-Flavian style of construction which might indicate an even earlier period of Roman occupancy. Between AD 52 and 57 Didius Gallus was known to have campaigned against the northern Brigantes tribe and between AD 47 and 52 Ostorios Scapula campaigned against the tribes of North Wales who were supporting the rebel warlord Caractacus.

The king of the Catuvellauni people, Caractacus, had continued to fight the Roman invasion of Britain right from the start and following the death of his father had been seen as the head of British resistance. Under constant military pressure from the legions, he had been forced further west to the lands of the Silures in modern-day Glamorgan, but had failed to stop the Roman's advance. Forced further north, he eventually came to the tribal homelands of the Ordovices in North Wales and tried once again to hold the Roman forces, but again was unsuccessful. By now Caractacus and his family were on the run and being relentlessly pursued by the Roman forces. He and his family finally managed to escape to the lands of the Brigantes people in the north of England, but unfortunately for him their queen, Cartimandua, was a client-chief of the Romans and was therefore obliged to hand Caractacus and his family over to the Roman General Ostorios Scapula, which she reportedly did.

Shackled and chained Caractacus, along with his wife and daughter, was then transported to Rome to be publicly paraded through its streets and exhibited before the thousands of fascinated citizens who came to catch a brief glimpse of the infamous British warlord. Finally he was brought before the Emperor Claudius and after making an impassioned and eloquent speech that so impressed the awkward Caesar, Caractacus and his family were freed and allowed to settle and live the rest of their lives in Italy.

Between AD 69 and AD 70 a civil war erupted within the empire between the supporters of the Roman General Vespasian and the Emperor Vitellius that caused major factional disputes between the various legionary forces and it was considered ill-advised to use any of these troops for any further military campaigns. The restless native tribes of Britain were not slow to exploit these problems and the northern Brigantes were said to have seized complete control of their tribal lands in both Lancashire and Yorkshire. It was only at the end of this turbulent period that Rome decided to adopt a new policy of total conquest of the British Isles, which would ultimately lead to the establishment of the first permanent military presence at Chester.

The policy of total conquest would be implemented by the 'hammer' of Rome, the legendary legions that had successfully conquered much of the known world and brought the 'civilising' influence of Rome to some of the most barbaric lands and peoples that had ever existed. Their ability to march long distances and to fight a hard battle at the end of it was one of the unique features that made them so difficult to defeat, as was their comradeship and *esprit de corps* which threaded each of these individual military units together.

The Roman centuria represented a military unit of 100 men which in earlier times had been the standard. However, in later years each centuria comprised only 80 men, with each of these larger units divided into 10 centubernu, or eight individuals. Within a legionary force there were 60 centuria, comprising a total of 4,800 men, plus their officers. The First Cohort of any legionary force was made up of 160 men: twice the normal number and so brought the full legionary compliment to 5,400 men in total. In addition to this there were reported to have been an equal number of auxiliaries for each of these regular legionary units.

Each of these 60 centuria was commanded by a centurion who was assisted by a number of NCOs and other subordinates. Typically, these centurions were housed in slightly better conditions than the men they commanded. Within his command each eight-man unit, or centubernu, was led by the most experienced soldier in the group, who would organise his comrades and teach new recruits the rules and regulations which governed their lives. The eight men would often spend much of their service together, eating, drilling, fighting and also possibly dying as a unit.

Once they had completed their basic military training, recruits would be posted to their regular units which was where they could spend the next 25 years of their lives, assuming of course that they lived that long. It was at their home garrison that they would learn to fully hone their fighting skills and consolidate the team work that would help them to accomplish their various tasks. New legionaries would also have to become adept in working with various building materials, including wood and stone which were common components of their forts and camps. The techniques involved in building earthen ramparts and erecting wooden palisades, in building bridges and roads, were all skills that a soldier of the legions was required to master, along with the more mundane tasks like keeping his kit clean as well as having to undertake regular patrols and sentry duty. Typically, experienced legionaries were thought to be able to march around 30 miles a day and at the end of it build a marching camp that could hold the entire military force within a few hours of having stopped.

As military service was a highly popular source of employment for the empire's young men, the Roman army could afford to be extremely particular about those who it accepted to serve. Only free men could apply and they were generally young males between the ages of 18 and 21 years who were in excellent physical condition and known to be of good character. The saying that an army marches on its stomach was well understood by the commanders that led the legions into battle and although basic field rations were fairly limited, there was always plenty of wheat and barley for the soldiers to utilise. On the march there were opportunities for the units to forage in the local area for rabbit, hare or wildfowl which could be added to the cooking pot. When they were garrisoned, food was not such a problem with regular shipments of wheat, barley and green vegetables, including cabbage and celery. Protein levels were sustained with legionaries eating mutton, beef, pork and occasionally goat as well as wildfowl and fish.

When they were not patrolling or campaigning against the native tribes of Britain, life for a legionary was fairly mundane, their days taken up with building or refurbishing their garrison, general maintenance and keeping their own equipment in good order. When they were off-duty they occupied themselves with gambling or spending time in the legionary bathhouses and occasionally a visit to the local prostitutes or their womenfolk who may be located outside of the defensive wall.

For those that infringed army rules, punishments could range from being put on unpleasant duties like cleaning the camp's latrines or the company's barracks, through to 'decimation' where every tenth man in the force was executed as an example to the remaining legionaries.

Chapter 3

THE FIRST PERMANENT SETTLEMENT

The result of the bitter civil war which had temporarily incapacitated the empire was that Vespasian was now emperor and he almost immediately set in motion the new military policy towards Britain – that of total conquest. A new military governor, Petilius Cerialis, was appointed in AD 71 and around the same time the Ninth Legion was moved forward from Lincoln to York, as a prelude to their final pacification of the troublesome northern Brigantes tribe.

The 20th Legion Valeria Victrix, under the command of the General Julius Agricola, was moved into Cheshire to deal with the native tribes that presented a potential threat to their plans. One of their first targets would have been the series of Iron Age hill forts which lay to the east of the county, all of which were systematically attacked and destroyed by the Roman forces. In AD 74 Cerialis was replaced as military governor by Julius Frontinus, who immediately set about the pacification of the Silures in South Wales. Following their defeat, Frontinus then set his sights on the Ordovices people in North Wales. In order to properly contain and prevent their escape into other more northern territories, the new governor is reported to have ordered the construction of a new and permanent military base at Chester.

The river site, lying as it did between the northern Pennines and the mountains of North Wales, was an ideal location to establish a protective gateway to both regions. This new base would also offer a launching point for later campaigns undertaken by Julius Agricola against both the Brigantes and the Celtic heartland of Anglesey. The Roman name for this place, 'Deva', was thought to be derived from the native Celtic name for the river, 'Goddess' or 'Holy One', reflecting both civilisations' beliefs that large bodies of water were holy or sacred. Several of the religions of the time believed that rivers, streams and open stretches of water represented the portals to, and boundaries of, the spirit world. This was often reflected in the practice of depositing valuable items in watercourses as offerings to the gods and spirits that lived within them.

Archaeological evidence found at the Chester fortress tends to support this timeline for the construction of the fortress. Lead ingots which have been dated from AD 74 are thought to have come from the lead and silver mines in Flintshire which was the tribal homeland of the Deceangli people. Also, fragments of lead water piping stamped with Agricola's name have been found at the site and have been dated to around AD 79.

The fortress, with its potentially excellent harbour facilities and access to the Irish Sea, was an ideal location for any proposed invasion of Ireland and also offered a base from where the Roman army could keep watch on the local native tribes. Sea power was a vital arm of the Roman military force and it is notable that the Second Legion Adiutrix was the first military unit to actually garrison the base at Chester and was a force that seems to have had extensive naval experience. Much of their early work, however, was dedicated to helping to construct the military base at Chester and its related installations, overseeing the mining of lead and silver in the Flintshire mines and patrolling the outlying areas of the settlement. The Second Legion was recalled to the continent in around AD 86 to help support the Roman forces based on the Danube which were being threatened and attacked. It is unlikely that the departure of the Second Legion left the fortress either deserted or unprotected until such time as a replacement unit arrived. It is far more likely that the base was protected by a small number of regular troops who were deliberately held back as a rearguard unit and which were themselves supported by a number of auxiliaries.

The legionary unit that replaced the Second Legion in around AD 87 was the 20th Legion Valeria Victrix, who had been under the command of Julius Agricola in his Scottish campaigns. They had been the garrison unit at the military fort at Inchtuthill in Scotland for a four or five year period prior to their new posting at Chester, where they would ultimately spend the next few centuries. Later excavations at Inchtuthill have discovered that the fortress buildings had been systematically demolished by the 20th Legion prior to leaving for their new posting and building timbers that could be reused later were taken away by the legionaries.

Thought to have been raised in the reign of the Emperor Augustus, the 20th Legion was reported to have fought its first actions in the Cantabrian campaigns which took place between 25 and 12 BC. It was later employed in the Balkans by Tiberius and under the same commander the legion was used to restore order in a series of Germanic campaigns. They also helped to suppress a rebellion in Gaul and during the reign of the mad emperor Caligula were once again used in a second series of military campaigns in Germania.

The legion was reported to have been present at Illyricum, under the command of Valerius Messalinus and following the loss of three legions by Quintilius Varus in central Germany the 20th was said to have been one of the replacement units sent to avenge this defeat. Under the command of Germanicus, records of the 20th Legion have been found at both modern-day Bonn and Cologne.

Having helped to restore order in the region, members of the 20th were then reported to have mutinied and the rebellion was only finally quashed when a number of the ringleaders were executed. Offered assurances about their future treatment by their commander Germanicus, the legion later appears to have become one of some note and held in high regard, often being trusted to undertake the most hazardous and arduous of tasks on behalf of the empire.

Perhaps because of their experience and reliability, the 20th Legion was chosen as one of four to help spearhead the invasion of Britain ordered by the Emperor Claudius in AD 42. Under the command of Suetonius Paulinus, they were engaged in the subjugation of the native tribes of southern Britain, and around AD 60 units of the 20th were instrumental in finally crushing the revolt of the Iceni leader Boudicca.

During the civil war which erupted in AD 69 between Vespasian and Vitellius, the legion was reported to be under the command of Julius Agricola, a soldier well suited to handle the formidable and highly experienced force. It was reported that Agricola himself declared for the cause of Vespasian and in all likelihood the bulk of his command did the same.

Twelve months later and with the empire once more settled, the legion was thought to have remained under the command of Agricola for a two-year period, from AD 69 to 71. When their former commander was appointed as British Governor in around AD 78, they were once again reunited against the tribes of North Wales and northern Britain during Agricola's military campaigns. Initially the 20th were supposed to have been stationed at Inchtuthill in Scotland and later excavations suggest that the construction of their new base was well underway, until events elsewhere brought about their sudden redeployment.

At its height, the legion was thought to consist of 5,400 men with an equal number of auxiliaries, including a naval contingent which has often been suggested as being based at Chester, given its port and easy access to the sea. During military campaigns the fortress would probably have been manned and protected by a reserve force which continued to maintain its functions until the main body of troops returned. In times of peace most of the legionary force would have been occupied rebuilding their home station, with its auxiliaries guarding and patrolling the wider region.

By about AD 80 the new Roman fortress at Chester had reached the absolute limits of its construction in terms of the area that it would actually cover. Comparable fortresses of the time invariably covered some 50 acres of land, yet at Chester the enclosure measured just short of 60 acres, which can only begin to suggest the increased importance the site had to its Roman builders. One possible explanation for this additional space was to accommodate a separate naval detachment within the fortress. An inscription later found within the base may have actually referred to a sailor rather than a soldier and it is entirely plausible that a naval contingent would have visited and stayed at Chester on a regular basis. The Dee estuary was an extremely important transport link for the emerging fortress and its inhabitants would have relied heavily on imported stores being shipped in to the base.

The risk of losing such goods to pirates or local tribesmen would have made it essential for the garrison to protect the river at all costs and it is therefore likely that a Roman fleet of some kind would have operated within the area.

The base was built in a manner which was typical of the period: a turf-covered rampart some 20 feet from front to back, around 10 feet high and fronted by a ditch which itself was around 10 feet deep and 20 feet wide. On top of this grassy rampart stood a wooden palisade which was approximately 10 feet high and backed by a walkway on which sentries patrolled. Each of the four walls included a gateway, which in turn were guarded by a pair of timber watch towers. Additionally, along the length of each wall it is likely that there were individual guard towers that provided extra protection to the fortress. The actual line of these original defences has subsequently been

The foundations of the Roman Fortress's eastern wall remain in place today.

White Friars Street is thought to mark the line of the Roman Fortress's missing southern wall.

Features of Chester's 2,000-year-old Roman amphitheatre, which was thought to have first been raised in the first century AD and rebuilt several times. Only half of this 7,000-seat theatre has been exposed since it was first rediscovered in 1929.

identified through archaeological excavations. The northern and eastern walls were sited at their present locations, with the western wall running slightly to the east of the present-day Linenhall Place and Nicholas Street. The southern wall is known to have run along a line between present-day White Friars and Pepper Street, intersecting modern-day Bridge Street and Lower Bridge Street.

Within this defensive enclosure many of the buildings were initially constructed of wattle and daub, with the exception of the more important structures, such as the legionary bathhouses, temples, etc. Despite the relatively simple level of construct, some of these buildings were furnished to an extremely high standard

Chester's Roman amphitheatre constructed by the troops of the 20th Legion Valeria Victrix.

The Roman garden at Chester is located close to the site of the city's still partially covered amphitheatre.

Roman artefacts found at Chester have been gathered together and displayed at a central point.

and included elaborately decorated walls and tiled roofs. A permanent fresh water supply had been in place for a lengthy period of time, utilising local wells and springs and a well-developed sewage system existed which drained the waste and water from both the military bathhouses and latrines.

Outside of the south-east limits of the fortress was the Roman amphitheatre which is thought to have originated from around AD 76. Initially it was a timber-built structure designed for use as a weapons training area, for performing plays and holding large-scale sports events. There is some evidence to suggest that this original timber building was itself replaced by a stone-built amphitheatre within a few years of its initial construction. No actual date has been clearly identified for this reconstruction but it has been proposed that it was designed to mark the arrival of one of the resident legions. A shrine to the deity Nemesis was found on the site, which was appropriate given the actual purpose of the building. The later stone construction was thought to have had a seating capacity for around 7,000 people, which would have accommodated the full legionary compliment and also had room for a large number of auxiliaries and civilian spectators.

Slightly to the west of the western defences lay the Roman harbour, located on the site of the modern-day Nuns Road and Roodee racecourse. At the time of the Roman invasion the Roodee was no more than a small flooded island surrounded by the original course of the River Dee, which ran directly beneath what are now the city's walls in that area. The Roodee derives its name from a combination of much later Saxon and Norse words. 'Rood' reflects the Saxon word for cross and 'Eye' was a Norse suffix for isle or island, so the literal meaning of Roodee is 'island of the cross'.

It is not entirely clear whether or not the Roodee itself was such a feature at the time of the Roman settlement. It is just as likely that it lay beneath the then much deeper and stronger River Dee and only became a substantial feature as the river began to weaken in later centuries. The massive stones of the original Roman harbour wall which once secured Roman galleys and merchant ships of the empire are still evident to the present day, but are largely obscured by modern construction and vegetation. In 1874 a Roman tomb dating to about the year AD 90 was found near the south end of the main public grandstand. It contained two skeletons, one of which was wearing a gold ring and lying beneath a tombstone, and both are now held in the care of the local museum. Later constructions and developments have resulted in this particular area of the Roman settlement either being buried or partially destroyed over the course of the past two millennia. The present-day Watergate is perhaps more representative of the true ground level of the Roman harbour area as it was then, rather than the artificially heightened area that we see today.

A little way south of the fortress's southern wall lay the River Dee and the suggested route for the arrival of the first Roman legions. The site of the present Old Dee Bridge is thought to mark the point of the first timber-built structure erected by the Roman settlers to ford the River Dee. Later evidence does seem to indicate that the original timber bridge may actually have lain along a slightly different alignment to its current successor, with its southern end located slightly to the east of its present position. Once across the river in Handbridge, troops and travellers could then move southward from Chester to Eccleston along the main Roman road called Watling Street and on to their southern settlements. They could also travel westward skirting the Saltney marshes through to Hawarden and then on to Flint and the North Wales coast.

The Roodee was originally a tidal flood plain which at the time of the Roman settlement would have only been visible at low tides.

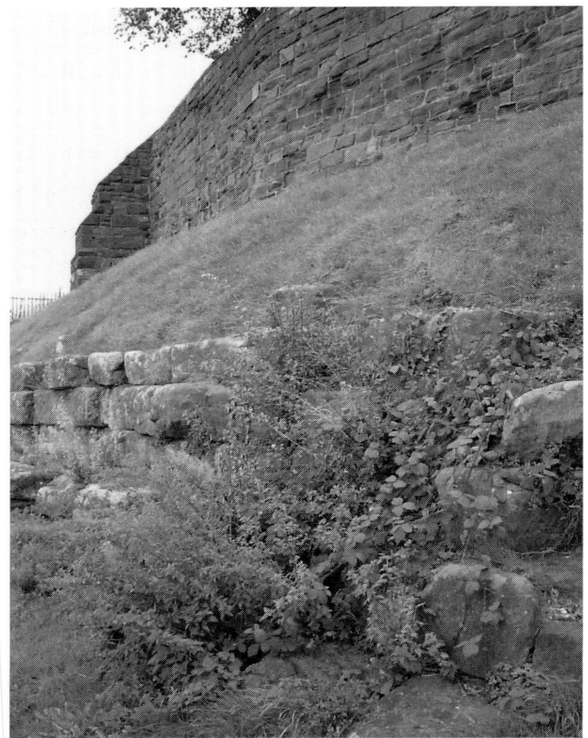

The Roman harbours and quays which helped to sustain the legionary fortress at Chester are largely hidden by later habitation, but the Roodee racecourse retains indications of its former existence.

On its way to Eccleston the road would have passed through the Roman settlement at Heronbridge, located some two miles south of the fortress. Close to the River Dee, the site is thought to having been a staging post for the supplies of tiles and pottery produced at the Roman works depot at Holt. It was at Heronbridge that these supplies were transferred from the river to the road for the final part of their journey to Chester. Later excavations at the site have since yielded evidence of continuous Roman occupation there, including the presence of a quayside and burial tombs. The site is also known to have been used for corn-drying and bronze-smithing and was thought to have remained in existence until around the fourth century.

Outside of the northern defences of the fortress lay the Roman road called Blake Street leading to the Wirral Peninsula and the major supply depot located at Meols. Today much of this route follows the line of the modern Parkgate Road as it runs out from the city to the village of Mollington. The north gate was also thought to be the route by which the legions travelled north-east from Chester to Wilderspool, the site of an auxiliary fort, via modern-day Hoole, Bridge Trafford and Helsby. Each of these vitally important thoroughfares may well have been used and protected by regular Roman patrols that set up temporary marching camps along their length. A number of such camps were clearly identified by the use of aerial photography between the 1980s and 1990s and were located around Christleton, Guilden Sutton, Hoole, Manley, Picton and Upton-by-Chester.

Although only temporary constructions, the marching camps employed by the troops were generally rugged and well-made fortifications. Shaped along the playing card lines of a more permanent base, these camps would have been protected by a defensive ditch at the front and backed by an earthen rampart topped by a wooden palisade. Access in and out of this enclosure was by way of gateways which were themselves protected by sentries.

Often these camps would have been constructed in advance of the patrol, or of the legion itself, by members of the unit who had preceded the main force. Once built, it seems likely that these protective enclosures would be used repeatedly, as and when they were required by the military.

The papihones, or leather tents, were generally used by legionaries when they were away from their permanent quarters on campaign or while patrolling. Within a Roman camp these tents were erected in a line of eight at the end of which would be the centurion's, allowing him easy access to his troops. Each papihone could accommodate eight men, making a total of 64 bed spaces for the troops. The remaining legionaries would be on guard duty, protecting their comrades from attack, suggesting that bed spaces were swapped around as men came on and off duty.

Given the time that has passed and the limited record-keeping of the period, it is little wonder that we have such meagre details about the men that made up the bulk of a Roman legion. Often such information is found as a matter of luck, rather than by design. A large number of tombstones, altars and legionary stones which have been recovered through archaeological excavations at Chester can offer us the slightest of insights into the lives of the men that they honour:

Aelius Claudian was recorded as an Optio, or second in command to a centurion at Chester, who dedicated an altar to the Guardian Spirit of the Legion.

Antiochus was thought to have been a doctor with the Roman legions at their Chester fortress and has been credited with dedicating a red sandstone altar to the 'all surpassing saviours of men'. The altar, which was unearthed in 1968 during excavations at Chester's old market hall, was unusual in that the actual dedication is written in Greek script, which may or may not indicate the origins of Antiochus himself.

Aulus Julius Marullinus was a soldier with special duties within the legion and he may well have served as a bodyguard or attaché to one of the legion's senior officers. His memorial stone at Chester records his age as 45 years old at the time of his death.

Caecilius Avitus was as a veteran who had seen 15 years of service with the 20th Legion and was a deputy to a centurion within the legion. He was also reported to be a religious seer who could interpret questions asked of the gods simply by looking at the entrails of sacrificed animals.

Decimus Capienus Urbicus was recorded as a native of Vienna who served as a standard bearer or 'signifer' with the resident legion and who had 24 years of service in the army. At the time of his death he was 44 years old. Typically his duties would have included those of paymaster, paying the individual soldiers and ensuring the security of the legionary pay chest which was held in a strongroom within the *principia* or headquarters building. He would have also been responsible for keeping the legionary accounts and would have probably been based within the *principia*.

Decimus Titianus was known to be a veteran of the 20th Legion Valeria Victrix who dedicated an altar to the spirit of his former comrades at the Chester fortress.

Festinius Probus was thought to have been the two-year-old son of a Roman administrator or trader who died at the Chester fortress. His memorial stone was paid for by his father Lucius Probianus.

Flavius Callimorphus was possibly a member of the fortress's civil administration, assuming that a Roman officer or soldier would not have his young family stationed with him. His memorial stone, dedicated by his brother Thesaeus, mentions not only Flavius himself but his three-and-a-half-year-old son, Serapionus, who was interred along with his father.

Flavius Longus was a military tribune stationed at the Deva fortress during the occupation of the 20th Legion. He was attributed with building an altar to the honour of the Emperors's Diocresian and Maximian, which was erected in the area of modern-day Eastgate Street. The dedication was also shared by his son Longinus, who along with his father was a native of Samosata, a town close to the border of modern-day Iran.

Gabinius Felix was recorded as being 40 years old at the time of his death and was said to be a soldier in the Second Augustan Legion, which had been raised by the Roman Emperor Antonine. The memorial stone dedicated to him was arranged by his family.

Gaius Juventius Capito was a soldier of the Second Legion Adiutrix, who served under a centurion called Julius Clemens and had completed 17 years of service with the army. He was 40 years old at the time of his death and his memorial stone suggests he was a native of modern-day Bulgaria.

Gaius Valerius Crispus was a veteran of the Second Legion Adiutrix who dedicated a memorial stone to his former unit in the city. The Second Legion left the Chester fortress around AD 80 to return to the continent.

Marcus Aurelius Alexander was recorded as the Prefect of the Camp for the 20th Legion Valeria Victrix and was thought to be responsible for the day-to-day running of the legionary fortress. The dedication stone states that Alexander was 72 years old and was formerly a Syrian citizen.

Publius Rustius Crescens was an Italian-born legionary who had served 10 years with the 20th Legion Valeria Victrix and who was 30 years old when he died. His heir 'Groma' arranged for a memorial stone to be erected at the Chester fortress.

Quintus Valerius Fronto was a veteran of the Second Legion Adiutrix; he was 50 years old at the time of his death and had completed his 25 years of service with the army. A large number of veterans chose to settle close to their former comrades and either received a parcel of land to do so or entered into a civilian occupation. His memorial stone suggests he was a native of modern-day Slovenia.

Quintus Vibius Secundus was a Roman soldier who served under the command of a centurion called Octavianus from the 20th Legion. According to his memorial stone Quintus was a native of Italy.

Titinius Felix was stationed at Chester with the 20th Legion Valeria Victrix and was 45 years old at the time of his death. His stated rank suggests that he was a specialist within the legion and might well have served as a bodyguard or attaché to one of the fortress's officers. His life was commemorated by his wife Julia Similina and the remaining members of his family.

Voltimesis Pudens was a horse trooper in the Second Legion Adiutrix Voltimesis and had served 13 years with the army; he was 42 years old at the time of his death.

In addition to the fairly anonymous soldiers that were recorded to have died at Chester, it has also been suggested that a small number of relatively famous individuals would have visited the military fortress as part of their 'state' visits to the Roman province. These included:

Emperor Hadrian who was reported to have visited Britain in around AD 120 to tour the province and is perhaps best known for the defensive wall that bears his name. Milestones which have been unearthed during excavations in the north-west region suggest that the emperor visited the Roman fortress at Chester as part of his itinerary.

Julius Agricola was thought to have been born in southern France around AD 40 and was the son of a local Roman administrator and the daughter of a minor aristocratic family. Not surprisingly he chose to pursue a military career and at around the age of 20 was said to have been a tribune under the command of Suetonius Paulinus while he was in Britain. He was reported to have been actively involved in the suppression of the Iceni people following the revolt of Queen Boudicca.

A decade or so later, during the bitter civil war which erupted between the rival factions who supported competing candidates for the imperial throne, Agricola openly declared for Vespasian, the man who subsequently became emperor. Legend suggests that his mother had been killed by forces loyal to Vitellius, the alternative candidate to Vespasian, and that this event alone had decided Agricola's choice for emperor.

Perhaps as a reward for his support of the new Caesar, he was soon appointed as commander of the highly experienced 20th Legion in Britain under the governorship of Petilius Cerialis. Almost immediately Agricola was employed in military campaigns against the native tribes of North Wales and northern Britain, including the Ordovices and Brigantes. His resulting military successes saw him transferred to both Aquitania and Rome and added to his already growing reputation as a leading military commander of his day. It was also around this time that his daughter married the noted Roman writer and historian Tacitus.

Around AD 78 Agricola was appointed as the military Governor of Britain and it was during the next six years that he was thought to have planned and implemented the final defeat of the troublesome British tribes and ordered the construction of numerous bases and forts. In North Wales he set about conquering the Ordovices tribe, including their religious and military centres on the isle of Anglesey. It was during these campaigns that Agricola was thought to have ordered that the earlier military base at Chester be more fully developed and enlarged to act as a gateway between the lands of North Wales and northern Britain. It has been suggested that during the winter months the Chester fortress was used as Agricola's military headquarters.

Having substantially subdued most of north-west Britain, Agricola now moved further north and into the Scottish border region. He managed to advance the Roman Empire to the very banks of the River Tay and consolidated the line between the Forth and the Clyde by constructing a series of manned military bases to protect his gains. Initially the 20th Legion under Agricola's command was to have been a part of these plans but events elsewhere in the empire prevented their use. The strategic withdrawal of the Second Legion Adiutrix from their base at Chester left the relatively new fortress on the Dee without a legionary force, so Agricola was reported to have assigned his former comrades-in-arms that particular task.

Around AD 84 Agricola was reported to have fought a decisive battle against the Caledonian tribes of Scotland at Mons Graupius where he crushed the Scottish forces. This success, along with his many other victories, brought him to the attention of the emperor Domitian who, jealous of his governor's fame, ordered Agricola to return to Rome. Although Agricola was accorded a great welcome by the emperor, senate and the people of Rome, his return effectively marked an end to his glorious military career. Forced into early retirement by the emperor, he lived the rest of his life on his family estates until his death in AD 93 at the relatively young age of 53.

Agricola's son-in-law, Tacitus, recorded the rise of the Roman Empire and in doing so he immortalised his father-in-law for future generations. Whether or not Agricola deserved the plaudits accorded to him is unclear, but there is little doubt that he was a remarkable and skilled militarist who helped to consolidate the Roman province of Britain.

Ostorius Scapula was the Roman Governor of Britain in around AD 49. He has been credited with building the first Roman military settlement at the Chester site and is considered by some to be the founder of the city. This early settlement was thought to have been a logistical centre, constructed to supply Scapula's legions in their military campaigns against the Ordovices, Deceangi and the Brigantes tribes. The store's depot may have been protected by a smaller military fortress – the predecessor of the much larger camp which remains in evidence today.

Septimius Severus was the Roman Emperor in around AD 208 who was reported to have visited the British province, along with his son Caracalla. Milestones excavated at Llanfairfechan were said to have praised the three Emperors, Severus and his two sons Caracalla and Geta. Given that the imperial party were in North Wales, it seems highly likely that they would have visited and perhaps based themselves at the Chester fortress.

When the Roman legions first invaded Britain they found that the country's road system was nothing more than a collection of individual paths and tracks which were often disconnected and tended to lead from one individual settlement to another. For the Roman commanders the most important function of a British road network was the rapid movement of troops and supplies away from their landing areas on the south coast through to their new military centres and their front line legionary forts. The first major road that they constructed extended from Lincoln through to Gloucester and was known as the Foss Way. Their later military campaigns pushed this initial road network forward from Lincoln through to York, then on to Wroxeter and finally the new legionary fortress at Chester. By around AD 82 this new Roman road network had been pushed forward to the Clyde and the Firth of Forth in Scotland and had over 60 front line forts running along its 1,000-mile length.

Chapter 4
A Future Set in Stone

Following the arrival of the 20th Legion Valeria Victrix at Chester in around AD 87 there began a period of substantial building and refurbishment at the fortress which was set to last for the next 200 years or more. The most obvious improvement was the replacement of the outer wooden defensive palisade with a much more substantial sandstone wall. This rich red sandstone was quarried from outcrops on both sides of the river, including the area of what is now Edgar's Field in Handbridge and from the northern bank of the river in the area now occupied by the modern-day county hall and around Chester's castle complex.

The front of the original earthen rampart was thought to have been cut back to produce a vertical face against which the sandstone wall could be set. It was laid upon a foundation trench cut into the natural bedrock and then filled with crushed rubble, some 18 inches deep and six feet wide, which would help carry the enormous weight of the stones. The outer face of the wall rose to a height of about 22 feet from ground level and was made up of individual blocks, each four feet in length. This outer wall was supported to its rear by crushed rubble packed directly between it and the existing earth and timber rampart. The rear section also carried the walkway, along which Roman sentries patrolled, and was thought to have stood at a height of some 16 feet. The remaining six feet was made up of a defensive parapet, behind which the defenders could monitor the wider area and the civilian settlement which had grown up immediately outside of the fortress.

Fronting the perimeter of the fortress was the fossae, the defensive ditches which surrounded each Roman settlement or camp and which were reported to have been typically V-shaped constructions. The average dimension for such ditches was 10 feet deep and 20 feet wide, with the spoil being used to construct the associated defensive rampart which stood at its back. The number of ditches depended on both the local conditions and the geology, with the distance of these ditches from the defensive palisade being determined by the calculated throwing distance for spears and ballistae bolts.

At each corner of the fortress and along the full length of its defensive walls, rectangular sandstone towers were erected at regular intervals of approximately 200 feet. These were built at the same time as the wall itself and were thought to be around 22 feet wide and have defensive walls some four feet thick at their base. One or two of these towers were reported to have been employed as platforms for ballistae or large catapults, the artillery of the time. Of the 22 towers which it has been suggested lined the walls of the fortress only six of them have subsequently been located, as well as the remains of one of the corner towers which now lies below the much later King Charles's Tower sited near Deanery Field. Set into each of the four walls was a gateway, of which only two are apparent today. The eastern gate was known to have stood approximately on the site of its later mediaeval and modern-day replacement but was substantially different to the gateway that we see today. Early illustrations show it as a pair of arched gateways through which military and civilian traffic would have flowed and which was flanked on either side by a stone-built guardroom.

The northern gate of the fortress was also sited near to its present-day location and was reported to have been flanked by a similar pair of stone-built guard towers. Construction of the present gateway around 1810 revealed the foundations of its Roman predecessor and excavations in the early 1970s suggested that the mediaeval and modern-day replacements may actually have lain well in front of the original Roman defences. It was impossible to

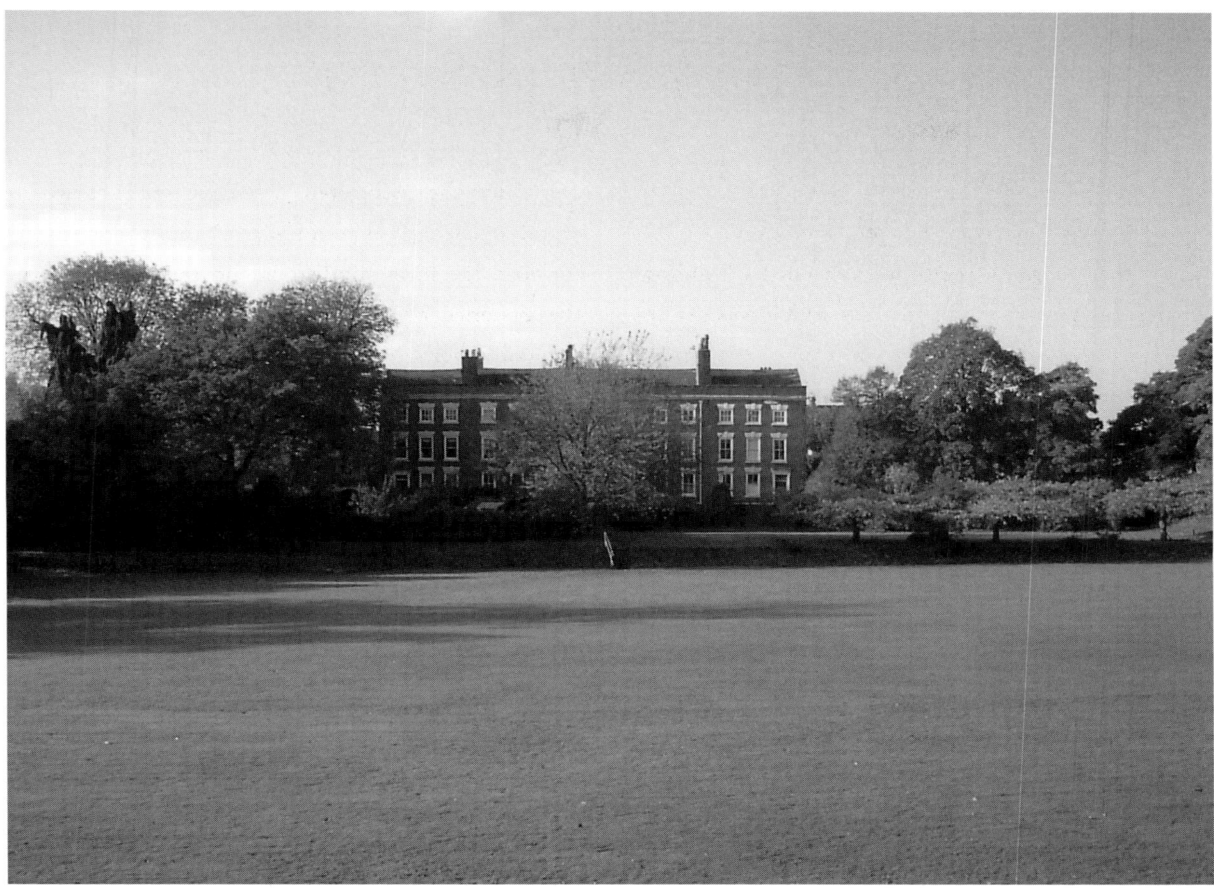

The Deanery Sports Field covers the remains of Roman ovens, bake-houses and workshops.

verify this though, due to the presence of other buildings located nearby which inhibited more extensive investigations. The southern gate was known to have been located at the junction between present-day Bridge Street and Lower Bridge Street, on the site of the modern-day Chester heritage centre, formerly Saint Michael's Church. Excavations in 1908 apparently partly revealed the foundations of this missing gateway, but little more than that is known. Finally, it is thought that the western gate was located at the junction of what is today Watergate Street and Nicholas Street, with its foundations lying below what was the Holy Trinity Church and which now serves as the city's guildhall.

Immediately behind the defensive stone wall of the fortress was an open area called the *intervallum*, which housed the circular legionary ovens which backed onto the rear of the wall's earthen ramparts. In addition to the ovens there was a line of long narrow buildings each 24 feet deep and 70 feet long that were constructed along each of the fortress walls and thought to have been used as store rooms, kitchens or possibly trade workshops. When tools, weapons or other manufactured items were required by the legion, their garrison workshops, or *fabrica*, would produce such items, as and when they were required. These workshops were generally manned by skilled blacksmiths, carpenters or masons, who were often drawn from the ranks of the legion itself but possessed the additional specialist skills required to meet its everyday needs. The intervallum was the space between the settlement's outer defences and the internal living accommodations which housed the legionary troops. Often this area could be as little as 60 feet wide, but could be anything up to 200 feet, depending on the overall

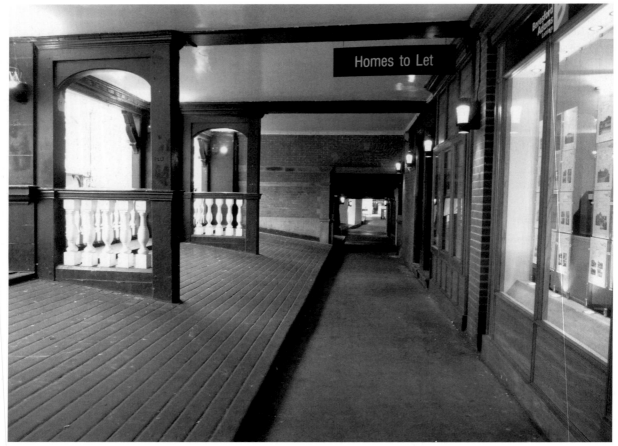

The Bridge Street Rows are thought to overlay the route of the first Roman streets.

size of the Roman station itself. This area of space allowed for free and easy access to the defensive walls and reduced the potential for burning projectiles to be launched over the walls and hitting either living quarters or important legionary buildings.

The Via Sagularis roadway which also ran behind the full length of the fortress's defences was thought to have been around 30 feet wide and bordered on either side by three-foot-wide sidewalks. Both sides of the road were defined with sandstone kerbstones laid vertically and a drainage system which ran along its full length. This particular feature was thought to have been used almost exclusively for the movement of military traffic, including patrols and materials used within the fortress and thus avoiding the need to move them around the centre of the base.

Running through the centre of the intervallum and along the full length of the defences the Via Sagularis also contained the main drains which drew rainwater from the centre of the camp and from the roofs of buildings which backed onto the defensive

From Roman times, Chester's High Cross marks the convergence of the city's four main streets.

During the time of the Romans, this thoroughfare was called the Via Decumana, leading to the fortress's northern gate.

wall. Typically running down a slight gradient, this accumulated water was then used to flush the settlement's latrines which were generally located at the lowest point of the camp.

The routes of the main Roman roads that lay within the confines of the fortress are still fairly evident in the city today. Eastgate Street and Watergate Street clearly mark the line of the Via Principalis. Close to its western end it meets the Via Decumana, or Northgate Street, at the site of the present-day High Cross. Bridge Street, or the Via Praetoria, on its original line would have run northward to join Northgate Street and intersected with the other two roads around the junction of the Roman headquarters building, the *principia*, which lay at the southern end of Northgate Street and which today lies beneath the much later St Peter's Church. Today's obvious lack of a direct north/south alignment between Northgate Street and Bridge Street is almost certainly due to later redevelopment and construction in both the Bridge Street and lower Northgate Street areas. If, as has been reported, the southern gate of the fortress now lies below the site of the Chester heritage centre, then it seems sensible to conclude that part, if not all, of the original Roman road lies slightly to the east of its present route and below the famous Bridge Street Rows, which were first constructed at a much later date.

The *principia*, or headquarters building, represented the administrative and judicial centre of every Roman settlement and as their most important building was invariably sited at the junction of the Via Principalis and Via Praetoria. Excavations at Chester have clearly demonstrated the phased development of this particular building throughout the entire Roman occupancy of Chester. In the early years of the fortress the *principia* was known to have been constructed of timber and was much smaller in size than its later stone-built replacement. In light of this it has been suggested that the earlier route of the Via Principalis was itself some 22 metres north of its present location. However, expert opinion is highly divided on this issue with many believing that such an idea is at best highly speculative. The later stone building was thought to be part of a much more extravagant construction, said to have been a major rebuilding project undertaken during the early part of the second century. The *principia* was known to have included a large open courtyard area, behind which lay the judgement hall, offices and the shrines which were dedicated to various Roman deities. Below the level of the building and cut into the natural bedrock was a strongroom which held the legionary pay chest and other regimental valuables. A small section of this room can still be seen today through a viewing window which was built into the

This covered row was known as 'Shoemakers Row' and was designed by John Douglas in around 1899. It covers the remains of the Roman *principia*.

south side of the Forum shopping centre, itself replacing the earlier market hall. The total length of the *principia* building was determined to be in excess of 300 feet and over 230 feet in width. The structure was supported by a series of massive stone columns and the south-facing entrance of the building was deliberately built-up with terracing to further enhance its already imposing façade. Excavations which took place in 1897 at No. 23 Northgate Street and those in Goss Street between 1948 and 1949 have helped to confirm these dimensions, while at the same time exposing the bases of a number of the building's massive support columns.

To both the west and the east of the *principia* lay a range of barracks, of which there were many within the fortress. Throughout the first two centuries of occupation these legionary barracks were thought to be of a mainly timber construction, with later versions built on much more permanent stone sills. With over 5,000 men to house and feed, much of the fortress's space and resources would have been given over to these particular purposes. Also to the west of the *principia* building in what is now Goss Street lay a stable block, thought to have been used by a small detachment of cavalry that were said to have been based in the fortress. In a later period of development these same buildings appear to have been altered and reused as living quarters or offices.

To the north of the *principia*, in what is today the market hall area of Chester, there were a number of important Roman buildings, including one with a central elliptical courtyard which has continued to defy identification and explanation since it was first discovered in 1939. Thought to date from around the third century it has been suggested that this building may be entirely civilian in nature rather than military and could have served as a theatre or as a shrine, but as yet no definitive evidence exists either way.

Immediately behind the *principia*, at its northern end, was the *praetorium*. This building was the residence of the legionary legate, the fortress's commander and the man who implemented both Roman planning and policy for the area and therefore the most important person residing within the base. Separated from the *principia* by a road some 20 feet wide, the *praetorium* was estimated to have measured over 200 feet from east to west and a similar distance from north to south. It appears to have been originally built of stone but was continuously redeveloped over time, including the widening and partitioning of various rooms and the rebuilding of internal and external entrances. A Roman altar thought to have come from within this building was unearthed in 1851 and is now held by the Grosvenor Museum. Doubts were subsequently cast on the identification of the site as the *praetorium*, in view of the apparent low level of decoration and finishing that were found during its excavation. One suggested alternative was that the building was in fact the *valetudinarium* or hospital. This theory was

Grosvenor Museum designed by T.M. Lockwood.

Dating from 1093, Chester's Norman abbey has remained relatively undisturbed for the past 1,000 years.

partly supported by an altar found in 1851 which had been dedicated in Greek by a doctor called Hermogenes. The finding of a second altar during the excavations of 1967–68 dedicated to another doctor called Antiochus seemed to further strengthen the hospital theory. However, those that believed the site to be the *praetorium* and not the legionary hospital pointed to the fact that this altar had almost certainly been moved from its original position and that the building itself did not correspond to known hospital plans taken from other fortresses. It was not unreasonable therefore, in their view, that the doctors would have lived within the legate's residence and would have dedicated the altars within that building.

Further west of the *principia* and *praetorium*, lying just within the western defences, were more barracks and workshops and outside of the wall was the legionary cemetery, an area that would later be occupied by Chester's Royal Infirmary buildings. Back inside the walls and north of the elliptical building, towards the northern defences of the fortress, were a series of buildings, including a water tank, workshops and legionary barracks. Much of this north-west quadrant of the city has been the subject of massive redevelopment during the 20th century, particularly in the late 1960s and early 1970s. Evidence of many of these major Roman buildings was completely removed during construction of the Forum shopping centre and its associated underground parking areas. The Roman archaeology that does remain intact does so because it has been protected by other later structures, such as pubs, private housing and the city's imposing town hall.

The north-eastern quadrant of the city has suffered much less development than its western counterpart, perhaps as a direct result of its later history as a religious precinct of Chester's cathedral which has stood, in one form or another, for well over a thousand years. Apart from infrequent excavations that have allowed identification of Roman ovens, workshops and sections of defensive ramparts the area remains largely undiscovered. In 1868 restoration work on the lady chapel within the cathedral revealed a Roman concrete floor, a drain and traces of a road which ran diagonally under the

These properties date from the 18th century and during their construction Roman bathhouse foundations were discovered, although little was saved.

Commonhall Street was the location for the Roman fortress's *Horrea*, or grain stores, which formed a large part of the legionary diet.

south-eastern buttress some nine feet below present ground level. As little or no substantial archaeological work is anticipated within the immediate cathedral grounds, it is virtually impossible to know exactly what Roman architecture remains there and perhaps we never will.

Almost the opposite is true of the south-east quadrant of the Roman fortress positioned in the area of the Grosvenor shopping precinct and its associated underground car parking and delivery bay system. Within this particular area of the fortress, known as the *praetentura*, lay a basilica – a large aisled hall – to the south of which lay rooms with tessellated floors heated by a hypocaust. Further observations of the site proved that this was the location for the main legionary bathhouses within the camp and reflected to some degree the very centre of fortress life and leisure time. The northern third of the complex was thought to be the covered exercise hall, called the *palaestra*. Generally, such halls were open-roofed but the cold climate probably caused the hall in Chester to be covered. In the south-east corner of the site it was speculated that a large water tank had stood supplying water to the complex's baths, saunas and latrines.

In 1863 two fragments of inscribed marble were found, which later study proved to be from the time of the Emperor Vespasian and dated the bathhouse to around AD 79. Later archaeological evidence also proved that the bathhouse had been constructed during the first phase of occupation at the fortress and that both it and the exercise hall were in use up until the third century. The baths part of the complex was estimated to measure some 275 feet along its north/south alignment and was approximately 265 feet wide, making it a wholly substantial feature within the fortress and perhaps indicating its very importance.

Unseen sections of the complex are thought to have been located below the modern street frontages in Bridge Street, including the *natatio* or swimming baths. Given the level of later development however, it is unlikely that much remains of these sections of the original Roman complex. Typically though, such a leisure centre would have included a changing area, the *apodyterium*, where the bather would have got undressed and stored their clothes. They would then enter the *frigidarium*, where they could initially wash themselves, before moving on to the *tepidarium* where the sweating process began. Bathers then went into the *caldarium*, in which they could immerse themselves in hot baths and scrape their skin clean using a strigil. Finally, they would return to the *frigidarium* in order to cool themselves off before getting dressed and returning to their duties or quarters.

During the early 1960s preliminary testing of the area for the proposed development of the Grosvenor shopping precinct clearly identified this site as being one of great importance in terms of Chester's archaeological past. Time constraints imposed on the site's contractor by the developers and the lack of intervention by the national inspectorates resulted in a minimal amount of time being given to study the remains and to fully understand the site as a whole. Recollections from the time suggest that many of the remains were in fact in excellent condition and that in some areas of the site Roman walls remained up to 12 feet high and would have offered local archaeologists an unparalleled opportunity to study this particular period of Roman occupancy. Sadly, this opportunity was lost forever when much of the site was quickly subjected to intensive machine-based excavation which completely removed the archaeological evidence that had managed to survive largely intact during the preceding 1,900 years.

Over in the south-west quadrant of the fortress there appears to have been only small-scale development of the base, with the *horrea* or fortress granaries being sited close to the present-day Commonhall Street area of the city. These structures were vital as grain was the staple diet of the legionaries. They were known to be long rectangular buildings, raised up from ground level enabling circulation of the air to prevent dampness from contaminating the stores. Their close proximity to the harbour area through the western gate implied that much, if not all, of these stores were imported into the fortress by ship. As with other areas of the city, extensive exploration of this section of the former Roman fortress has been extremely limited by the presence of later buildings. Bounded as it is by Watergate Street to the north and Bridge Street to the east, many of the later shops and elevated rows undoubtedly hide many of the Roman artefacts that still lie below them.

Outside of the fortress itself a number of buildings were constructed continually throughout the whole of the period of Roman occupation. The actual purpose of many of these sites has not yet been clearly defined, but in all likelihood they were civilian in nature rather than military. These were in addition to the *vicus* or civilian settlements that regularly established themselves outside the precincts of large legionary bases. The main civilian settlement at Chester was known to have been located in the present-day Foregate Street area and would have included traders who made their livings from the military, ex-soldiers who wished to remain close to their former comrades and the legionary's womenfolk. Later building during the Middle Ages has obscured much of this earlier Roman activity, but pottery and coin finds have confirmed the existence of the vicus lying between the outer fortress wall and the Love Street area of Chester which is located further east. Excavations around 1966 also identified the fortress's former parade ground lying slightly north of the eastern gate and separated from the defensive wall by a section of

Nicholas Street's Georgian terrace fronts: evidence of extensive building and rebuilding over several centuries.

open ground. Much of this area is now covered by modern retail units and car parking spaces.

In the south-west corner of the fort, remains of an unknown structure which included an altar were found during later excavations. In around 1976, in the area of Chester Castle, the remains of a formerly unknown Roman complex were uncovered. Further investigations suggested that the building had stood in one form or another from the first century through to the fourth. Comprising a central courtyard which was surrounded on three sides by a number of individual rooms, the building was thought to be 60 metres long and lying on an east to west alignment. Two Roman wells were found within its precincts, as was evidence of its timber predecessor dating to between AD 75 and AD 100. The actual day-to-day purpose of the building is uncertain, but it has been speculated that it was a relatively high status residence and may well have been a *mansio* or guesthouse that was built to accommodate important guests or travellers.

To the north-west of this building, lying outside of the western gate and towards the harbour area, evidence of a second early Roman complex was discovered during the 18th century. Excavations in around 1779 exposed the remains of a suite of rooms in the area of the present-day Lower Watergate Street and City Walls Road junction. The building contained a hypocaust heating system and a patterned mosaic floor and was almost certainly destroyed shortly after its actual discovery. It has since been speculated that the building was an officers bathhouse or *thermae*, but this has not been proved definitively.

Further remains, thought to be related to this same building, were then discovered in various excavations undertaken between 1894 and 1959 and subsequently recorded and preserved. Remains of a furnace room arch, the remnants of a terrace revetment wall and stable block have all been investigated by local archaeologists. It appears that some, if not all, of these buildings were constructed of timber in or around the first century and then replaced in stone at a later date. The presence of stabling for draught animals further reinforces the idea of large quantities of stores being imported into the fortress from supply ships that berthed at the nearby quays.

The Grey Friars area of Chester identifies the location of the religious house for the Franciscan Order who settled in the city around 1240.

There is more than enough evidence to suggest that a number of other equally substantial buildings existed within this particular section of the city. At the rear of modern-day Nicholas Street there are the remains of heavy stone walls which clearly indicate extended phases of building and rebuilding during several centuries of Roman occupation. This is duplicated at the southern end of the site, around the Grey Friars area where similarly substantial buildings are known to have existed. Much of this whole area was later reused during the mediaeval period by a number of the city's religious orders who located their houses there, and in the process utilised much of the earlier Roman materials and foundations that had remained in place.

It is perhaps significant that these particular buildings and the one located near to the castle lie alongside or close to the main routes leading into and out of the military fortress. It has been speculated therefore that each of these buildings, despite being civilian in nature, were actually maintained by the military and this may reflect their daily use. Initially it had been assumed that these buildings were entirely for the use of the military and were themselves the location for the legionary bathhouses. Following the 1964 discovery of the actual legionary baths and exercise hall within the precincts of the fortress proper, the purpose of these other sites has had to be reconsidered.

No completely definitive explanation for these buildings to the west of the fortress has yet been offered, but it is conjectured that they might have been used to accommodate merchants or wealthy citizens that were visiting the area. Alternatively, given their proximity to the busy harbour area of the fortress, they might equally have served as accommodation for the administrative personnel who controlled the port. In either event, only future excavations and definitive finds would help to clearly identify their actual layout and purpose, which, given the current commercial and residential status of the area, are not anticipated in the near future.

Chapter 5

DISPUTES, DECAY AND DEVELOPMENT

As with all great civilizations, the fortunes of the Roman Empire constantly ebbed and flowed throughout the whole of its existence and often these various peaks and troughs were directly reflected in their 300-year occupation of Chester. During these three centuries the fortress was subjected to extensive periods of decay and destruction, followed almost immediately by phases of development and renewal to the actual fabric of the base. These regular changes in the fortunes of the fortress also tended to reflect the ever-changing priorities within the empire itself, as well as the prolonged restlessness of the many native peoples whose homelands had been invaded by the legions and who continued to resist this ongoing occupation.

In order to more clearly identify potential reasons for these obvious periods of decay and development within the fortress itself, it is probably useful to both clarify and elaborate on the known chronology of events that were particularly relevant to Chester throughout the period of the Roman occupation. Almost all of these reported events are generally large-scale and national in their nature; no actual records exist that might offer specific details regarding local disputes which may also have had a serious impact on the continued development of the fortress.

Between AD 47 and AD 60 the native Welsh tribes waged a series of fairly successful guerrilla campaigns against the Roman army which compelled the legions to establish a series of temporary bases in the region. The Ordovices of North Wales, led by the ousted tribal warlord Caractacus, were central to this opposition, as were the leaders of the Druidic religion based on the island of Anglesey. In around AD 51 Ostorius Scapula, the Roman commander, met and defeated Caractacus and his Welsh army at the battle of Caer Caradock, and thus effectively ended the tribal warlord's military threat against the Roman forces.

Between AD 58 and AD 59 Suetonius Paulinus, the new governor of Britain, launched a major military campaign against the tribes of north-west Wales and the Druids on the island of Anglesey. The Romans considered the Druids to be little more than uncivilized savages who practised human sacrifice as part of their rituals and exerted a rebellious influence on the native peoples. Towards the end of AD 59 Paulinus, after finally crossing the Menai Straits which protected the island and its inhabitants, then set about obliterating all traces of the Druidic religion by massacring its priests and destroying all of their sacred sites.

In around AD 60 Boudicca, the wife and widow of the late Iceni King Prasutagus, was reported to have been publicly flogged and her daughters raped by the Roman forces that had been sent to acquire the lands and possessions of her late husband. The Iceni were a proud, war-like people and in response to this unforgivable insult they rebelled against Roman rule and their allies with unimaginable ferocity. At Colchester Boudicca and her army attacked and burnt the town and massacred all of its inhabitants, later routing the Ninth Legion which had been sent to intercept them. Moving on to London, the Iceni army easily overcame the relatively unprotected settlement and forced the Roman governor Paulinus to retreat, leaving the town to be totally destroyed and all of its inhabitants murdered.

St Albans was the next settlement to suffer a similar fate, with old tribal scores being settled at the same time. In the meantime Paulinus had managed to regroup his forces and joined with two other legions and their auxiliaries to face Boudicca's army in a battle which would determine the fate of Roman Britain. Although he was vastly outnumbered, Paulinus and Roman military discipline eventually won the day with some 80,000 British casualties reported against several hundred Roman losses. Rather than be taken prisoner Boudicca was said to have taken poison in order to escape certain Roman revenge.

From around AD 69 through to AD 70 a civil war raged within the Roman Empire which had the potential to divide, if not completely destroy, the very fabric of its influence and power. Two diametrically opposed parties vied with one another for political control of the immensely rich and powerful empire and in doing so, threatened to bring about its very end. The Roman legions, the source of the empire's power, began to take sides in the dispute and this would ultimately lead to questions being asked as to their loyalty and also to a general level of uncertainty within the army itself. Rather than risk any potential mutiny or unrest among the legions, Roman commanders were thought to have scaled back military campaigns throughout the period and recalled units to their established bases within the British mainland.

The native tribesmen of Britain were not slow to fully exploit these temporary withdrawals. The Brigantes tribe who inhabited large parts of Lancashire and Yorkshire found their pro-Roman Queen Cartimandua usurped by her ex-husband Venutius, who was fiercely opposed to the Roman occupation and who attempted to break away from their control. The Roman General Petilius Cerialis, commanding two legions and supported by Julius Agricola who led the 20th Legion, began a series of campaigns against the Brigantes which would end with the death of Venutius and the establishment of a legionary fortress at York. While Cerialis was leading his two legions in the east of the region, Agricola and the 20th Legion were located on the western side of the Pennines making their way northward to finally meet up with Cerialis's forces at Carlisle.

These early native rebellions and the subsequent legionary retaliatory strikes all preceded the actual building of the permanent fortress at Chester by some years and consequently would have had no direct effect on its construction. The burial urn which was discovered at the Chester fortress and said to date from around AD 60 was almost certainly deposited by the military garrison of a temporary base which pre-dated the much later permanent fortress. It is entirely possible that this earlier base was first built in support of Didius Gallus in his campaigns against the northern Brigantes tribe between AD 52 and AD 57.

The later campaigns which commenced in AD 71 and were undertaken by Julius Agricola and the governor of Britain, Petilius Cerialis, probably marked the period when the site at Chester was once again identified as a possible location for a permanent military base. Given later archaeological evidence, such as the lead pipes assigned to Julius Agricola, it seems likely that a defensive position was constructed near to the River Dee, if only to support the Roman forces that were campaigning in the region around that time.

Some three years later, between AD 74 and AD 77, a new governor, Julius Frontinus, was known to have begun a series of campaigns against the Welsh tribes that would finally lead to the establishment of much more substantial and permanent legionary fortresses at both Chester and Caerleon. In subsequent campaigns against the Silures of South Wales and the Ordovices of North Wales Frontinus effectively secured the whole of the region with the construction of these two new bases, adding to the one which was already being constructed at York.

Twelve months later Julius Agricola, who had now been promoted to provincial governor, had returned to Britain and set about reinforcing the gains made by Julius Frontinus in the preceding three years. Following the destruction of a Roman cavalry contingent in AD 78 he finally crushed the troublesome Ordovices of North Wales and virtually exterminated the whole tribe in the process. In the following year Agricola led a rapid and hard-hitting campaign against the Brigantes tribe and as a result effectively ended all opposition in north-west Britain and Wales. In around AD 84 Agricola was said to have begun a series of campaigns against a number of Scottish tribes including the Votadini, who were a sub-tribe of the much larger Gododdin. Records suggest that he was supported in these campaigns by his former comrades in the 20th Legion Valeria Victrix, who would later garrison the fortress at Chester.

The 20th Legion arrived at their new garrison in around AD 87, following their three-year campaign against the Caledonian tribes of Scotland. The base that they inherited was in relatively good order, but many of the timber-framed buildings were now showing the effects of the region's extremely damp conditions and nearly 20 years of general wear and tear. Allied to the need for decent long-term accommodation, there appears to have been a great mood of confidence within the empire itself and this was expressed both in the scale and design of buildings from the period.

By AD 102 the timber defences of the fortress were gradually being replaced by a much more permanent and formidable sandstone alternative. Throughout the next 18 years several major rebuilding phases were to take place within the fortress, but seemingly on a relatively ad hoc basis. This piecemeal approach may be explained by regular absences of particular army units for other military duties throughout the province and within the region. This reduction in the fortress's manpower would almost certainly have resulted in building projects being strictly prioritised, with the more important military structures built first and the less vital ones put on hold indefinitely, or until such time as the absent units returned to their home bases.

Between AD 120 and AD 140 there was thought to have been a much reduced garrison at the Chester fortress because of the additional manpower required for the construction of Hadrian's Wall from AD 122 until AD 136 and the later, more northerly Antonine Wall completed in around AD 154. The 20th Legion was also thought to have garrisoned part, if not all, of this latter defensive structure for an extensive period of time. This reassignment of part of the legion's force was generally reflected in the curtailment of many of the major building projects that were taking place at Chester. It has been suggested that the amphitheatre fell into a period of disrepair sometime before AD 150. In addition some parts of the base such as former residences and legionary accommodations were regularly being used as refuse tips or latrines or were semi-derelict.

A new period of rebuilding and restructuring at Chester around AD 160 suggests that the garrison had substantially recovered its numbers, possibly due to the return of the 20th Legion from the northern frontiers of the empire. In around AD 196 there appears to have been some slight destruction of the vicus, the civilian area which was just outside of the fortress's eastern defences, but the cause of the destruction has never been clearly identified and could have simply been due to the outbreak of disease or possibly civil disorder.

Following the assassination of the Emperor Commodus around AD 196 another internal dispute occurred within the empire, when Albinus, the Roman governor of Britain, directly opposed the rule of the Emperor Severus and took troops from the province to settle his argument by force of arms. Sadly for Albinus he was defeated by Severus in AD 197, but not before a northern tribe – the Maeatae – and other allies of the Brigantes had attacked and overran the defences at Hadrian's Wall and destroyed everything in their path up to the Roman fortress at York. As part of this 'British Force' it is almost certain that units of the 20th

Legion would have been used by Albinus in his unsuccessful challenge and records suggest that his forces suffered heavy losses, which would have seriously depleted the fortress's legionary manpower.

Following the defeat of Albinus's forces and the suppression of the Maeatae, the new governor Virius Lupus, who had been appointed in AD 197, set about restoring order within the province. The 20th Legion was eventually restored to its full strength, possibly through the introduction of other military units from the continent, and the fortress's defences were substantially strengthened around AD 200. The Emperor Severus campaigned in Britain and it was during his reign that the systematic refurbishment of the Chester fortress was started and continued for subsequent generations. It was also during his rule that major reforms in military policy were introduced which permitted legionaries to marry and to quarter their families in and around the area of the fortress. This new phase of rebuilding ordered by Severus was continued through to the first part of the third century by the soldiers of the 20th Legion, but it is thought that men from the Second Legion Augusta were also present at the fortress around this time and may have taken part in the actual refurbishment of the base. Elsewhere in Britain, such mixed garrisons were fairly commonplace and were often used as a method of supplementing an under-strength legionary force.

By the middle of the third century, around AD 250, the 20th Legion was still garrisoned at the Chester fortress, in name at least. Detachments were known to be active in northern Britain, the Rhine and the Danube and in about AD 260 men from the

The Roman amphitheatre at Chester was subject to extensive periods of development and decay.

legion were known to have been stationed around Hadrian's Wall. Other units from the Valeria Victrix were also thought to have been part of the military forces of the usurper Carausius towards the end of the third century in around AD 283.

By around AD 285 large areas of the fortress were known to have been fully paved and there seems to have been a reduction in the actual numbers of military buildings within the fortress. It has been suggested that the actual military garrison at this time had itself been reduced in number and that the wives and children of the legionaries were now quartered within the fortress proper. Buildings such as the *principia* and *praetorium* were still occupied at the time, but it is uncertain whether their purpose was now military or civilian. Coins paid to legionaries who served under Carausius have been found at the fortress and these strongly suggest that elements of the 20th Legion were still present in the fortress around this time. The northern defences of the fortress were thought to have been completely rebuilt in around AD 300, perhaps as a direct result of earlier troubles, but this rebuilding has been attributed by some experts to the later mediaeval period. Tombstones from the nearby Roman cemeteries were used in the rebuilding of the north wall, but fail to help identify the actual period of reconstruction.

Constantius Chlorus undertook a series of campaigns against the Picts in around AD 306 and it is thought that military units from the Chester fortress formed part of his Roman forces. It is not entirely clear, however, whether or not these detachments were legionaries in the strictest sense of the word, or merely an auxiliary force of some description. Some experts believe that Chlorus may have been responsible for actually disbanding or merging the remaining units of the 20th Legion during his British campaigns and this might help to explain their sudden later disappearance.

Towards the end of the Roman military occupation of Britain, a series of internal disputes within the empire once again resulted in the serious depletion of legionary manpower throughout the province. Although these power struggles were in themselves not unusual, their coinciding with a resurgence of raiding by bands of Scottish and Irish tribesmen who were poised to take advantage of any distraction on the part of the Roman forces, resulted in the situation being far more critically important.

In AD 367 the north-west region of Britain was reported to have been attacked by marauding Scottish tribesmen allied to a people called the Attacotti, who had swept across the Irish Sea and began assailing Roman settlements all along the western coast of Britain. After several unsuccessful attempts these raiders were finally driven out of the area by a Roman general called Theodosius and although it seems unlikely that the fort at Chester was actually taken by these raiders, the very fact that they were able to infiltrate and ransack the area would seem to indicate the absence of a substantial military force at the base.

Around AD 383 a Spanish-born Roman general called Magnus Maximus, serving in Britain, was elevated to the status of emperor by his soldiers and immediately set about opposing the will of the legitimate western Emperor Gratian who was based across the channel in Roman-controlled Gaul. Maximus withdrew military forces from Britain in order to confront his opponent and after defeating Gratian established his new court at Trier. He was recognised by the other emperors, Theodosius in the east and Valentinian II in the south, as an equal and ruled over the territories of Britain, Gaul and Spain.

For the next four years Maximus was content to rule over and consolidate his new kingdom and was even converted to Christianity. Unfortunately for him, after this fairly peaceful interval he began to feel that his rule was under threat from Gratian's younger brother, the southern Emperor Valentinian, and he began to make preparations to oust his counterpart. Mobilising his forces, Maximus invaded Italy and quickly took Milan and then moved on to besiege Rome itself. For nearly a year he held the city captive and it was only with the arrival of additional forces that he was finally able to capture the city, although he failed to detain Valentinian himself which would prove to be a fateful mistake.

The ousted Valentinian managed to make his way to the court of Theodosius, the eastern Emperor, who was so outraged by the actions of Maximus that he raised an army to settle the matter by force of arms. Twice defeated at Illyricum, Maximus was finally killed, along with his son Victorius, at Aquileia in AD 388.

Legend has it that Maximus was married to Elen, the only daughter of the British king Eudaf Hen, and following the death of his father-in-law he had succeeded to the throne and had been known by some as Macsen Wledig. It has also been said that Maximus was supported in his military campaigns by a nephew of Eudaf Hen who was known as Cynan Meriadog. Although little is known about him, his name is associated with the later Welsh king Cunedda Wledig, who brought the Scottish-based Votadini people to Wales some 40 years later.

In the 20 years following the death of Magnus Maximus Britain was under the control of a series of weak western emperors who failed to properly reinforce the legions that were stationed there and were unable to prevent the increasing number of incursions that were taking place in the provinces of Gaul and Spain.

It was as a direct response to these attacks that the second and final withdrawal of Roman troops from the British province took place. A native Briton, whose name and date of birth is not known, was once again raised to the status of emperor by the army. Taking the title of Constantine III, he rallied the majority of the troops in Britain and crossed the channel to drive out the bands of Vandals, Burgundians and Huns that were regularly raiding the continent. Having successfully quelled these hordes Constantine quickly gained recognition from his two reigning counterparts and established his court at Aragon in Spain.

Although remnants of the Roman military and administrative classes remained in Britain, the withdrawal of troops by Constantine III in AD 407 is widely regarded as the final Roman evacuation of Britain, effectively ending 400 years of occupation. The relatively sudden departure of the legionary forces left Britain at the mercy of the numerous bands of sea-borne raiders that had plagued the country for many years. Serious incursions had been prevented by the presence of the highly disciplined legions and their immense defensive structures, such as Hadrian's Wall, as well as their series of military fortresses which protected large parts of Britain.

The small number of Roman commanders that had been left behind following the final withdrawal were now compelled to seriously reassess their own positions and in some cases took the decision to establish their own personal kingdoms within the former Roman province. Without the manpower and command structure of the legions, however, these relatively sparse military forces were not a very effective deterrent against the large numbers of Irish and Scottish-based raiders that now seemed to be infiltrating the country at will. The wealthier, more economically developed southern settlements of Britain were a prime target for these marauding bands of pirates, but few areas of the country escaped their attentions, including the lands of Wales and what is now north-west England.

Apart from these fragmentary Roman forces, much of mainland Britain was once again held by the native tribes whose ancestors had pre-dated the occupying armies of Rome and who were once again able to control their homelands militarily. However, many struggled to resist the Scottish and

Irish invaders who systematically raided and sacked large areas of the country. It was as a direct response to these increasing threats that both British and Welsh tribal leaders actively began to seek out new allies that would help them to defend their home territories.

The British king Vortigern Vorteneu, who held court in Kent, was thought to have been instrumental in inviting the first Saxon people to settle in these islands, a decision his people would later have cause to regret. It was considered to be in similar circumstances that the northerly Votadini people were invited to settle and defend the northern region of Wales which was being attacked and held by Irish raiders originating from around what is now modern-day Northern Ireland.

By around AD 368 local records suggest that the 20th Legion were no longer the garrison force within the fortress at Chester and that they had been completely withdrawn from the region. A Scottish tribe called the Votadini, under their leader Cunedda, was reported to be protecting the city from raiders, having been asked for help by the newly emerging British leadership. Skilled metal-workers, horsemen and warriors, the Votadini people were thought to have been a subordinate tribe of a much larger confederation of native Celts, the Gododdin, who inhabited the territory of Manau Gododdin near the modern-day Firth of Forth. Following the arrival of the Roman legions and the eventual subjugation of the native British tribes, the Votadini were said to have been employed by Rome as a paid auxiliary force on the northern frontiers of the empire. They occupied the lands immediately north of Hadrian's Wall and acted as a deterrent or buffer to any of the northern tribes that might think about attacking the Roman defences.

As a retained auxiliary force, it seems likely that the Votadini would have liaised, trained and campaigned with both the regular and irregular units that were used by the empire on its northern borders. Some historians have suggested that as a primarily cavalry-based force they may well have trained and shared tactics with the Sarmatians, a mobile auxiliary unit known to have been employed by the Romans in their British campaigns.

These foreign units were reported to have carried hollow metal dragon heads into battle with them with flowing windsocks, which trailed behind giving the impression of real dragons flying above the cavalrymen as they charged towards their enemies. These hollow standards were also said to have emitted a loud hissing noise as the wind flowed through them and no doubt added to the terror of the opposing native forces. Another feature of these 'heavy' cavalry units which may well have been adopted by the Votadini horsemen was the wearing of chain mail by both the rider and horse, which would have offered a high degree of protection to both.

Although there appears to be little, if any, documentary evidence that the Votadini actually adopted these 'Draco' standards as part of their own military tactics, it seems reasonable to assume that such an 'oriental' or 'eastern' emblem can only have come to Britain as part of the Roman invasion itself through one of their own foreign military units, such as the Sarmatians. These Thracian horsemen were said to have formed a large part of Rome's legionary cavalry units and it has been suggested that the dragons' heads that they carried into battle actually represented one of their own native deities. Historical records also suggest that a number of the Roman emperors including Severus and Aurelianus actually adopted the dragon motif as part of their own personal imperial standard and indicates that perhaps the emblem did eventually become a commonplace design among the legions of Rome.

Modern-day archaeological research would appear to indicate that the lands of the Votadini contained numerous hill forts and well-defended settlements, while at the same time having individual homesteads that offered little or no defence to any attacking force. This might suggest that their people relied on having the time to withdraw to one of the many defensive positions when danger threatened, or it might simply indicate an extremely secure and well-defended territory where there was little chance of attack by an outside enemy force. The tribal capital of the Votadini was located at Trapain Law, a 40-acre hill fort standing some 500-feet high in what is now the present-day Lothian area of Scotland, and was an extremely well-defended site with earthen ramparts on all sides. Large quantities of Roman silver and general wares found on this site indicate the level of day-to-day trading that existed between the Votadini and the occupying forces of Rome. The silver itself may represent payment for services offered to the empire in helping to secure their northern borders.

Born towards the end of the fourth century, the tribal leader of the Votadini was a warlord called Cunedda. As with many early British leaders very little is known about him. One ancient poem called the *Marwnad Cunedda* is said to record the Votadini's wars against the forces of Coel Hen, a former commander in the Roman army, and to be the origins for the Old King Cole nursery rhyme character. Legend has it that Cunedda was descended from Roman stock on his father's side and that his maternal grandmother was a daughter of Cynan Meriadog, who fought alongside Magnus Maximus and was a nephew to the then British king Eudaf Hen. It has been suggested that Cunedda's ancestors had originally come from Wales and were in fact political refugees fleeing the occupation of their country or possibly the vengeance of Valentinian II. Whichever reason is true there seems little doubt that Cunedda and his highly experienced military forces were approached by King Vortigern or another British leader, Ambrosius Aurelianus, to help defend Wales against the Irish and Scottish threat that was facing the region. In return for their help the Votadini were promised lands to settle and sometime around AD 425 Cunedda and his forces made the long journey from their home in the Scottish borders to the lands of North Wales.

Such was their military prowess that before too long, the majority of the Scottish and Irish invaders had been expelled from much of Wales and only retained possession of small areas of the country and the isolated island of Anglesey. With most of the northern region secured, Cunedda then set about driving the remaining raiders out of Powys and Dyfed and effectively securing all of the lands that lay between the River Dee in the north and the River Taff in the south of Wales. For the next 800 years or so Wales, in one form or another, would be ruled over by various dynasties all of which claimed direct descent from Cunedda and his heirs.

Having rid the country of the invaders and established an effective military force within the borders of Wales, Cunedda then set out to consolidate his new kingdom of Gwynedd and located his new court at Rhos, in the heart of his new lands. At that time the former legionary fortress at Chester lay within the borders of Wales and was regarded by the Welsh kings as being subject to their rule. It was only following the near total conquest of Britain by the Saxon peoples, bringing about the repositioning of the borders between Wales and the kingdom of Mercia, that saw Chester finally captured by the Mercian king Egbert and later incorporated into a unified England.

Cunedda was awarded the title *Gwledig* or *Wledig*, which it is said could be interpreted as prince or ruler over the kingdom of Cunedda's Land or Gwledig-y-Cunedda. This has been suggested as the derivation for the name *Gwyneddia*, a title which sometimes appears on old maps of the region. There is little evidence of internal opposition to Cunedda's arrival in Wales, suggesting a widespread acceptance of his right to rule and perhaps reinforcing the idea that he was indeed related to the original Welsh nobility that had ruled there prior to the Roman invasion. This rapid re-adoption of traditional ways, language and subservience to ancient nobles illustrates the lack of real social change which was perhaps indicative of Roman military control in the northern areas of the province. In southern Britain there appears to have been a much greater level of Romano-British integration, which managed to survive for a much longer period following the final withdrawal of the last Roman legions.

Compiled around AD 400, the *Notitia Dignitatum* was a list of Roman officials, dignitaries and military units that were still present in Britain at that time. This official record does not mention Roman troops being based at their Chester command in the north-west region of the province or that any elements of the 20th Legion were still operating anywhere within the islands of Britain.

Later archaeological excavations have not been able to clearly identify all of the latter stages of the Roman occupation at the Chester fortress but some reports suggest that by AD 417 much of Britain was being run by local magistrates or civilian authorities and this could possibly be the case in Chester. Later investigations of the fortress seem to indicate that there was no widespread or haphazard use of its buildings or inner precincts and perhaps suggests a highly organised and well-administered settlement. The Roman legions left behind them a legacy of culture and development that sadly did not last much beyond their withdrawal from Britain. Within a short period of time the entire province was under constant pressure from competing tribal groups and began to revert to a fragmentary state where many of the improvements in communication, construction, hygiene and civil government would not be seen again for well over a thousand years.

Chapter 6

A Journey into Darkness

As the fortress at Chester was likely to have been an entirely military post, it has been suggested that the Roman influence lasted only for as long as their actual presence in the region. Once the legionaries were gone, the local population would have simply reverted back to their native languages and tribal customs, soon forgetting their former occupiers' influences.

This does not appear to be the case at Chester and it is likely that the fortress was governed by some sort of civilian administration for a relatively short period, which was able to maintain a degree of law and order over the settlement. However, it is just as likely that the fortress remained as a military base under the control of the native British force such as the Votadini, who filled the void left by the Roman withdrawal. Either of these possible scenarios is supported in part by later archaeological evidence, which tends to indicate an increased level of habitation and cultivation in areas immediately outside of the fortress's defensive walls, rather than inside them.

A relatively modern walkway which is thought to overlie a 2,000-year-old Roman defensive structure hidden below Duke Street.

The centre of modern-day Chester is littered with any number of historic buildings that help to completely conceal the settlement's Dark Age history, the 500 years or so which marked the departure of the legions and the arrival of its Norman occupiers. The very importance of the buildings themselves tends to inhibit any detailed exploration of these earlier periods of habitation and activity, resulting in gaps in our current knowledge. Post-Roman building which is likely to have taken place alongside the main internal roads of the fortress were in all likelihood later covered over by the city's world-famous shopping rows, its churches and its cathedral.

One fact that is not in any way disputed was the continuing importance of the fortress site, both in terms of its geographical location and the security of its defences. Both of these reasons would inevitably result in the city being fought over for centuries by the native Britons, marauding Scottish tribes, sea-borne Vikings raiders and finally the Anglo-Saxon people that would settle there. These continuing changes in ownership of the fortress site would only finally be resolved at the beginning of the 10th century when it was eventually incorporated into the British kingdom of King Alfred the Great.

The Mercian king responsible for creating the system of burghs which protected his kingdom from the Viking menace. Chester was one such stronghold.

Much Dark Age materials are thought to lie beneath the modern-day Rows.

Following the withdrawal of the legions in the fifth century the native Britons seized control of much of the north-west region of England and sought to incorporate the whole area into their individual tribal kingdoms. At that time much of northern England was still under regular attack from sea-borne Irish raiders and the Picts from further north, who ransacked the native settlements and carried away their livestock, food stores and treasures.

British leaders such as Ambrosius Aurelianus and Vortigern are thought to have rallied the local tribes to oppose these raiders and the latter was said to have brought the Votadini tribe from Scotland in order to help protect the north-west region of Britain. Sources suggest that these forces, under their leader Cunedda, were actually based at the Chester fortress around the beginning of the fifth century and were primarily employed as a local mercenary force to help protect both the city and its outlying areas. This tribe was formerly part of the Gododdin people from southern Scotland and as previously mentioned they would subsequently rule the Gwynedd region of Wales for the next 800 years.

Sometime around AD 428 these same British tribal leaders are said to have requested the aid of the Saxon peoples who lived in continental Europe to help defend England against the various raiders that were attacking the country. Under the command of their leaders, Hengest and Horsa, the Saxon forces landed in Kent and in return for land and supplies set about expelling the Irish and northern raiders from the country. Having completed the task, however, the Saxons were quick to capitalise on their gains and instead of returning home, they requested additional forces from their homeland and set about conquering the lands of their former

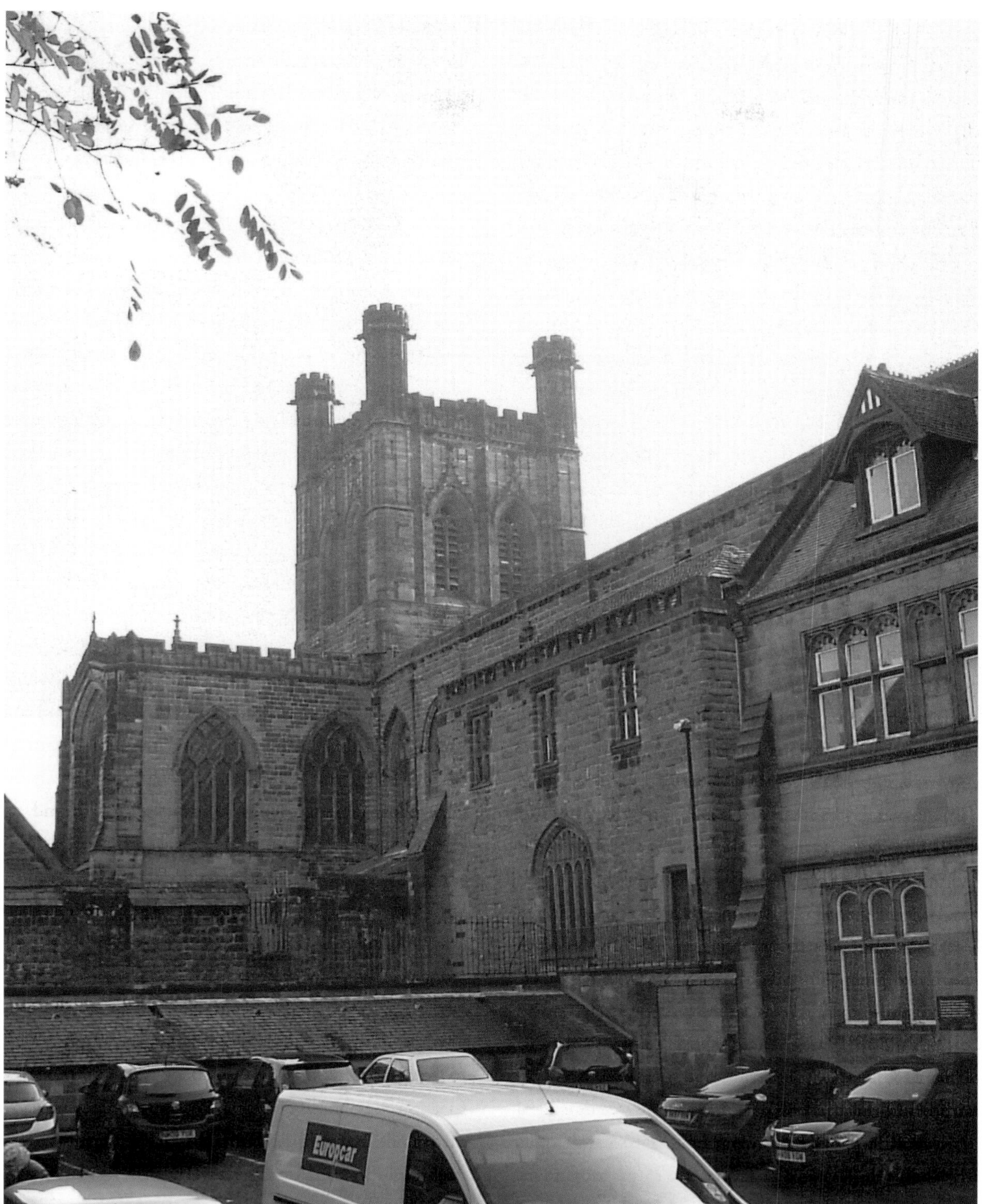

A good deal of Chester's early history will no doubt lie beneath the foundations of the city's cathedral.

employers. The native Britons who were unable to resist the onslaught of the Saxon invaders found themselves pushed westward and back into Shropshire, Cheshire and to the borders of Wales.

At the same time the Christian faith and its very interpretation was the subject of a great deal of controversy and dispute throughout much of Britain. The Roman Emperor Constantine had converted to Christianity around AD 312, later adopting it as the imperial religion and it continued to spread the length and breadth of the empire from that time onward. In around AD 413 Pelagius, a native of Roman Britain, had dared to question the doctrine of 'original sin' which was one of the founding principles of the Christian faith itself. His teachings were then adopted by Agricola, the son of the British bishop Severianus, causing Pope Celestine I to send Germanus and Lupus to Britain in AD 428 to try and heal the divide within the English church that these heretical and blasphemous beliefs had caused.

It was reported that Germanus of Auxerre had led an army of orthodox British Christians to victory over a force of Pelagian heretics at Maes Garmon near Mold in around AD 429. A related Chester legend has it that a man called Gormundus, a 'Roman Cap'tayne', had built a set of fortifications at Heronbridge, a former Roman site just outside the fortress at Chester, and beat the 'Saxons' in a major battle. This is notable for the fact that Germanus, the agent of Pope Celestine I, had indeed been a Roman military officer prior to his entering the priesthood and is likely to be the 'Gormundus' noted in the legendary tale.

It would be tempting to believe that this event, real or not, somehow connects the two major disputes of the period and may well have occurred in the region of the former legionary fortress at Chester. Historical records do suggest that the native British tribes were eventually forced out of Shropshire and into Cheshire by the Saxon incomers who had occupied much of southern Britain.

An alternative interpretation of these events might be possible if one assumes that the 'Saxons' referred to in the legend were actually the inhabitants of Chester, rather than an outside force. There is a suggestion that in the last years of the Roman occupation the regular legionary units at Chester were actually reinforced by foreign auxiliaries from the continent, some of whom originated from the Saxony region. The discovery at Chester of small dwellings with timber walls, thatched roofs and sunken floors appear to be similar to those found in Germanic settlements on the continent and might further support this hypothesis.

The fortress at Chester was said to have been held by the local native Britons from the time of the Roman departure in AD 407 through to AD 607, when it was wrested from the Welsh rulers of Powys by the king of Northumbria, Aethelfrith. Brief details of these events were noted in the much later *Saxon Chronicles*, which have since been attributed to the ninth century and were known to have often reported from a highly questionable Saxon perspective.

Brochfael, reputed to be a war band leader from Powys, was said to have attempted to defend the city of Chester from the Northumbrian army of King Aethelfrith. However, it was reported that Brochfael's forces were defeated and the Welsh leader only just managed to escape the battle with a small band of his followers. Selyf ap Cynan, said to be the son of the Welsh ruler Cynan Garwen (Cynan White Shanks) from the royal house of Powys, was one notable individual reported to have been killed during this battle.

Early and modern-day excavations at Heronbridge have revealed the remains of 20 or more burials that are thought to be battle casualties from this 'Battle of Chester' and which may well have included members of the Votadini people who had previously been in attendance at the Chester fortress. Legend has it that the Northumbrian army slaughtered some 200 monks from the monastery at Bangor Isycoed as they prayed for a British victory. The Northumbrian king was reported to have said of the monks: 'Whether they bear arms or not, they fight against us by crying to their God.'

Chester was also considered to be the seat for the British Church Synod from around AD 600 and would have included the church based at the nearby

One of the many features of Chester's cathedral, founded as a Norman abbey by Earl Hugh Lupus in 1093.

village of Eccleston. Aethelfrith was thought to be fulfilling a prophesy uttered by Augustine which said: 'If the Welsh will not have peace with us, then they will perish at the hands of the Saxons.'

Some time after this 'Battle of Chester' it was reported that a number of native British princes gathered their forces and marched on the city and in their turn defeated Aethelfrith, forcing him to retire to his native Northumbria. In around AD 617 Aethelfrith himself was said to have been killed while fighting the East Angles who, following their victory, took over large parts of the country.

The Welsh leader Cadwan, or Cadfan, was reported to have been the son of Iago ap Beli, the king of Gwynedd from AD 599 through to AD 613. Cadfan was also noted as being the father of Cadwallon ap Cadfan, the ruler of Gwynedd who would become one of the most notable and important figures in mid-seventh century Britain. Cadfan was recorded on a memorial stone at Llangadwaladr on Anglesey as 'King Cadfan, the wisest and most renowned of all kings', suggesting that his power base was actually centred on the island. His son Cadwallon ap Cadfan was said to have succeeded to the throne of Gwynedd in around 625 and may have been besieged on the isle of Anglesey by Earl Edwin, heir to the kingdom of Deira, who had earlier defeated the king of Northumbria, Aethelfrith. Eventually Cadwallon was forced to abandon the isle of Anglesey and retreat across the Irish Sea to Ireland in around 627. However, having finally allied himself with Penda, the Mercian king, Cadwallon later met and defeated Edwin and was subsequently crowned as (Welsh) King of the Britons at Chester sometime around AD 630.

The fortress was thought to have changed hands many times throughout the next 200 years or so. In AD 869 Aethelred, the king of Mercia, was thought to have dedicated a church to St John in the city. Located outside of the south-eastern defences of the fortress, close to the site of the former Roman amphitheatre, this ecclesiastical centre was granted extensive lands and privileges by the monarch. At some time prior to 1102 this church would become the cathedral for the then Norman city but it would prove to be an unlucky building, suffering at least four collapses and standing today in a fairly ruinous state – its many past glories forgotten with the passage of time.

Directly descended from King Egbert's bloodline, Aethelred was reported to have ordered the construction of St John's Church at Chester as the result of a dream. Legend has it that the king, who was an uncle to Werburga, later St Werburgh (daughter of the king of Mercia), was visiting his niece at her abbey in the city. While there he had a vision which instructed him to build a church where he would see a white hind. Having instructed his entourage to search the area for such a beast, a white hind was said to have been seen at the spot where the church was eventually built.

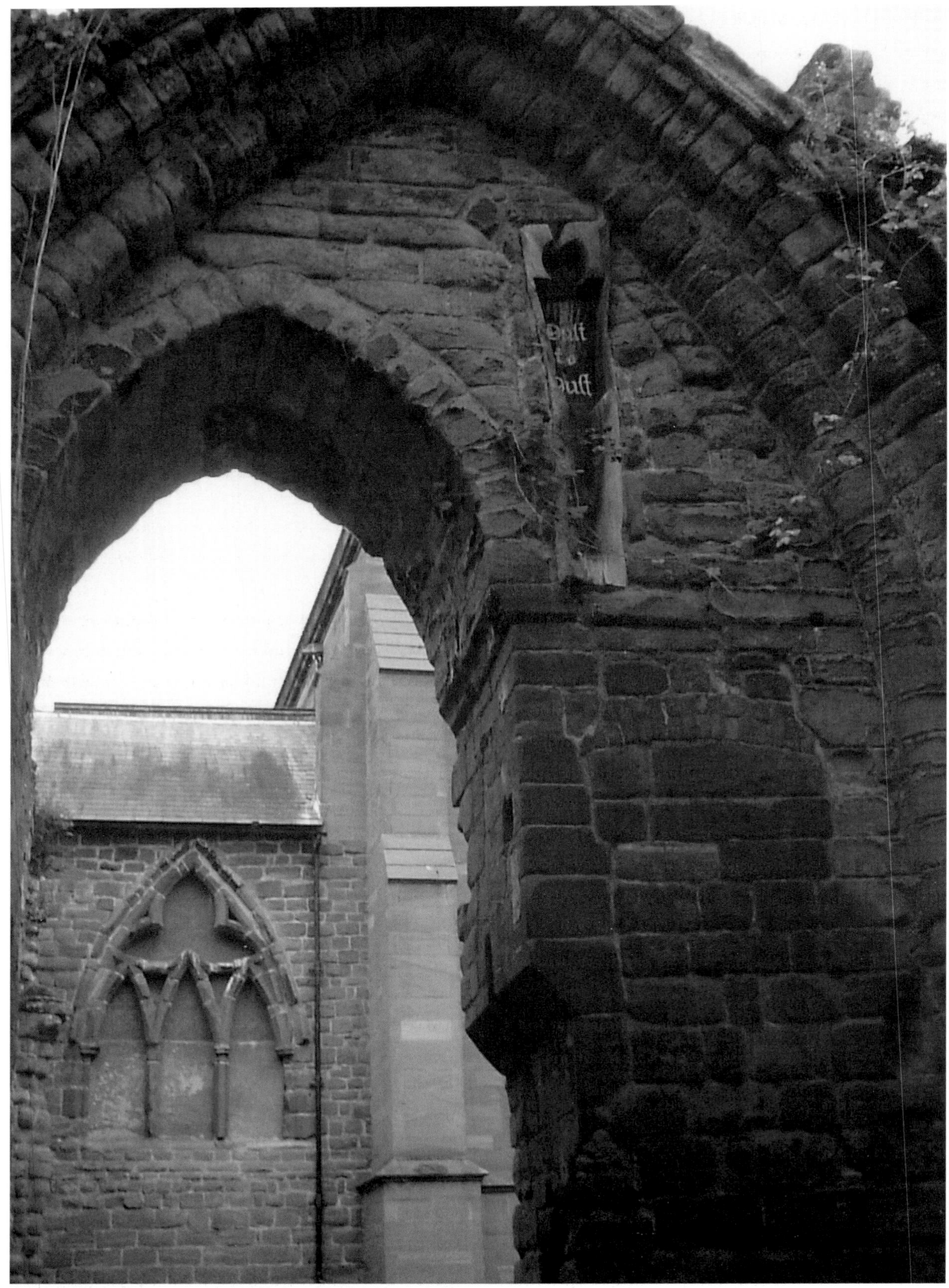

St John's was said to have been constructed as the result of a dream by King Aethelred.

There has been much heated debate over the actual age of St John's Church, with some suggesting that the building dates from around AD 689 – a full 150 years or so before the reign of Aethelred. Others believe that its first construction does indeed date from around the mid-ninth century and was built on the orders of the Saxon king, regardless of the legend that has been associated with its first building.

It is not clear whether or not the city reverted back into Welsh ownership or if it was overtaken by some other force in the following hundred years or so. What is known, though, is that a church dedicated to the memory of the Irish saint Bridget was founded by King Offa in around AD 797 close to the site of the later St Michael's Church, which today houses the Chester heritage centre.

Offa was the king of Mercia around AD 757 and was responsible for the construction of 'Offa's Dyke', which marked the boundary between England and Wales and replaced the earlier 'Wat's Dyke'. This later structure ran from Chester in the north through to Bristol in the south.

Throughout the period of the fifth and sixth centuries the western provinces of Britain were regularly swept by plague and famine which was thought to have decimated the local population, restricting both economic and civil development. The permanent recording of such events was minimal and had it not been for a Welsh priest called Gildas in the sixth century and the Venerable Bede in the eighth century, then even less of the island's history from these periods would exist today. Latin literature and language survived the fall of the Roman Empire and helped form the basis of many of the modern European languages that exist today. It continued to represent a common thread between the emerging nation states and allowed the well-educated and professional classes to communicate across borders and boundaries.

At the same time skill levels among the general working population were thought to have declined in both the manufacturing and construction trades since the end of the Roman period. Non-basic items such as glass and ceramics lacked markets, and building techniques which had been common during the occupation were forgotten or simply unknown to the later generations of artisans. It always was and continues to be a common practice for people to reuse and recycle materials from disused and derelict buildings and it would be fair to assume that this was the case at Chester. In the three centuries following the departure of the Romans it would seem likely that at least some of the internal stone buildings would have been dismantled and taken away for use in other projects or cleared away to allow the land to be reused for general agricultural use and for small-scale domestic habitation.

Where evidence of human habitation has been found, both inside and outside of the fortress's defences, it suggests a relatively modest level of habitation and cultivation. A number of sites have been discovered, all of which indicate isolated pockets of ploughed land and meagre buildings constructed with simple timbers and covered with thatched roofs. One of these sites, which was located behind the modern western frontages of Lower Bridge Street, close to the river, suggested that there had been limited use of the land followed by a period of abandonment and then a further period of use.

The Lower Bridge Street area of the city which has produced evidence of early post-Roman settlement outside of the military fortress.

Such irregular use of the land surrounding the former fortress may support the contention that its people partially abandoned the city and were soon dispersed to other parts of the region, until the city became much more economically active and secure. This may in part be true, but it seems highly unlikely that a total abandonment of the fortress would have taken place given that it would have offered shelter and a degree of security within its walls. Local springs and wells would have also provided the inhabitants with fresh water and the nearby River Dee would have represented an ideal food source.

In addition to all these local benefits and resources, the river itself offered much in terms of trading and of course transportation. Chester was still ideally located to benefit from the continuing trade between the ports of Britain, Ireland and continental Europe. The lead and silver mines of Flintshire, so heavily exploited by the Roman Empire, were still producing their precious metals and Chester was the obvious place from which to export such materials.

It is entirely plausible therefore, that in these uncertain and turbulent years a proportion of the civilian population actually moved into the surrounding areas which bordered the river and which would later develop into the suburban communities of Handbridge, Saltney and Blacon. It was here that they could found their settlements, safe in the knowledge that the fortress defences remained nearby should the area become insecure.

It is also likely that Chester survived the withdrawal of the Romans and the subsequent centuries of wars and disputes with a much reduced civilian population that managed to coexist with whatever military force happened to be in power at that particular moment. Given the nature of the fortress's inner precincts at the time of the Roman departure, it seems unlikely that any resident force or population would be willing or indeed able to make wholesale changes to either the shape or fabric of the base itself, given their limited skills, knowledge and manpower. The remains of the legionary bathhouses apparently resisted all civil development up until the early 1960s and were only finally removed when they was attacked with modern machinery. The apparent lack of evidential materials for this period may just as likely be caused by the city's inhabitants occupying a much smaller area of the fortress which has thus far escaped identification. It is also a possibility that extensive restructuring and building in later centuries has completely removed or destroyed many of these Dark Age materials.

Following its inclusion into the kingdom of Mercia in the middle of the ninth century and the foundation of the Christian religious orders in both the eighth and ninth centuries, Chester enjoyed a period of steady development and growth for the best part of a hundred years or so. The growth of its churches and monasteries, coupled with its economic resurgence as a result of its international trading, all combined to enhance the influence, reputation and prosperity of the former Roman fortress. This success, however, had not gone unnoticed and towards the end of the ninth century the city was regarded as a prime target for the greedy ambitions of the much feared Vikings.

Ingimund was the leader of a band of Norse-Irish people that had been expelled from the Dublin area of Ireland and landed in Wales around AD 860 seeking a place to settle. The Welsh tribes were less than welcoming and it was reported that the sons of the great Welsh leader Rhodri Mawr drove Ingimund and his people from their lands. It appears that the refugees then approached the Saxon leader Aethelflaeda who controlled Chester and requested the gift of lands where they might finally settle and build a community. It has been suggested that Ingimund and his people were granted lands around the Heronbridge area, the site of the former Roman settlement and where there does appear to be evidence of Viking construction. Other accounts suggest that Ingimund and his followers were actually granted lands on the Wirral Peninsula to the north of Chester, but no definitive evidence either way has come to light which might fully settle the matter.

Having settled peacefully in the area for a number of years, it then appears that Ingimund and his people began to cast an envious eye on the apparently wealthy city of Chester which lay nearby and began to plan for its capture. He was reported to have colluded with other leaders to demand the surrender of the city under the threat of force, but, unfortunately for Ingimund and his comrades, Aethelflaeda had heard rumours regarding the planned raid and ensured that the city's forces and defences were substantially strengthened before any raid could actually take place.

York was captured by the Danish invaders in around AD 867 and within the next 10 years they had managed to overrun much of the Mercian kingdom, including the Midlands and East Anglia. The north-western part of the kingdom though remained relatively unscathed by the troubles, including the vitally important seaport and fortress at Chester. Around AD 893 however, the Danish army finally turned its full attention to the city and after marching across the country from Essex they seem to have easily taken Chester from its Saxon defenders. Within the city's defences there was known to be a small Norse community who traded there and it has long been suspected that members of this community were instrumental in allowing the Danish army access to the city.

Records in the *Anglo-Saxon Chronicle* for the period describe the city as 'Waste' Chester, which implies the city was partially deserted or derelict as a result of the Viking incursion. However, some historians suggest that this description is purely the result of a corruption of the word for 'West' Cheshire and that in reality the city remained in relatively good order. A Mercian mint was known to have existed in the north-west of England in around AD 890 and it was reported to have been sited at Chester, which would not have been the case if the city had been deemed to be economically unsound or insecure.

The Danish raiders were thought to have held the city for the winter months only and then deserted the fortress in the early part of AD 894 after being starved into submission by the local Anglo-Saxon forces who had removed or destroyed all the available food stores from the immediate area. It has also been suggested that the local Anglo-Saxon forces around Chester were supplemented by a large number of Welsh troops provided by the ruler of Gwynedd, Anarawd ap Rhodri, the third son of the late great Welsh King Rhodri Mawr. When Anarawd died in around 916 he was reported to have been buried as King of the Britons (Welsh) according to the Welsh Chronicles and was then succeeded by his two sons who took control of much of the North Wales region.

A direct result of this major incursion was the building of a defensive network within the Saxon kingdom that would ultimately protect all of its towns and cities from the Danish army and at the same time totally isolate the Norse invaders. Alfred, the young king of Wessex and later Mercia, was said to have developed a series of defensive settlements or burhs that would help secure the borders of his kingdom. To further counter the threat which came from the nearby Wirral Peninsula and the Danes that were based in Ireland, Alfred was said to have agreed a treaty with their leaders, which guaranteed them land to settle in return for a continued peace.

To help finally neutralise the threat from both the east and the north a refortification of the kingdom's northerly border at the River Mersey was undertaken and the old hill fort at Eddisbury to the east of Chester was rebuilt and strengthened. The defences of the fortress itself were rebuilt and extended so that they would now fully enclose both the southern and western areas of the city which had grown up outside of the original compound since Roman times.

The northern defences of the fortress were extended further westward until they met the banks

The southern defences which at one time would have protected Chester from Welsh tribesman attacking the city from Handbridge.

of the river. In modern-day Chester this represents the length of the city walls between the later Morgan's Mount, past Pemberton's Parlour and terminating close to what is the site of the later water tower. This extension to the original defences effectively secured the whole of the western flank of the buhr, simply by employing the river as an additional natural barrier to any invading force.

A defensive palisade was thought to have run south from the northern wall, parallel to the remaining length of the earlier Roman western fortress wall and incorporating the modern-day areas of King Street, Princess Street and Watergate Street. It then continued on, past the south-west corner of the fortress walls towards the river and enveloping the area of the Saxon earthwork defences, later the Norman Castle which in turn was itself replaced by the modern-day Chester Castle and county hall. Much of the land which now lay within the city's western flanks was said to be open and undeveloped and was generally used as small-scale agricultural plots by the local inhabitants. The ruins of the former Roman buildings which had once existed outside of the main fortress and continued to stand in these areas were almost certainly demolished around this time and their materials reused for other local construction projects. The defences then continued eastward, a little north of the line of the river and past the developing business communities which were starting to establish themselves in the south of the settlement. This southern wall then continued to run on to a meeting with the original eastern defences of the Roman fortress which had been newly extended southward towards the river. It seems likely that these extensions to the northern and eastern defences and the relocation of the western and southern defences were constructed using part or all of the materials from the original Roman fortress. Both the original western and southern walls of the former Roman defensive compound are known to have disappeared at some point in time and it seems reasonable to assume that this was due in part to a later extension of the defences by its then Saxon inhabitants.

The construction of such formidable defences would have taken a considerable period of time and despite their being generally credited to Aethelflaeda in AD 907 it seems likely that the continued protection of the city was undertaken on a fairly long-term basis. That the raiders of AD 893 are thought to have required help from a 'fifth columnist' who helped to gain entry into the city suggests that the site itself was adequately defended during the period, further supporting the notion of a defensive palisade or wall being in place before that time.

The *Saxon Chronicles* record that Chester was rebuilt by AD 907 but this may only reflect the final phase of the reconstruction work which was undertaken as a direct result of the earlier incursion. King Alfred, the actual architect of the buhr system, was dead by AD 899 and this work appears to have been continued by his successor Edward the Elder. It now seems far more likely that the development of these defences was the result of continuous upgrading, which had started with the Danish invasion of York in AD 867 some 40 years earlier.

Around AD 875 the earthly remains of St Werburgh were reported to have been brought to Chester in order to protect them from the Danish army that had invaded the country and her final resting place soon became a place of pilgrimage for many Christians. The daughter of King Wulfhere and a niece to King Aethelred, she had devoted her life to the founding and development of convents throughout the kingdom of Mercia. She died at Hanbury in around AD 690 and was initially buried within the precincts of the convent that was located there. When her remains were removed to Chester they were re-interred in the existing church of St Peter and St Paul's in the city centre. The church itself was enlarged and rededicated to St Werburgh by Aethelflaeda, Lady of the Mercians, in around AD 907. A new church was constructed within the city,

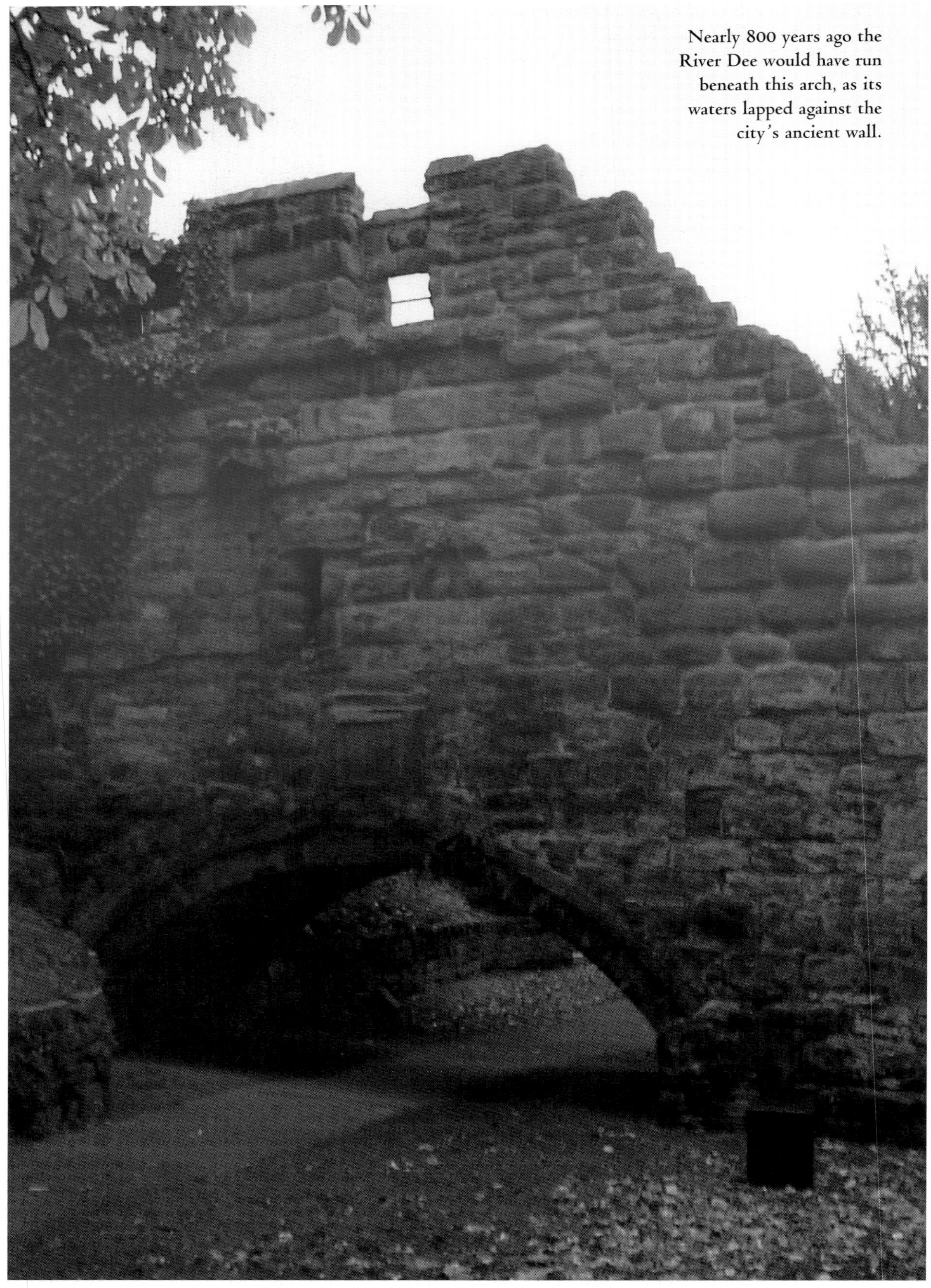

Nearly 800 years ago the River Dee would have run beneath this arch, as its waters lapped against the city's ancient wall.

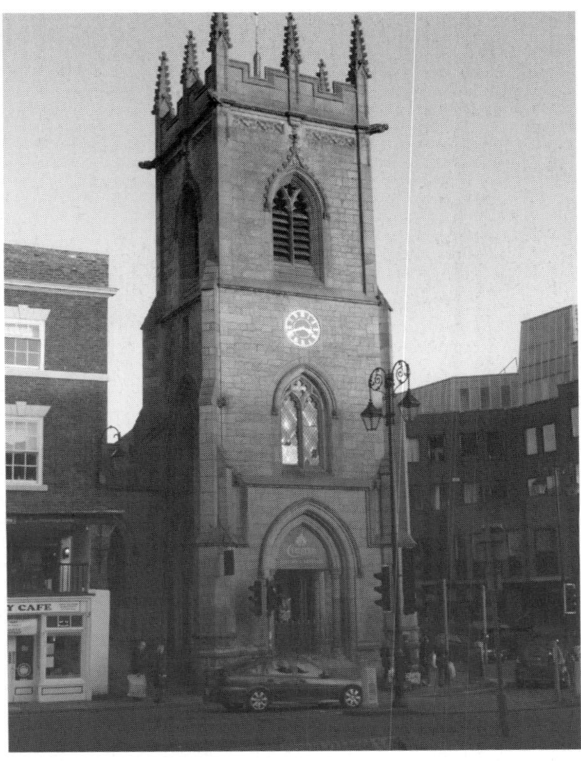

St Bridget's Church stood opposite the modern-day St Michael's Heritage Centre and originally dated from the eighth century.

above the remains of the Roman *principia* building and was itself rededicated to St Peter. A little over 200 years later the second Norman Earl, Hugh Lupus, who ruled Cheshire after the Norman Conquests, would devote an abbey to the memory of St Werburgh which would later become the city's magnificent cathedral.

Later relationships between the inhabitants of Chester and those that lived on the Welsh side of the border were not always so agreeable, however, and around AD 916 Aethelflaeda was said to have attacked the Welsh kingdom of Brycheiniog as a warning to its ruler Tewder ab Elise. Idwal Foel, the ruler of Gwynedd from AD 916 to 942, was reported to have organised a revolt at Chester in AD 924 in an act of defiance against the English monarch Edward the Elder. In AD 925 Edward's successor, Athelstan, made peace with the leaders of the Welsh tribes including Hywel Dda and Owain, the king of Gwent, and together they would meet and defeat a Danish force at Bromborough on the Wirral Peninsula in around AD 937.

Aethelflaeda, the Mercian queen and daughter of the late King Alfred, was reported to have died in AD 922 at Tamworth. She is known to have been vital to the security of her kingdom and was instrumental in the rebuilding and refortification of many towns and cities throughout the whole of Mercia and Wessex. Some 17 years after her death Britain would receive a new name from the kings of Wessex, Engla Land – a title that would survive for over a thousand years and remains with us today.

The 50 years of relative peace that had passed by was finally ended in around AD 965 when a new wave of incursions by the Danes began. They established their bases on the Wirral and throughout the next 20 years or so would devastate much of the Cheshire area. However, Chester was obviously fairly safe from the menace of these invaders as the then king, Edgar, was reported to have visited the city by sea around AD 972. Nominated as 'The Peaceable', the Anglo-Saxon monarch was reported to have visited Chester in order to receive tribute from the eight subordinate kings or *reguli* that were subject to him, and to build alliances with rulers whose lands bordered the Irish Sea where many of the Viking raids originated from. Legend has it that these eight *reguli* rowed him upriver from the site of Edgar's Field in Handbridge to the ancient church of St John's on the opposite bank of the River Dee. While the other monarchs rowed Edgar was said to have steered the boats rudder, indicating his right to steer the 'ship of state' perhaps? Once at St John's these subordinates were required to swear a sacred oath of allegiance to Edgar before once more rowing the king back down the river to the journey's starting point. The subordinate kings were reported to have included: Kenneth, King of Scotland; Malcolm, King of Cumberland; Maccus, King of Anglesey; Dunmael, King of Strathclyde; Siferth and Hywel, Princes of Wales; Iago, King of Venedotia and finally Nichil, King of Westmoreland. Iago ab Idwal, the sole ruler of

Formerly a tavern dating from the 16/17th century but now a private dwelling, this building was possibly associated with King Edgar whose 'Edgar's Field' is located on the southern bank of the River Dee.

Gwynedd (Venedotia) was later forced to share his kingdom with his nephew Hywel ab Ieuaf and as a result was said to have entered into a plot with a band of Viking raiders in AD 974. However, things did not work out as Iago expected and he was thought to have been kidnapped by his former employees in AD 979 and was never seen again.

In AD 976 there was a great famine in England which, despite the wealth that many of its inhabitants had accumulated in the past decades, would have some effect on the city. Then, in AD 980 a further tragedy struck the fortress when it was raided by the Danish forces from the Wirral who plundered the wealth of the city.

Despite these troubles and setbacks, Chester remained a vital geographical location for the trade and defence of the kingdom. In AD 1000 King Aethelred II sailed his navy to and from the city in support of his army that was campaigning in Cumberland at that time. The monarch's unfortunate designation as 'the unready' appears to have been well deserved, as he seemed to have lacked both the skill and vision of many of his forebears throughout his life. His failure to control events, both inside and outside of his kingdom, would ultimately have dire consequences for the future of the country, both in the short and long term.

The Danes, under their king, Sveyn Forkbeard, landed in England in 1003 and began their conquest of the country. Within a decade large swathes of land were under his control and its native people were subject to his rule. By the time of his death in 1014 Sveyn had subjugated much of England. In 1017 one of his sons, Canute, ascended to the throne, his brother Harald becoming the king of Denmark at the same time. The period between his father's death and

Canute's actual succession were turbulent years with opposing groups wreaking havoc throughout the whole of England. Chester was recorded to have been attacked and then plundered by marauding Northumbrian forces in around 1016 – an event that does seem to have been fairly typical of the time.

The new king tried to consolidate his position in England by marrying Emma who had been queen to the late Saxon king, Aethelred II. During his reign Canute also became king of both Denmark and Norway and during his often regular absences in Scandinavia he used powerful English and Danish earls to assist in the government of the country. To help in this process he split England into four separate earldoms, Northumbria, Wessex, East Anglia and Mercia, and he arranged that each one should be ruled with common government and laws.

Following the reigns of Harold Harefoot (1035–40) and Hardicanute (1040–42), the English crown finally returned to the House of Wessex when Edward the Confessor ascended the throne in 1042. Although an astute ruler and statesman it was said to be Edward's political manoeuvrings that ultimately led to the later Norman invasion of Britain by the illegitimate son of the Duke Robert of Normandy, the man more commonly called William the Conqueror. It was also during Edward's reign that Aelfgar, the son of Leofric of Mercia, inherited his father's titles, including control of the historic fortress at Chester which lay within the earldom of Mercia. This title and possession was later passed to his eldest son Edwin, who succeeded to his father's estates on Aelfgar's death.

Along with his brother Morcar, the Earl of the Northumbrians, Earl Edwin remained in control of these lands throughout the period leading up to and beyond the Norman conquest of England and was instrumental in leading and coordinating later Saxon opposition to William's continuing rule of the country. The brothers were also said to have offered their protection to King Harold's widow, Ealdgyth, who was their sister, following the fateful Battle of Hastings. William's subsequent 'Harrying of the North', which saw the northern regions subjugated by the French invaders, also saw Earl Edwin assassinated by his own men in 1071 and his brother Morcar captured and imprisoned by William the Conqueror.

It is worth noting that Harold's widow Ealdgyth had previously been married to the ruler of Gwynedd, Gruffudd ap Llewellyn ap Seisyll, who had been an ally of Ealdgyth's late grandfather, Earl Leofric of Mercia. With his lands under threat from rival noblemen and the emerging kingdom of Wessex, Leofric had turned to his nearest neighbour, Gruffudd, in order to build military and political alliances which might guarantee the security of his lands and the inheritance of his family. As part of this alliance his granddaughter Ealdgyth was betrothed to the Welsh ruler in around 1057, further strengthening the bond between the two families.

However, sometime around 1063 Harold Godwinson, the ruler of Wessex, attacked Gruffudd's lands and laid waste to his stronghold at Rhuddlan. In an often bitter campaign the Welsh ruler was forced back into the interior of his homeland and with little hope of a Welsh victory his own forces turned against him and killed him. Harold was later reported to have taken Gruffudd's widow Ealdgyth as his wife, thereby securing a relationship with the northern kingdom of Mercia and receiving the submission from Gruffudd's successor in Gwynedd.

Such were his close ties with his new wife's family that Harold was reported to have deliberately put them before his own brother in at least one particular instance. Morcar, the brother of Ealdgyth, was said to have dispossessed Harold's brother Tostig of the earldom of Northumbria, an act that does not appear to have been objected to by his new brother-in-law. It has also been stated that Earl Morcar was aided in his Northumbrian campaign by troops supplied by the new ruler of Gwynedd, Bleddyn ap Cynfyn – the same monarch who had made submission to Tostig's brother Harold.

In the year 1066 Edward the Confessor, the Saxon King of England, died without an heir to succeed him and Harold Godwinson of Wessex immediately proclaimed himself King Harold II. The lands in Northumbria, Mercia and East Anglia were then claimed by Canute's successor in Denmark, King Sveyn II, but these same lands were also claimed by Harald 'the ruthless' Hardrada in Norway and by William, Duke of Normandy, the illegitimate son of the late Robert of Normandy.

Later that year Harald Hardrada of Norway set sail for England to settle his claim on these lands and was met at Stamford Bridge by the forces led by Harold Godwinson, who subsequently defeated the Norwegian invaders. It has also been reported that Hardrada's forces included Harold Godwinson's brother Tostig who had a personal score to settle. The king's two brothers-in-law were thought to have been absent from the Battle of Stamford Bridge and the later fateful Battle of Hastings, having been required to remain at home and secure their respective earldoms in the north of the country.

As Harold II was busily occupied in settling the terms for the withdrawal of the surviving Norwegian army, William, Duke of Normandy, was able to land and establish his Norman forces at the port of Hastings. Having regrouped his army, Harold Godwinson was then forced to march his men over 200 miles to meet this new threat to his authority. Having raced across country to meet this new enemy, Harold was subsequently defeated by the forces of William, close to their landing site. Following the death of Harold and the complete defeat of the native English forces the young Norman duke soon received his new designation as William the Conqueror, later crowned as King William I of England.

Despite his emphatic victory at Hastings William was not immediately accepted by the native population of England and found his occupation was strongly resisted in many parts of the country. Over the coming years he would initiate a reign of terror and a culture of control in which the fortress at Chester would play a vital part. The ruins of its Roman defences and buildings would be enhanced, its military and strategic importance would be increased and it would later come to achieve national status as one of the most important cities within the English kingdom.

Chapter 7

A City of Death and Divinity

The earldom of Mercia, the region to which Chester belonged, was still held by Earl Edwin who had first inherited it from his father Aelfgar and he in turn from his own father Earl Leofric. It was, and continued to be, regarded by him as his own personal fiefdom and a change of English monarch was unlikely to alter that. In view of this, and despite William's military victory at Hastings, Earl Edwin was not inclined to bow easily to the new king's authority. A number of contemporary reports have suggested that both Edwin and Morcar, his brother that held the earldom of Northumbria, had initially been prepared to accept William as their sovereign but were later persuaded otherwise by the Norman leader's actions and demands.

No doubt supported by a number of his tenant lords and neighbouring landowners, it appears that Edwin hoped that William and his forces would eventually be defeated by one of the number of individual princes and regional leaders that were disputing the Norman leader's right to rule England. The Welsh ruler of Gwynedd, Bleddyn ap Cynfyn, who was allied to Edwin and who had earlier supplied troops for Morcar's seizure of Northumbria was one such leader. In the two years following the Battle of Hastings the conquering French forces were thought to have met and defeated all those that had stood against them and in around 1068 they were finally able to turn their full attention to the north-west region of the country.

Because of their continued resistance to him and in order to perhaps make an example of them, William and his forces devastated the region, seizing lands, burning crops, slaughtering livestock and dispossessing the people of their properties. As they occupied each area of the region earlier fortifications were rebuilt and strengthened in order to fully control the lives of the local population. In a little over 12 months William's forces were said to have crushed all opposition to his rule in the region and despite a last ditch attempt at resistance in 1069, by 1070 the Normans were reported to have been besieging the city of Chester itself.

Here too, he was unrelenting in his persecution of all those who had stood against him. The city eventually fell to William's forces and once it had his army were said to have sacked its inner precincts and dismantled or destroyed its ancient defences. In the surrounding countryside Saxon lords and landowners, such as Leofine and Leofwine, were generally dispossessed at the cost of their lives with their properties granted to leading members of the new Norman administration. The three main protagonists that had marshalled the local Saxon opposition to William were thought to have met entirely different fates. Bleddyn ap Cynfyn was said to have made peace with William, Earl Edwin was reported to have been assassinated by his own men and his brother Morcar was held prisoner for the remainder of his life.

Leofine was reportedly a Saxon freeman who held the manor of Saughall (Salhare) just outside of the city. His compatriot Leofwine was thought to have been a major landowner in Chester during the reign of Edward the Confessor and was said to have held title to lands in the Handbridge area of the city. An ancient chapel, dedicated to St James, was said to have existed close to the site of the modern-day St Mary's Church in the township which may also have been the location of the Earl's Palace in Chester. This building was reported to have existed up until the 16th century but was then subsequently abandoned and disappeared without trace.

William Mallbank was reported to have been granted the lordship of the manor at Saughall (Salhare) following the Norman conquest of

Chester. Only two thirds of the manor was under the direct control of Mallbank himself, the remaining third was said to have been in the hands of the nearby St Werburgh's Abbey. In around 1080 the second Norman Earl of Chester, Hugh Lupus, was thought to have ordered the construction of a motte and bailey castle at Shotwick, which lay just to the west of the Saughall (Salhare) township. Lying on the eastern bank of the River Dee, this rugged defensive structure formed an important part of William's plan to protect his newly conquered lands from the native Welsh princes that at the time lay outside of his control.

With the city and the country fully secured William I was now able to focus his attention on other matters and within a year or so was to lead a mixed French and English force campaigning in France. The 'Conqueror' would subsequently die in the same fashion as he lived, as a warrior. On the 9 September 1087 William I, Duke of Normandy and King of England, died after succumbing to wounds that he had received at the French town of Mantes. He was succeeded by his second son, William Rufus, who would later be crowned as King William II.

Chester had originally been left in the charge of one of William's most trusted lieutenants Walter De Gerbod, who was appointed as the first Norman Earl of Chester. However, Walter seems to have grown tired of the arduous campaigning in Britain and shortly afterwards returned to his properties in Normandy. It has also been suggested that Walter was captured by his enemies on his return home and subsequently held prisoner, thereby preventing his return to Britain and taking up the post of earl of Chester.

Walter was then succeeded by one of William's other relatives, Hugh Lupus, who would later become known as Hugh 'The Wolf' or Hugh 'The Fat'. The latter name was possibly more appropriate for him as most records would describe him as being so fat that he could hardly walk. He was also described as being a persistent womaniser who fathered innumerable children, most of which would die in their infancy. The son of Richard of Goz, Viscount of Avranches in south-west Normandy, Hugh was reported to have inherited vast estates and wealth from his father. He acted as counsellor to the Conqueror, as well as providing ships for the actual Norman invasion of England. It has also been suggested that he did not fight at the Battle of Hastings but was left at home in Normandy in order to secure the estates of those knights that were away fighting.

As Earl of Chester Hugh was also appointed as the Sword Bearer of England which entitled him to carry the sword of St Edward, often called the 'Curtana' or 'Sword of Mercy' at state occasions. The sword is said to be inscribed on the hilt with 'Hugo Comes Cestriae', which translates as 'Hugh, our brother at Chester' and is today held in the care of the British Museum.

At the time of his receiving the earldom of Chester he was still a relatively young man, with some records suggesting he was only in his early 20s. The office gifted to him by William made Hugh the largest landowner in England and his rights as earl were equal to those of the king himself within the region. He was held responsible for the government and security of the kingdom in the North West of England and it was under his rule that a network of castles were built to protect the Cheshire region from the princes of North Wales and other Irish raiders. These motte and bailey-type castles were built at Dodleston, Shotwick, Shocklach, Aldford, Oldcastle and Malpas and were in addition to those constructed at both Chester and Beeston.

An early success for Hugh was the capture of the Welsh prince Gruffydd ap Cynan in around 1081. He was said to have succeeded to the rule of North Wales following the death of Trahaern ap Caradog, who had recovered the kingdom from an earlier Welsh ruler Gruffudd ap Cynan ap Iago. The unfortunate prisoner was reported to have been held in chains for 10 years or more for both the

The Grosvenor Park Lodge building was designed by John Douglas as his first commission for the Grosvenor family. The Lodge depicts a number of the Norman earls of Chester on its upper half-timbered walls.

convenience and amusement of the earl and his company. It was little wonder that Hugh was so despised by the Welsh people and their leaders. He was now able to fully exploit the power vacuum that his imprisonment had caused and his Norman lords were able to seize great tracts of lands within North Wales and bring them under their direct control. Gruffudd's successor in Wales during his captivity is recorded as Rhys ap Tewder, who was said to have met with William in 1086 and signed an agreement with the king which left him with control of much of Wales while accepting William as his overlord.

To aid him in his day-to-day governance of the earldom, Hugh was known to have been supported by a number of under-tenants or lieutenants who held both lands and rights of domain within the north-west region. The most important and influential of these was Robert of Rhuddlan who was the son of Humphrey of Tilleul, the man charged with erecting the temporary fortress at Hastings which had aided William's forces in their first vital battle on English soil. Robert himself was said to have been a favourite of the late English king Edward the Confessor and around 1073 was reported to have built a castle at Rhuddlan which would be instrumental in the pacification of the Welsh princes and their people. Robert was said to have been the Norman lord responsible for capturing the Welsh Prince Gruffudd ap Cynan in 1081 and had been in fairly regular conflict with various Welsh princes for a number of years.

Legend tells us that sometime around 1088 Robert was staying at a smaller fort located near Deganwy in North Wales. A band of raiders were reported to have attacked lands in the nearby area and Robert had gone out to deal with them without

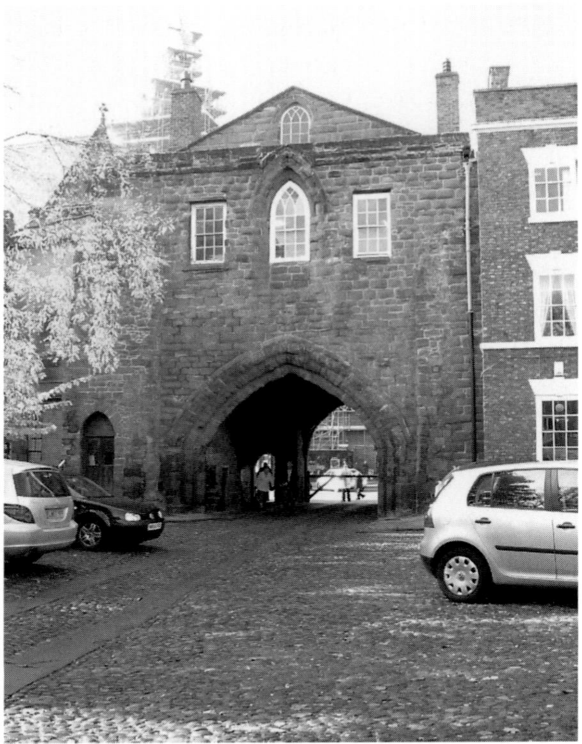

The main gateway of Chester's historic Norman abbey which was founded by Earl Hugh Lupus in 1093, succeeding an earlier Anglo-Saxon religious minster established by Aethelflaeda to house the earthly remains of St Werburgh.

having first properly prepared his own protection. Initially wounded by an arrow or bolt fired from some distance, it was said that the Welsh raiders then set about him and decapitated him before carrying his head away as a trophy. His remains were said to have been recovered by his friends and later carried to Chester, where he was buried at the Abbey of St Werburgh's.

Some two years before his 'reported' death however, Robert, along with the other Norman lords, would have been busy making arrangements for the assessment and recording of land ownership within England. The resulting *Domesday Book* remains as a permanent legacy of the Norman period and was the means by which landowners and citizens alike were assessed for tribute to the crown. The list had to include every animal, holding or asset held within a particular area, in order that its liability to the king could be properly assessed, demanded and paid.

Robert le Montalt was reported to have been granted Mold by Hugh Lupus to hold against his enemies. The town itself was in an important location, commanding as it did a vitally strategic approach to the city of Chester from North Wales. Robert was reported to have constructed a castle on the hill in the centre of the town which commanded the surrounding roads and countryside. Despite its rugged construction it failed to survive indefinitely and around 1147 was said to have been captured by the forces of the Welsh leader Olwain Gwynnedd and subsequently destroyed.

Shortly after the death of William the Conqueror and possibly around the time that Gruffudd ap Cynan was captured by Robert of Rhuddlan in 1081, large parts of the border area between England and Wales were taken under the control of a number of Norman knights. Huge tracts of both Gwynedd and Powys were thought to have been seized by the likes of Roger of Montgomery the Earl of Shrewsbury, Roger de Lacy and Ralph Mortimer. They were then said to have come into dispute with William Rufus who, rather than settle matters, was reported to have left England with a number of his leading knights and left the dispute to simmer. When he did finally return to England in around 1095 he found that these land seizures had led to a series of Welsh rebellions and uprisings, which were said to have lasted for a further two years.

Between 1094 and 1097 a native Welsh leader Cadwgan ap Cynan had led a determined resistance to the annexation of the Welsh border lands which had been seized by the Norman landowners. However, towards the end of 1097 these rounds of rebellion were beginning to wane and a sort of uneasy peace was starting to settle around the region. Welsh unrest in the area was once again reignited following the reappearance of Gruffudd ap Cynan, who was thought to have escaped his captivity at Chester Castle some three years later. Whether or not his escape had been just pure good fortune or was a deliberate act on the part of his Norman captors is not entirely clear but some historians have speculated that Gruffudd was purposely released in order to undermine the power and influence of his successor, Cadwgan.

No doubt some sort of immediate retribution had been wrought on the local population for Robert of Rhuddlan's death, but it was thought to be a full 10 years before Earl Hugh attempted any serious military advance into the province. In around 1098 Lupus and the second Earl of Shrewsbury, Hugh of Montgomery, were said to have launched a major military campaign into Wales to reclaim the lands of Gwynnedd from the Welsh princes Gruffydd ap Cynan and Cadwgan ap Cynan. The Norman earls were thought to have been aided in their military campaign by Owain ab Tewder, a leading Welsh landowner, who held extensive lands and assets in and around Chester which he was keen to retain should the conflict go against his fellow Welshmen. Fortunately for Tewder, things did not go that well for Gruffudd and Cadwgan and the Welsh princes were eventually forced back onto the Isle of Anglesey and when that was besieged they were finally forced to withdraw to Ireland in order to escape the Norman earls and their troops.

Despite the Welsh leaders' abandonment of their native lands the two Norman earls were not able to consolidate their gains immediately, which resulted in a military vacuum being created. Hugh's future plans for the region were thrown into turmoil when a Norwegian fleet under their leader Magnus Barefoot unexpectedly arrived in the area and began attacking the Norman forces. It has been suggested that the Viking fleet had been in the area to subdue a rogue Viking leader that was holding control of the Isle of Man, but having become aware of the conflict on Anglesey had decided to become involved in the dispute. Hugh Lupus's ally, Hugh of Montgomery, was reported to have been killed during one of the many skirmishes with Barefoot's forces, and Lupus himself was forced to withdraw from the region.

Following the Norman retreat from Wales, Gruffydd and Cadwgan were able to return from Ireland and recover their lands virtually unopposed. Legend suggests that rather than launch any new campaigns against the Welsh and risk a similar result, Lupus came to an agreement with Gruffydd and Cadwgan which allowed the Welsh leaders to hold title to their native lands in return for recognising the earl's overall authority. Despite this formal agreement with Gruffydd and Cadwgan, Hugh seems to have been largely despised by the majority of his Welsh subjects. As part of the treaty which was agreed in 1099 Cadwgan was said to have been given the Welsh regions of Powys and Ceredigion and Gruffudd was granted parts of Gwynedd as well as the Isle of Anglesey.

Back at Chester, and in order to enlarge and repopulate the city, Hugh was reported to have created three asylums in and around the city where criminals and wanted men could live without fear of the law. Hoole Heath, Over Marsh near Farndon and Rudheath near Middlewich were said to have been repopulated by these outlaws, making Cheshire one of the most colourful and dangerous places in the

A stained-glass window in Chester Cathedral depicting Earl Hugh Lupus and related characters. Earl Hugh died in 1101 and was interred within the abbey.

country. These asylums were thought to have existed for nearly 600 years and were only finally abolished during the reign of James I.

When he died in 1101 Hugh Lupus was said to have been a member of the abbey community for three days prior to his demise. His remains were initially interred beneath the chapter house of the abbey although it has been suggested that his body was removed at a later date and relocated in another part of the building.

Hugh's legitimate heir, born to him and his wife Ermentrude, was his son Richard who inherited the title at seven years of age in around 1101 when his father, the second earl, died. He was reported to have been educated in France and raised alongside the children of the monarch, Henry I, and was very much a favourite of the royal family. However, Richard was later thought to have drowned, along with the king's son, Prince William, in the *White Ship* (*Candida Navis*) which foundered on 6 December 1120. Richard's wife Maud, who was the daughter of Earl Stephen of Blois and Adela, a daughter of William the Conqueror, was also drowned in the disaster.

At around the same time that Hugh Lupus passed away, a Norman noble, Richard Pincerna, was said to have gifted the church of St Olave's to the Abbey of St Werburgh. This relatively small church was reported to have been dedicated to King Olaf Haroldson, the Norwegian monarch who was killed at the Battle of Stiklestad in 1030. He later became a cult Christian figure in his homeland and a large number of foreign churches were known to have been dedicated to his memory. The church in Chester was thought to have been built by members of the large Scandinavian community which had existed in the city from around the beginning of the eighth century. Known to have always been a highly impoverished church, throughout its history it only just managed to eke out a meagre existence. In 1393 it was temporarily amalgamated with the much larger parish of St Mary's which stood alongside Chester's historic castle, but by the end of the English Civil War, along with much of the city, it was said to have been in a fairly ruinous condition and as a result was effectively closed down for the next 100 years or so.

It was only from around 1750 that the church was said to have been reinstated as a city parish in its own right, but this only lasted through to around 1840 when the parish of St Olave's ceased to exist within Chester. In the same year the church building

St Olave's Church was dedicated to King Olaf and is now associated with the city's early Hiberno-Norse community.

was closed as a place of worship and its parish turned over to the nearby church St Michael's.

Even today the *Domesday Book* continues to offer an almost complete list of every community in existence at that particular time in Britain. There are two interesting facts that are illustrated in this regional record. The first is that the Wirral Peninsula was at that time regarded as being part of Cheshire with large areas of the region held by the ill-fated Robert of Rhuddlan, who was reported to have died shortly after its completion. Secondly, the *Domesday Book* indicates that the vast majority of lands were not only held by Hugh Lupus himself, but also by the Bishop of Chester and the monks from the Abbey of St Werburgh's. These records support the idea that the main religious centres within Chester had become extremely powerful and wealthy under both the Saxon lords and their Norman successors. It was a situation that would only finally be altered some 500 years later when the church chose to directly oppose the wishes of a reigning monarch, a decision that would eventually cost them much of their accumulated power and wealth.

The canons that ran the early Saxon minster of St Werburgh are recorded to have held substantial lands in and around the city of Chester and particularly at Saigton, a few miles outside the city limits. Under the later Benedictine monks these lands would be turned into a 1,000 acre park which provided both food and cereal crops for the brothers at the abbey. The markets and fairs held within the city limits, one at Abbey Gate close to the current town hall square and the other at the High Cross, would have also provided the opportunity to sell any excess products to the local population and so generate extra income for the abbey's coffers. The monk's ownership of the park at Saigton was said to have lasted for over 500 years until the dissolution of the monasteries by Henry VIII. Around 1249 the monks were reported to have fortified their grange at Saigton in order to defend the building and its lands from bands of marauding Welshmen and in 1490 its gatehouse was rebuilt and marked with the image of a black dog, along with the motto 'Advance Boldly'.

Originally granted their charter in 1092 by Earl Hugh, the Abbey of St Weburgh replaced the earlier Saxon monastery which had also been dedicated to the same saint. Hugh requested that the abbey pray for him and his family after their deaths and its foundation was so important to him that he invited Anselm of Bec, who would later become Archbishop of Canterbury, to witness the granting of the charter. From around 1093 to 1116 there was an extensive program of church building and religious dedication throughout much of England, with most church services conducted in either French or Latin.

Richard of Bec was the first recorded abbot of Chester's new Norman abbey and had been appointed by Anselm of Bec, who had been invited to witness the abbey's foundation charter by Hugh Lupus – the second Norman Earl of Chester. Richard held office between 1093 and 1116 and on his death was interred in the abbey. The presbytery and the north and south transepts of the abbey were the first sections to be built and by the time of Richard's death in 1116 were thought to have been largely completed.

Abbot William was appointed as head of the abbey in 1121 and on his death in 1140 was buried within its precincts alongside his predecessor, Richard of Bec. During his tenure as abbot the monks' living accommodation at the abbey was constructed and by around 1129 the chapter house had been completed. The abbey's cloisters and refectory were also thought to have been started during the period, although their construction was undertaken in a series of managed stages. At the time of Abbot William's death, the abbey's north-west tower was also thought to have been completed.

Abbot Ralph held tenure from 1141 to 1151 and was thought to have supervised the construction of the two west towers as well as the abbey's western façade. He was followed to the office by Robert Fitz Nigel, abbot from 1157 to 1174, who was thought to have overseen a phase of remedial construction

Chester Cathedral's north-west tower was largely completed by 1140 when Abbot William died.

work at the abbey, undertaken to correct earlier mistakes. St Anselm's Church, the abbot's private chapel, was also said to have been built during his tenure.

Abbot Geoffrey was the head of Chester's Norman abbey from 1194 through to 1208 and it was during his tenure that the choir was said to have been started and the Saxon bell tower replaced. It was also reported that the earlier presbytery and transepts were replaced and a new entrance to and from the cloisters was constructed. Lucian was reported to have been a 12th-century monk at the abbey and was thought to have been educated at the nearby collegiate church of St John the Baptist in the city. Much of his work seems to have been undertaken during the tenure of Abbot Geoffrey.

Hugh Grylle was abbot from 1208 to 1226 and was responsible for the completion of the abbey's

The abbey's south transept was built during the early 12th century.

The cathedral's northern flank.

The inside of Chester's ancient cathedral.

choir and bell tower. His next project was the completion of the nave, thought to be incomplete at the time he took office. He oversaw the demolition of the earlier Saxon nave and its replacement with a new English style of architecture. Upon his death on 7 May 1226 Abbot Hugh was buried in the chapter house at the feet of Abbot Geoffrey, his predecessor.

His successor, William Marmion, was the abbot of St Werburgh's from 1226 to 1228 and it appears that there was a lull in the building activity at the abbey as his tenure as abbot was a relatively short one. He in turn was succeeded by Walter de Pinchbeck, who held tenure from 1228 to 1240 and was thought to have initiated the reconstruction of the monastery at the abbey sometime after 1230.

The abbots of St Werburgh were granted equal rights to that of Earl Hugh himself. The abbot's court would deal with both secular and religious matters, with trial by fire, water and combat being employed to resolve such cases. Those found guilty of a serious or capital offence would have their punishment carried out by the abbot's officers, including their execution if appropriate. Even following the dissolution of the monasteries in the 16th century, these courts continued to try cases and dispense their own brand of spiritual justice through the consistory courts.

The summary execution of prisoners for any number of crimes was a common feature of the English judicial system for hundreds of years. In Chester, as with most other towns and cities, people were found guilty on the most spurious of evidence and paid for it with their lives. Religious intolerance, the belief in witchcraft and sorcery, along with regular criminality all helped to condemn the poor, the mentally ill and those thought ill of, to the hangman's noose. Such was the power of the religious zealots that even the failure to attend church regularly could often lead to people being imprisoned and vilified by the rest of the community.

These religious courts were operating at the same time that the monks of the abbey were feasting on the game that they had caught in the forests of Delamere, where they had been granted rights by the Norman earls of Chester. Instead of being dressed in plain, functional material, records suggest that these men of God were often attired in the very best apparel and with all the fashionable accessories of the age. The scraps from their well-laden tables were not given to the poor of the parish, but were generally fed to the hounds and terriers that accompanied them on their regular hunting trips. It was little wonder, perhaps, that Henry VIII would later look at these religious houses and wonder about their true merit.

From the date of its Norman foundation the physical fabric of the abbey was continually rebuilt and extended around the original Saxon monastery that it had replaced. As each replacement section of the abbey was built, the corresponding area of the Saxon building was demolished and by about 1211 much of this work had been successfully completed. The lady chapel itself was begun in around 1265 and from 1350 onward a new phase of building was undertaken which would last until Tudor times. The cloisters were finally completed at the beginning of the 16th century, barely 10 years before much of the property was seized by the Crown.

From the time of the city's final capitulation to William in 1070, its defences were gradually rebuilt and refortified along similar lines to the original Saxon settlement. The earthwork defences of Aethelflaeda which were thought to have been located on the top of sloping ground in the south-western section of the settlement overlooking the river and harbour were rebuilt and strengthened by the Normans. In the next few decades these same earth and timber fortifications would eventually be replaced with walls of hard sandstone, much of which was quarried and transported from the nearby Alvanley Cliffs in Cheshire. The resulting motte and bailey Norman castle would offer the city protection for the next several hundred years and help to protect and pacify the whole of North Wales and Cheshire from the threat of invasion and rebellion.

By the end of the 12th century much of the castle and the city's defences were completed and Chester was thought to be one of the most heavily defended cities in Britain at that time. The Agricola Tower, the gatehouse to the inner bailey, is all that remains intact today and houses a chapel dedicated to St Mary de Castro (St Mary of the Castle). The wooden tower that stood on top of the motte was replaced by a later square stone tower which would eventually become known as the Flag Tower. Some time after its first construction an outer bailey was added to the castle which, although initially surrounded by a timber palisade, would be replaced with an extremely high stone curtain wall in 1246. To the north of the castle itself, a great hall, later to be called the Shire Hall, was constructed. This first hall was used as both a meeting place and as a court and was thought to have been built in around 1247.

The ruined Flag Tower at Chester Castle is thought to be the remains of the original Norman defensive redoubt built in the early 12th century.

Dating from the 12th century the tower was the main gateway to the inner bailey of Chester's Norman castle and contains the Chapel of St Mary de Castro.

Replaced in around 1570 the building was reported to have stood on the site of the modern-day crown court building.

Outside of the city's defensive perimeter and lying between the castle and the river, in what is now the modern-day area of the Little Roodee, was the site of the city's leather industries. A highly lucrative industry, it was also one of the most unpleasant and this goes a long way towards explaining why it was located on the periphery of the city. As well as the site close to the castle, later archaeological excavations have also found evidence of the industry in the eastern sector of the suburbs, near to the present-day Foregate Street in Chester.

Much of the Norman castle's existing curtain wall has been rebuilt and refaced in later centuries, but parts of the 13th-century structure still exist.

The leather industries which lay outside of the castle were thought to represent the 'lighter' leather crafts, including leather dressing and glove-making. These, along with the much 'heavier' leather crafts, were thought to have been in existence since Saxon times and in mediaeval England such industries were a vital part of the local commercial economy and were common in most large towns and cities. The existence of glove-makers in this particular area is reaffirmed by the presence of the glover-stone, which lay outside the precincts of the castle's outer bailey. In later years this stone was known to have marked the boundary between the crown and city authorities and was where convicted felons who had been tried by the Crown or its representatives would be passed over to the city officers for sentencing to be carried out. From here, prisoners would be taken by cart through the city streets to Boughton and the site of the public gallows, where they would be dispatched by the city sheriffs or public executioner. Alternatively, other more fortunate felons might be whipped through the streets of Chester or placed in the city's stocks which stood at the High Cross and subjected to the punishments or entertainment of the passing crowds.

Thought to have been originally constructed towards the end of the 11th century, the Dee Weir was built to power the waterwheels of the newly emerging Dee mills. This mill dam is thought to be the oldest of its type in the country and was constructed during the rule of the second Norman Earl, Hugh Lupus. Everyone but the monks of St Werburgh's were compelled to bring their corn to be ground at the mills and the fees charged represented an extra form of revenue for the earl and for the Crown. By the end of the 17th century there were thought to have been 11 waterwheels operating on the Dee and they have been blamed in part for the later silting of the River Dee by restricting the actual flow and natural scouring action of the river.

Chester's High Cross – where miscreants would often be placed in the public stocks.

The 12th century was extremely eventful both for the city and its citizens. Ranulph de Ghernon, or Randal II, succeeded to the title of fifth Earl of Chester following the death of Ranulph de Meschines in 1128 and became a pivotal figure during the reign of King Stephen. De Ghernon strongly disapproved of the king's decision to grant the earldom of Carlisle to Henry, the son of King David of Scotland. Responding to the king's decision Ranulph chose to support the cause of the Empress Mathilda who was in dispute with Stephen and was the aunt of Ranulph's wife.

During this turbulent period for the Norman dynasty, the rulers of North Wales were busily enlarging and rebuilding their kingdoms. The two sons of Gruffudd ap Cynan had taken over the day-to-day control of their father's kingdom and, being aware of the fractious nature of the Norman position, raised a rebellion in the region which saw numerous Norman settlements burnt and destroyed. In 1137 Gruffudd himself was reported to have died and his sons Owain ap Gruffudd and Cadwaladwr ap Gruffudd succeeded him as joint rulers of the kingdom.

At the Battle of Lincoln De Ghernon and his forces helped to capture the king, an act that would not soon be forgotten by the monarch. Following a settlement between Mathilda and Stephen it seemed that the kingdom had fallen back into some sort of peace and harmony. However, when Ranulph visited the king in around 1146, seeking assistance in battling Welsh rebels, he was immediately arrested and held captive until he offered certain guarantees to the monarch. It was during the earl's enforced absence that forces belonging to Owain ap Gruffudd (Owain Gwynedd) were said to have captured the vitally important Welsh border town of Mold.

In 1150 Owain Gwynedd once again came into conflict with Earl Ranulph after De Ghernon had allied himself with Madog ap Maredudd, the ruler of Powys who was in dispute with Owain. The warring parties were reported to have met at Coleshill, a battle that Owain Gwynedd was said to have won. It was also around the same time that Gwynedd was thought to have imprisoned his own son Cynan and seriously injured another relative called Cunedda. Finally, in order to consolidate his position within the region he was also said to have displaced his younger brother Cadwaladwr from power and forced him into exile in England.

Earl Ranulph De Ghernon was recorded as having died in 1153 with some reports stating that it was poison. Whatever the cause, at the time of his death he was thought to be one of the most powerful men in the country and held title to around one third of all lands in the kingdom. In 1154 a new king succeeded to the throne of England; Mathilda's son Henry II took the crown with a grim determination to re-establish royal control over England as well as the troublesome region of Wales.

Hugh Kevelioc or Hugh II was the sixth Norman Earl of Chester who held the office from 1153 and 1181 and was the son of Earl Randal II (Ranulph de Gernons). His surname was thought to derive from Cyveliok in Merionethshire, Wales, and in 1147 Hugh was reported to have married the daughter of Simon, Count of Monmouth and Evreux. As the king's representative at Chester Hugh would have been directly involved with Henry's military campaign against Owain Gwynedd, which was launched in 1157 and included a number of exiled Welsh noblemen such as Owain's ousted brother Cadwaladwr. Despite his formidable force Henry was unable to decisively beat Gwynedd and was thought to have only reached Rhuddlan Castle before his advance was completely stalled. Resigned to not defeating the Welsh ruler militarily, Henry eventually settled for a peace treaty between the two parties and guaranteed Owain Gwynedd's position provided that the Welsh prince accepted Henry's status as his overlord. Owain was also required to reinstate his estranged brother Cadwaladwr and return the lands and titles that had previously belonged to him.

Despite this enforced settlement, and in common with his father, Earl Hugh II was in almost continuous conflict with the Welsh and around 1170 was reported to have killed a 'multitude' of Welsh men at the Bridge of Baldert. Following this battle, legend suggests that the earl built a mound at Boughton with the decapitated heads of his enemies. When he died at Staffordshire in 1181 Hugh was succeeded by a relative, Ranulph III of Whitchurch, who was also known as Randal Blundeville.

Ranulph or Randal Blundeville was the seventh Norman Earl of Chester and was thought to be responsible for the construction of Beeston Castle in Cheshire. He also founded the hospital of St John the Baptist outside the city's Northgate, which occupied the site of the modern-day Bluecoat School. This hospital was reported to have been established for the sick and 'silly' people of Chester and perhaps illustrates the earl's recognition that madness within a person was indeed a mental illness, rather than some sort of divine curse.

Reported to have taken part in the Crusades against the Saracens, Earl Randal was said to have been involved with the capture of Dalmietta shortly before returning home to England in around 1220. Randal was recorded as having fought at the second Battle of Lincoln where the forces of Louis VII were apparently extremely disparaging about his lack of physical stature. It was an insult that they would ultimately be forced to regret, as Randal's unrivalled military instincts and skills subsequently led to his enemies being defeated.

Blundeville was renowned as a well-educated and pragmatic individual who was also an astute politician. He was so popular that bards and poets were reported to have written songs and poems in his honour throughout England. Holding the title of Earl of Chester for over 50 years, Randal was a counsellor to four separate English monarchs, including Henry II, Richard I, King John and Henry III. Shortly before his death in 1232 he vehemently opposed the final king's demand for monies to offset his debts incurred as a result of his military campaigns. Randal also refused to pay a papal tax known as 'Peter's Pence' that was being imposed on the country, and threatened dire consequences on any tax collector that tried to collect the charge within his jurisdiction.

During his time as earl his main military opponent was the Welsh prince Llewellyn ap Iorwerth, who ruled the Gwynedd region of North Wales. The son of Iorwerth Drwynchwn, who was a son of the notable Welsh ruler Owain Gwynedd, Llewellyn was thought to have spent his formative years in the border region of Wales following his mother's remarriage to a Norman marcher lord. Around 1190 he was reported to have launched his bid for control of the still-divided Gwynedd region of Wales and by 1201 had captured the remaining north-west part of the kingdom following the death of its ruler Gruffudd ap

Owain. Later the same year Llewellyn was said to have reached an agreement with the English monarch King John which allowed him to keep almost all of his gains. He was also thought to have cemented this new political arrangement with England by agreeing to marry John's illegitimate daughter Joanna and as part of the settlement was said to have received Ellesmere in Shropshire as part of his new wife's dowry.

Regardless of these new relationships, dealings between Llewellyn, the Crown and its agents in the region continued to be highly fraught affairs. Earl Randal's decision to rebuild Deganwy Castle was just one instance which provoked a response from Llewellyn, who saw the position as a direct threat to his rule and ordered his forces to attack the castle and ravage the nearby Norman settlements. The English king's patience soon ran out and in 1211 John was said to have ordered his knights and subject Welsh lords to meet with him at Chester, from where they would launch a military campaign against Llewellyn to finally bring him to heel. Such was the level of threat posed by the Welsh leader that John's military force was thought to have included two former allies of Llewellyn, Hywel ap Gruffudd ap Cynan and Madog ap Gruffudd Maelor – both of whom regarded their former ally as a direct threat to their own positions. Faced with such an enormous force, Llewellyn's troops were no match for the English army and in a relatively short time he had been forced back into the wilderness of Snowdonia. Besieged in this inaccessible and mountainous region of Wales, within 12 months Llewellyn had been forced to come to terms with the king. However, such was the severity of the penalties that were levied against Llewellyn and his allies that by the following year they were once again in open rebellion with the king.

Throughout much of England King John's reign was a period of regular disputes between the monarch and a number of his leading noblemen, which were often to do with the arbitrary nature of royal rule. At the same time that the Welsh ruler Llewellyn and his allies were once again rebelling against him, John also had to deal with a number of English barons disputing his rights and powers, preventing him from quelling this second Welsh rebellion. Llewellyn was not slow to exploit the king's difficulties and by 1215 he and his allies were said to have regained most of the assets and lands which John had taken from them three years earlier. By 1216 the Welsh prince was regarded as the pre-eminent ruler in Wales and following the death of King John in the same year he was the Welsh leader that the new English king, Henry III, met with in 1218 in order to bring about a settlement.

Having agreed terms with one another the two warring sides began a period of relative peace and even Llewellyn and Earl Randal Blundeville at Chester eventually settled into an uneasy relationship of distrust but mutual respect of one another. With one eye to the future perhaps, both leaders arranged a match between Randal's nephew, John, and Llewellyn's daughter, Elen, which was designed to cement and formalise this new-found friendship. Another of Llewellyn's daughters was also betrothed to a marcher lord, William de Lacey, who held lands in the Welsh Marches and in Ireland.

This later cordiality between the two masked a previously uneasy relationship between the two men and their followers. Legend relates that Earl Randal was besieged at Rhuddlan Castle by the forces of Prince Llewellyn and could not escape from the residence. Realising his predicament he urgently sent a messenger back to Chester informing his constable, Roger de Lacy, that he was trapped and needed help. De Lacy was said to have rushed to the city's marketplace where a fair was taking place and rallied local men to come to their earl's rescue. A good number of those that answered the call were either extremely drunk or were simply minstrels entertaining the crowds in the city. Regardless of this, De Lacy assembled his army of 'musical irregulars' and marched out of the city to begin their long journey towards the besieged castle at Rhuddlan and their lord who was imprisoned there.

The Welsh force that had trapped Blundeville inside the castle heard the approaching relief force and given the noise they were making assumed it was a much larger band of men than their own and quickly dispersed, lifting the siege on the castle. Randal was able to return to the city at the head of his victorious 'army' and immediately granted the fairs numerous privileges by way of thanks. To his constable he granted the custody and licensing of the city's minstrels, a right that was later passed to the Dutton family. (These rights entitled the family to regulate and charge admission to the city's minstrels' guilds and companies. They also led the annual pageant and parades when the company received the blessing of the church. The Dutton family's authority over the minstrels' companies was thought to have been in force right up until the reign of George II). Ralph Dutton was said to have played a large part in the rescue of Randal Blundeville, and was the main reason why so many Chester men joined the rescuing force. He was reported to have organised the unruly band of minstrels and performers into some kind of military formation that might make the Welsh besiegers believe that a large English force was on its way to confront them.

Although De Lacy was noted as having famously saved the Earl of Chester, history might better remember the constable for his admirable defence of the French fortress Chateau Gaillard, deemed by many at the time to be virtually impregnable. The chateau was a stronghold of Richard the Lionheart which was attacked by the forces of King Philip of France in around 1203. The defensive structure had been built on the orders of Richard I in order to protect his holdings as the Duke of Normandy and was reported to have been substantially completed by 1198, around 12 months after it had first been started. Unfortunately Richard died before the castle was finished and his successor King John was thought to have ordered a number of alterations to the building which would later prove to be fateful for the chateau and its defenders. His addition of an extra toilet and a chapel window would later offer King Philip's troops a way past the chateau's impenetrable defences, allowing them to lower the castle's drawbridge and enter the chateau's inner precincts. The defenders were caught totally unaware by the surprise attack and most of the castle's English garrison was subsequently massacred by their French adversaries.

The captain of Chateau Gaillard, Roger De Lacy, and a number of other nobles were thought to have escaped their troop's fate and were held hostage by the French monarch until such a time that a ransom was paid to secure their release. Records suggest that Earl Randal of Chester was the man who met the cost of freeing De Lacy from his captivity at a price of £1,000, with some £200 of the ransom being met by King John who had inadvertently brought about the disaster in the first place.

Blundeville was recorded to have died at Wallingford in Berkshire in 1232 and, having no male heirs of his own, was then succeeded by his sister's son, John. John (the) Scot was the eighth and final Norman Earl of Chester and legend suggests that he was the last Norman earl to carry the 'Curtana' or 'Sword of Mercy' when the monarch Henry III married his future queen, Eleanor. He was known to have held the title from 1232 to 1237 and died without a male heir to succeed him. There is a suggestion that he was actually poisoned by his wife, Elen, the daughter of Llewellyn ap Iorwerth – the Welsh prince who had so violently opposed English rule of his homeland throughout much of his reign.

On the Welsh side of the border Llewellyn ap Iorwerth was reported to have died in 1240, leaving his legitimate heir Dafydd ap Llewellyn as ruler of his extensive kingdom. The young prince's mother was Joanna, the illegitimate daughter of the late King John who Llewellyn had wed in around 1205 and which made Dafydd a cousin to the reigning English monarch, Henry III. However, as was perhaps typical of the time, Dafydd's inheritance was challenged by his illegitimate older half-brother, Gruffudd, who Llewellyn had fathered by one of his many mistresses. Despite this, Henry III had previously agreed with Llewellyn in 1222 that he would officially recognise Dafydd as his legal heir on the Welsh ruler's death. In spite of these assurances however, when Llewellyn died in 1240 Henry reneged on his word and chose to only recognise Dafydd as ruler of Gwynedd and not the other lands and territories previously held by his father.

By 1241 Henry and Dafydd were in open dispute with one another and the English king was said to have used the imprisonment of the Welsh prince's older half-brother Gruffudd as the pretext for invading the kingdom of Gwynedd later the same year. Although he would claim to be protecting the rights and inheritance of Dafydd's older sibling, in reality Henry was implementing a plan which would finally remove the semi-independence of the Welsh rulers and put much of Wales under the control of the English Crown. Ostensibly he claimed to be holding the illegitimate prince in order to restore him to his elevated position, but in reality he was holding Gruffudd as a hostage to guarantee Dafydd's future behaviour and more importantly to remove him as a future threat to his own long-term plans for Wales. As part of the agreement which was forced on Dafydd, Henry insisted that should the young prince die without legitimate issue, then the region of Gwynedd would automatically revert to the English Crown.

Gruffudd ap Llewellyn was thought to have been held as a hostage by Henry until 1244 when he was then killed, having fallen from a tower as he tried to escape. His younger half-brother, Dafydd, was said to have died two years later in 1246, having been in dispute with Henry for a full five years and reportedly having no legitimate heirs to succeed him at the time of his death. This effectively handed Gwynedd to the English Crown and put the region under the control of the monarch Henry III. However, the new English ruler of Gwynedd had apparently forgotten that Gruffudd ap Llewellyn had fathered four sons before his untimely death and it was the second of these heirs, Llewellyn ap Gruffudd, who would ultimately come to challenge Henry and his son Edward for dominion over the lands of Gwynedd.

Following the death of the eighth and final Norman earl without a legitimate heir, the earldom of Chester was said to have reverted to the Crown and to the eldest son of the English monarch, beginning with Henry III who awarded the title to his son, the then Prince Edward. The former Lodge building located in Chester's Grosvenor Park continues to display a permanently carved record for seven of the eight Norman earls that ruled Chester. This record, however, does not include the first holder of the title, Walter de Gerbod, who was presumably omitted because he failed to take up the title or role as the first Norman earl of Chester.

Chapter 8

Historic Walkways and Bitter Welsh Wars

In around 1140 there was reported to have been a major fire within the city which destroyed many of the timber residences and business premises which were still being built at that time. The mainly stone-built religious centres and those buildings belonging to the Crown probably fared better than most, but it seems that any lessons learned as a result of the conflagration were soon forgotten. Some 40 years later the replacement dwellings and business properties which had been built after this first fire were said to have once again been consumed by a major inferno in 1180.

The period seems to have marked a change in the practice of building commercial properties mainly of timber. On the western side of the Bridge Street area of Chester there is a stone façade consisting of three Norman arches thought to date from around 1274 and believed to be one of the oldest shopfronts in the country.

In the first few decades of the 13th century the castle at Chester was substantially enlarged and refurbished as its importance continued to grow and by the middle years of the century new royal apartments were being built to accommodate the king and his entourage while they were battling the two rebellious Welsh princes, Owain Ap Gruffydd and his younger brother Llewellyn. Owain had been held at Shotwick Castle by the king from around 1246 but had managed to escape his captors and rejoin his brother in their isolated Welsh homeland. The princes' continuing refusal to accept the king's authority, as well as their regular raiding and pillaging of English villages and settlements, would eventually and almost inevitably lead to continuous conflict between the two royal houses. In order to achieve some sort of settlement with the two renegade princes, Henry was reported to have reached an agreement with Owain and Llewellyn which recognised their right to rule the Gwynedd region. The resulting Treaty of Woodstock, which was signed in 1247, deprived the two brothers of much of their true inheritance, but nonetheless gave them a power base from where they could orchestrate future expansion of their lands.

During the next five years the brothers were said to have been busy building new political alliances and extending their influence well beyond the borders of their homeland. By around 1252 they had built a large number of coalitions with many of their neighbouring regions. It was around this time that a third brother, Dafydd ap Gruffudd, was said to have reached his majority and immediately demanded parity with his two older siblings with respect to his land rights in Gwynedd. The older brother Owain was said to have been inclined to meet Dafydd's demands, but his younger, more astute and ambitious sibling Llewellyn refused these demands and in doing so set the brothers on the road to conflict with one another. The resulting Battle of Bryn Derwin in 1255 between Owain, Dafydd and Llewellyn saw the latter defeat and imprison his two siblings before seizing their lands and assets. From around 1256 onward Llewellyn was recognised as the sole ruler of Gwynedd and continued the development and expansion of his North Wales kingdom.

In the same year he was thought to have begun a series of attacks on lands adjoining his own, driving the English settlers out of Wales. He was also said to have ordered the construction of Ewloe Castle, which was designed to protect the eastern part of his kingdom from any future English incursions. Within 12 months Llewellyn was reported to have recovered much of the territory that had been held by his late uncle Dafydd ap Llewellyn and had regained the loyalty and support of many of the

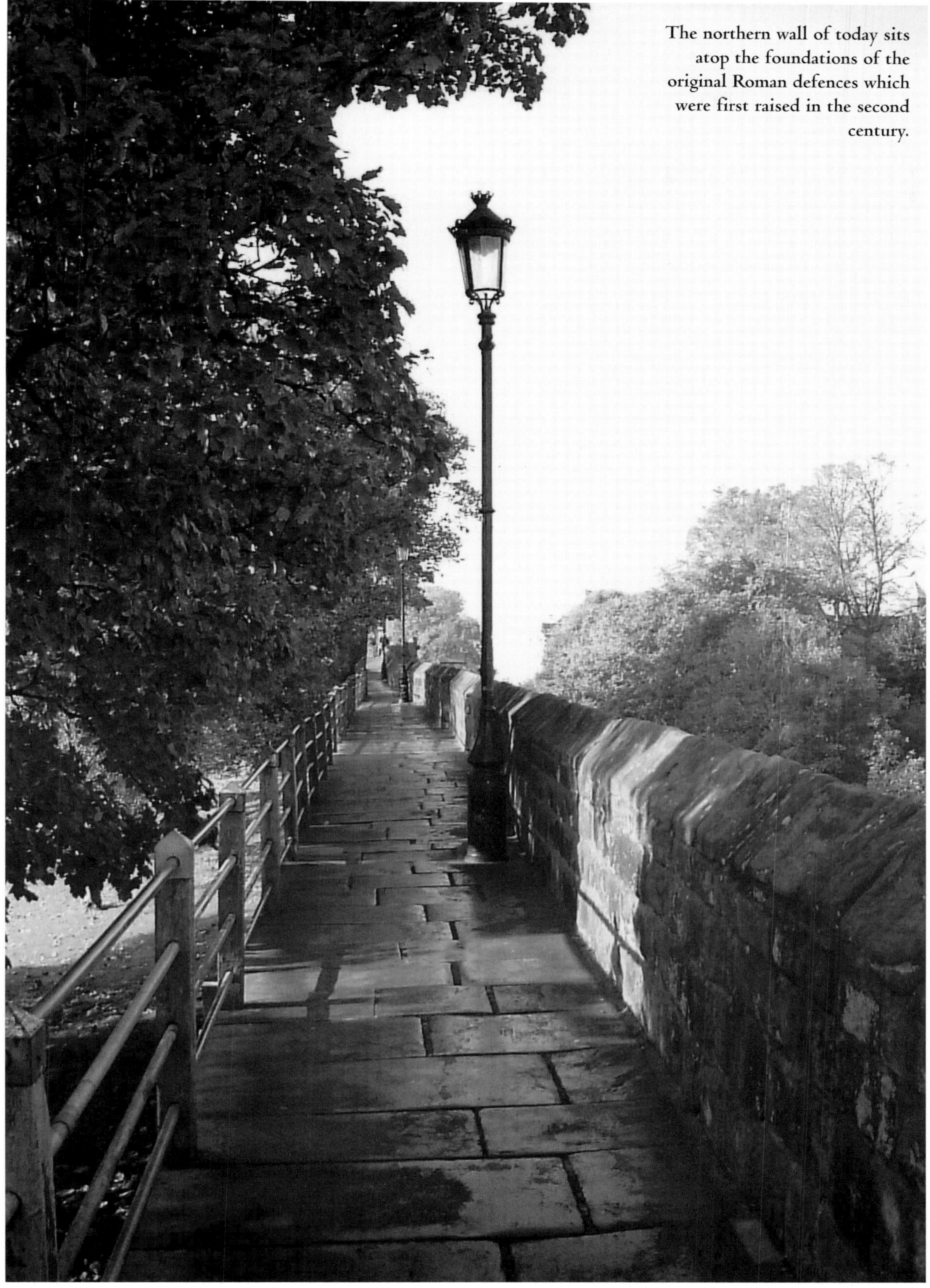

The northern wall of today sits atop the foundations of the original Roman defences which were first raised in the second century.

native Welsh lords who had previously been allied to the English monarch Henry III. Although Henry was thought to have launched at least two military campaigns in order to curb Llewellyn's ambitions they were generally unsuccessful affairs given that Henry was facing serious problems within the rest of England.

In the latter years of his reign Henry III was in almost constant dispute with a large number of rebel English barons, which finally resulted in the Battle of Lewes in 1264 where both he and his son Edward were taken prisoner by their enemies. As part of the agreement to secure their release Prince Edward was required to surrender the earldom of Chester to Simon de Montford, the Earl of Leicester, who was one of his captors. The Welsh ruler Llewellyn was said to have encouraged de Montford to appropriate the earldom of Chester from the English Crown in order to guarantee and fully secure his eastern border from further English invasions.

Twelve months earlier William La Zouche, a Cheshire baron, had taken control of the city for Edward and had constructed a defensive ditch outside of the city's northern wall which brought about the destruction of certain properties owned by the abbey of St Werburgh and causing friction between the two parties. He was reported to have been involved in a major incident with the religious community where he verbally assaulted the clergy which resulted in the abbey closing its precincts to the townspeople for an undisclosed period of time.

Having extorted the earldom of the city from Prince Edward, De Montford then tried to make it his own. In the following year his son Henry was said to have visited Chester for a 10-day period, during which time he received the homage of both its citizens and civic authorities. Neither of the De Montford's ever managed to return to Chester however, as they were later defeated by the king's forces at the Battle of Evesham in 1265 during which Simon de Montford was killed. Chester then reverted back to Edward's control and once again became a threat to Llewellyn's eastern border. Perhaps in order to pre-empt any hostile actions on the part of Henry or his son Edward, Llewellyn was thought to have ordered his troops to attack Hawarden Castle in September 1265 and the position was said to have fallen shortly afterwards. Despite this, the English monarchy was so busy trying to restore order throughout England that they had little time to deal with rebellions within the Welsh provinces and simply chose to negotiate a truce with Llewellyn.

This truce was formalised with the Treaty of Montgomery which was signed by the two parties on the 25 September 1267 and was intended to settle all outstanding grievances between the two families once and for all. Under the terms of the treaty Llewellyn was permitted to retain many of the land gains that he had acquired in the previous years but was required to surrender Hawarden Castle to English control. He was entitled to receive tribute from his subordinate Welsh lords but was required to pay an annual tribute to the English Crown of 25,000 marks as well as accepting Henry's authority over him. Given the restrictions that were imposed by the treaty Llewellyn was always likely to breach the terms of the agreement which had been made by the two leaders. Records suggest that within three years the Welsh prince was beginning to struggle to meet the annual charge which had been imposed on him and by 1270 was said to have been late in meeting his 25,000 mark obligation.

Around four years later, and still struggling under a mountainous debt, Llewellyn was thought to have been made aware of a plot that was being mounted against him, supposedly involving his younger brother Dafydd. Llewellyn immediately ordered his brother to attend his court in order that he could be questioned about the matter, but before any action could be taken Dafydd was said to have fled across the border into England and sought the protection of the new king, Edward I. Later investigation of the planned coup suggested that Dafydd, along with another marcher lord, had planned to murder Llewellyn and place his younger brother on the throne of Gwynedd. The plot itself, his younger brother's complicity and Edward's protection of the would-be assassins all contrived to fracture the tenuous relationship which had existed between Llewellyn and King Edward and inevitably led the two parties to outright conflict.

King Edward I, also known as Edward 'Longshanks', had succeeded his father, Henry III, to the throne in 1272 and immediately began to make plans to recover the Welsh lands. Llewellyn had absented himself from Edward's coronation in 1272 and generally made himself unavailable at the English Court, which Edward chose to regard as an act of rebellion. The final straw for the English monarch was Llewellyn's decision to marry Eleanor de Montford, a sister of the family that had seized Edward and his father during the civil war of 1264–65. The king was reported to have arranged Eleanor's abduction as she travelled to Wales to marry Llewellyn and openly declared that the Welsh leader was a rebel and should be treated as such. Edward was then said to have visited Chester in 1276 to formally receive tribute from Llewellyn, perhaps hoping that the Welshman might refuse him and giving him a reason to settle the issue by force of arms. Needless to say the Welsh prince did not disappoint him.

In the following year Edward gathered a large military force at Chester which was thought to consist of over 1,000 knights and 15,000 soldiers and marched into Wales to force Llewellyn to accept his sovereignty. He quickly captured Rhuddlan Castle and refortified its defences in order to prevent any further Welsh raids into the area. Llewellyn and his forces were eventually forced back into the wilderness of Snowdonia and subsequently starved into submission by Edward's enormous English army. The usual Welsh 'bolt holes' on the Isle of Anglesey had earlier been isolated from the mainland by a fleet of warships that Edward had dispatched for that specific purpose. With nowhere to go and with few other options open to him the resulting 'Treaty of Aberconwy', signed in November 1277, was a public humiliation for the Welsh prince, which left him virtually powerless within his own homelands. Not only was Llewellyn dispossessed of the many gains that he had made during his reign but he was refused permission to pass his remaining lands and titles on to his legitimate heirs. With that particular provision in place Edward was then reported to have released his captive Eleanor de Montford so that she could finally be married to Llewellyn, safe in the knowledge that any resulting offspring would no longer pose a threat to any future English rule of the principality.

Having subjugated and humiliated the most important and influential Welsh leader of his time Edward then set about initiating a round of land seizures and the submission of other potentially dangerous Welsh lords, all of which were designed to strengthen English control and dominance within Wales.

Much of Edward's martial success seems to have been founded on his more disciplined approach to the planning of military warfare than had been previously adopted by other commanders. Unlike his predecessors, Edward's army was known to have been comprised of a large number of professional soldiers who would stay in place until the job was done, or for as long as they were paid. Parts of Edward's forces were said to have included men from the town of Macclesfield in Cheshire who were the predecessors of the famous Cheshire Archers, possibly the finest fighting men of their age. Also in his vanguard, the king was known to have employed a large number of mercenaries from Gascony who were famed for their use of the crossbow.

By ensuring that his lines of communication and supply were both protected and remained effective, Edward was able to guarantee the smooth movement of men and materials throughout the region, both of which were vital to his continued military control of Wales. Enormous numbers of woodcutters, masons and other craftsmen were employed to construct a road network that gave the English king easier and much speedier access to the hinterland of Wales. The Welsh rebels, who at one time could have easily disappeared into the wild and rugged countryside, now found their hideaways easily accessed by the pursuing English forces. The later construction of the English-held castles at Conway, Beaumaris, Caernarvon and Harlech further ensured Welsh compliance with his rule and this was added to by the enforced 'colonization' of North Wales by large numbers of Englishman who owed their true allegiance to the English Crown.

Perhaps because of the terms contained within the Treaty of Aberconwy, both Edward and Llewellyn knew that such an unfair and enforced peace could not last. Some four years later, in 1281, Edward had to return to Chester once again to suppress a second Welsh rebellion which had been sparked by Llewellyn's brother, Dafydd ap Gruffydd. He ruled in eastern Gwynedd and was said to have launched an unexpected attack on the English-held castle at Hawarden, killing its garrison and its commander Roger Giffard. Within days a large number of native Welsh rulers were said to have rallied to his cause and many English holdings within the province, including Oswestry were raided and ransacked. Llewellyn had been reluctant to challenge the English king a second time but was forced to support his brother's rebellion all the same. In the first few weeks of the uprising the Welsh forces saw nothing but success and held control of the province, from the Bristol Channel in the south to the very gates of Chester in the north. By the middle of the year Llewellyn had become central to this new uprising, despite the fact that his wife Eleanor was reported to have died while giving birth to a baby girl who was named Gwenllian.

Once again Edward mustered a large military force at Chester and marched into Wales, intent this time on dealing a crushing defeat to the rebellious princes once and for all. Events elsewhere, however, forced the king to change his plans unexpectedly. One of Edward's leading supporters, Luke de Thaney, who had been charged by the king with occupying the Isle of Anglesey, chose instead to attempt an unsupported pre-emptive strike against Llewellyn's forces, which involved having to cross the treacherous Menai Straits and resulted in the English force being decimated by their Welsh opponents.

Having pushed the rebel forces back into North Wales, Edward had counted on De Thaney and his forces joining his own to finally crush the Welsh rebel army. Hearing of the debacle caused by his trusted lieutenant's rashness Edward was then forced to re-organise his troops and his strategy, finally having to settle for starving his opponents into submission once again. William de Beauchamp, the Earl of Warwick, was said to have commanded the forces of Edward I during his wars against the Welsh princes and was thought to have been based at the Chester fortress during these disputes.

Although much of South Wales was under English control, the regions of North Wales and Mid Wales were far more awkward for Edward and it is thought that by October 1282 the king was seeking to reach a settlement with the two Welsh princes, Llewellyn and Dafydd. However, the terms which were being offered by Edward were thought to be so unreasonable that the two brothers had little difficulty in refusing the king's offer. Edward was said to have demanded that Llewellyn and Dafydd leave Wales and to surrender any future claims to the throne of Gwynedd. Additionally he required the children of the two Welsh princes to be placed in his care and charge, as a guarantee against their fathers' future good conduct. It was little wonder that Dafydd and Llewellyn refused such unwarranted demands and chose instead to continue their rebellion against the king.

From the king's personal point of view, there was a highly unexpected silver lining to this particular cloud. Llewellyn was later reported to have been killed at the Battle of Orwen Bridge when he and his men were ambushed by an English force commanded by John Gifford and Roger Mortimer. A large number of leading Welsh retainers were thought to have died with their prince, whose severed head was said to have been displayed at the Tower of London. With Llewellyn dead, Welsh resistance was all but over and English rule of the province was substantially restored.

For a short time following his brother's death, Dafydd ap Gruffudd was reported to have taken sole charge of the remaining Welsh forces that continued to oppose Edward's invading English army. Unfortunately for Dafydd, as his military situation worsened and he was forced further and further back into the isolated areas of his homeland, a number of his supporters, perhaps with more than an eye on their own future prospects, were reported to have deserted him and made their own peace with Edward. By 1283 the king's army was said to have penetrated deep into Snowdonia and Dafydd's final defence, Castell Y Bere, was reported to have fallen to Edward's troops in April of the same year. Finally, and perhaps not unexpectedly, it was thought that Prince Dafydd was betrayed by one or more of his own retainers and delivered into the hands of his nemesis Edward I. He was taken in chains to the English border town of Shrewsbury where after a short trial he was found guilty of treason. In October 1283 Dafydd ap Gruffudd, the last native Prince of Wales, was duly executed by the English Crown, suffering the punishment of being hung, drawn and quartered and his severed head later being displayed at the Tower of London – sharing the same final humiliation as his brother.

Following Dafydd's execution the monarch was reported to have ordered the imprisonment of the Welsh prince's two young sons, who were said to have been held at Bristol Castle until their deaths. Llewellyn ap Gruffudd's one and only daughter Gwenllian, who was less than a year old at the time of her father's death, was delivered to a convent located at Sempringham and was thought to have stayed there up until her death in 1337 aged 54 years old.

Edward was said to have returned to Chester in 1284 and again in 1294 when he passed through on his way to suppress a Welsh rebellion led by a leader called Madoc, but by 1300 virtually all opposition to the English Crown in Wales had been crushed. John de Warenne, the Earl of Surrey, was said to have commanded elements of Edward's forces during the king's third campaign against the Welsh in 1294 and John Langton, the king's chancellor, was based at Chester in 1295.

This period was said to mark the first documented evidence for the elevated rows that would later become a world-famous feature of the city, the record dating from around 1331. A number of suggestions have been made as to the actual reasons for their initial construction and for their historical development. One suggested theory is that the amount of debris and standing remains that still existed from Roman times prevented any sort of extensive building program at or on street level. To overcome this problem, mediaeval builders were said to have been forced to create a new elevated ground level which was set above these earlier foundations. As well as the living accommodations and business premises which were built at this new first-floor level, walkways which linked these new accommodations together were necessary and would later develop into the rows that we see today. Many of the spaces or voids which lay below these new raised walkways were eventually cleared of the rubble and debris and developed into the street-level businesses that are still evident in the city.

An alternative suggestion as to how and why the rows developed was that they offered the inhabitants of the city better security from potential invaders. The theory suggests that businesses and living accommodations were deliberately built at an elevated level joined by a linked walkway and accessed by a number of stairways throughout their length. These staircases would then have been

The elevated rows in Chester were first recorded around 1331.

protected by shutters and gates which prevented invaders gaining access to the upper levels of the city and therefore protecting the local population.

This second suggestion seems far less likely, but no doubt there is an element of truth to both. It is known that the local historian Ranulph Higden, writing at the end of the 14th century, noted that Chester was *'filled with enormous foundation stones laid by the labor of the Romans.'* This does seem to support the idea that even after a thousand years of continual habitation certain areas of the city were still largely uninhabitable because of the continuing presence of much earlier Roman building foundations, which had defied all subsequent efforts to remove them.

Higden was a 14th century monk and local historian at Chester's mediaeval abbey, who wrote his history of the world, *The Polychronicon*, which detailed the period from creation through to his own time. His work is generally considered to be the only serious publication that was ever produced by members of the community in Chester. Higden recorded that:

'The city of the legions, Chester, which lies in the marshes of England towards Wales, lies between two arms of the sea, which are named the Mersey and the Dee. The city, in the time of the Britons was head and chief city of all Venedotia, which is North Wales. This city in British speech is called "Carthleon", Chester in English, as well as the "City of the legions".

'For there, lay a winter the legions that Julius Caesar sent forth to win Ireland. After that, Claudius Caesar sent legions out of the city to win the islands that he called "Orcades".

'The city has plenty of corn, flesh and specially Salmon. This city receives great merchandise and sends out as much. The Northumbrians destroyed this city sometime, but Ethelfleda, Lady of Mercia, rebuilt it and made it much more than it was.

'In this city wonderfully built, three chambered works lay underground with old names therein. This is the city that Ethelfrith, king of Northumbria destroyed and slew there, two

The Kaleyard Gate has existed from the 14th century, linking the inner precincts of the Norman abbey to their vegetable gardens which lay outside of the eastern wall.

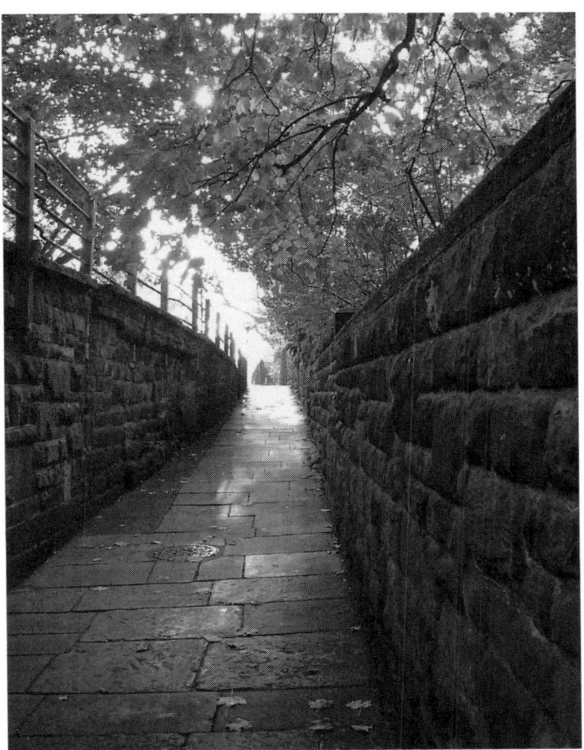

thousand monks from the monastery at Bangor. This is the city that King Edgar came to, sometime with seven kings that were subject to him.'

Higden's publication is thought to have been based on an earlier work written by a monk called Roger who was a member of the same Benedictine abbey earlier in the 14th century. Higden's Latin history was later translated into English by a clergyman called Trevisa, who was chaplain to the Earl of Berkeley in 1887, and was published some time later by Caxton.

Higden has also been credited with authoring a great number of the *Chester Mystery Plays*, which during the mediaeval period were a major part of the city's religious life. It was said that Higden had to travel to Rome in order to get permission from the Pope for the plays to be translated into and performed in the English language, as so few people that watched the plays spoke Latin. These 'plays' or 'interludes' had originated in the Middle Ages and were performed to help mark the intervals between separate church services. They were specifically written to help illustrate and convey important biblical messages to the local population in a format that was easy to understand.

Initially the church was known to have been actively involved in the performance of the plays, but as they became more popular they began to become more boisterous and noisy. Because of this the plays were moved out of the abbey itself and relocated to a site just outside of the church's main doors. Local monks, who had in the past been involved in producing and performing the plays, were forbidden from further involvement and it was because of this that the city's local crafts became involved and associated with them.

Most, if not all, of Chester's guilds actively participated in performing the city's historic *Mystery Plays* and there was thought to have been a highly competitive atmosphere between the various city companies. The drapers, wrights, tanners and smiths all tried to outdo one another in terms of their scenery, the costumes worn and levels of performance, to the extent that actors were often 'poached' by one guild from another. Each individual company would take responsibility for performing one particular scene or story from the Bible which was designed to reinforce the preaching of the Christian message. Eventually, these annual plays became so well known and popular that they had to be performed over a period of consecutive days in the city. This later led to a number of separate stages being erected throughout Chester so that the citizens and visitors had the opportunity to see each individual play performed. Eventually the guilds were said to have constructed mobile stages or floats which could be transported throughout the city, allowing each play to be seen all over Chester.

Following Henry VIII's suppression of Chester's Norman abbey in around 1540, there were deliberate moves to stop these annual *Mystery Plays* from being performed at all. In 1575 the city's Mayor, Sir John

Chester's Norman abbey was home to the likes of Higden and Bradshaw, notable writers and historians.

Savage, was cited by the English Privy Council for allowing the round of plays to be performed in the city. Following this intervention by the national authorities, Chester's council ordered their performances to be discontinued. Although it is not entirely clear if these performances were always called 'Mystery' Plays, which today we regard as some sort of mediaeval whodunit. Instead it has been suggested that Mystery is a corruption of the French word 'mystere', or guild, which would seem a far more likely derivation.

Higden has also been attributed as the source for the local legend that tells of King Harold's return to Chester following his defeat at the Battle of Hastings and his stay there as a blind hermit until his death. Higden was thought to have died at the abbey sometime around 1360 and his body was later interred within its precincts.

A noted contemporary of Higden's was thought to be Henry Bradshaw, a monk at the abbey in Chester, who was a renowned local historian and writer. Sometime before 1500 he wrote a history on the life of St Werburgh whose dedication the abbey carried during his lifetime. He has also been suggested as another possible writer of Chester's Mystery Plays. His second celebrated work, *De Antiquitate Et Magnificentia Urbia Cestriae* was first published in around 1513 and it has often been speculated that Bradshaw was a local Chester man who had been educated at the Collegiate Church of St John's in the city.

The writer and historian Henry Bradshaw was thought to have been a student at St John's in Chester.

It has been recorded that the city's rows were once far more extensive than those we can see today and are known to have extended well into both the Northgate Street and Lower Bridge Street areas of the city. Many of the open walkways that were once present on the western side of Lower Bridge Street were said to have been later acquired by the wealthier families who lived alongside them and who later incorporated these elevated thoroughfares into their private residences, causing them to be lost forever. It was reported that the first people in Chester to seek official permission to fully enclose these public walkways into their private accommodation were the Grosvenor family, who lived at the Falcon Inn at the corner of Lower Bridge Street.

A building in one form or another is known to have stood on the site of the modern-day Falcon since

The Falcon Inn was formerly the city home of the Grosvenor family, who are thought to have initiated the enclosure of Chester's elevated rows in some areas.

around the beginning of the 13th century. These earlier buildings were said to have been much more extensive than their modern-day counterparts and to have extended further south into what is now Lower Bridge Street. Reported to have included a great hall which ran parallel to the main street, the house was substantially modified shortly after its initial construction with an elevated gallery added to its frontage. As is typical with many of Chester's mediaeval buildings the Falcon's structure includes a stone undercroft, which in earlier times might have been used as workshops, warehouses or even living accommodations. Much of the existing building fabric is thought to date from around the late 16th and early 17th centuries, but timbers dating from around 1200 have been clearly identified by archaeologists and bear witness to the great age of the property.

Purchased in 1602 by the Grosvenor family from Sir George Hope, the property was known to have been used as a town house by the family during the English Civil War in which Sir Richard Grosvenor was a leading royalist supporter within the city. It was said to be around this time that the house was substantially altered in order to enlarge the actual living space and as a result the historic elevated gallery or row was fully enclosed and lost forever as a feature of the city.

Throughout the length of the city's existing streets and their elevated rows, its tradesmen tended to cluster their businesses and trades together. Bakers and cooks were primarily located in Eastgate Street, as were the gold and silversmiths. Ironmongers were to be found in Northgate Street, fishmongers in Watergate Street and the glovers in Foregate Street.

Generally, the craftsmen and merchants of the city were members of the Chester guilds, bodies which regulated and controlled the particular trades and industries in the city and which had formally

Watergate Street was the main area for the fish sellers of Chester to congregate.

existed since the beginning of the 13th century. Most guildsmen were also freemen of the city, a position that could be afforded them in one of four ways. They could earn it through a formal apprenticeship, or by being born as the son of a freeman of the city. Alternatively, membership might be bought, or they could receive it as a gift of Chester's assembly.

On the north side of Eastgate Street, at row level, the Boot Inn was a commercial centre for the city's visiting livestock traders. The modern premises are said to still contain the historic 'Horse Traders' seat which was reported to have been used for agreeing terms during the various mediaeval markets and

The Boot Inn was reported to be an early meeting place for livestock merchants and is said to contain an ancient chair called the Traders Seat. The building itself is thought to originate from between 1550 and 1640.

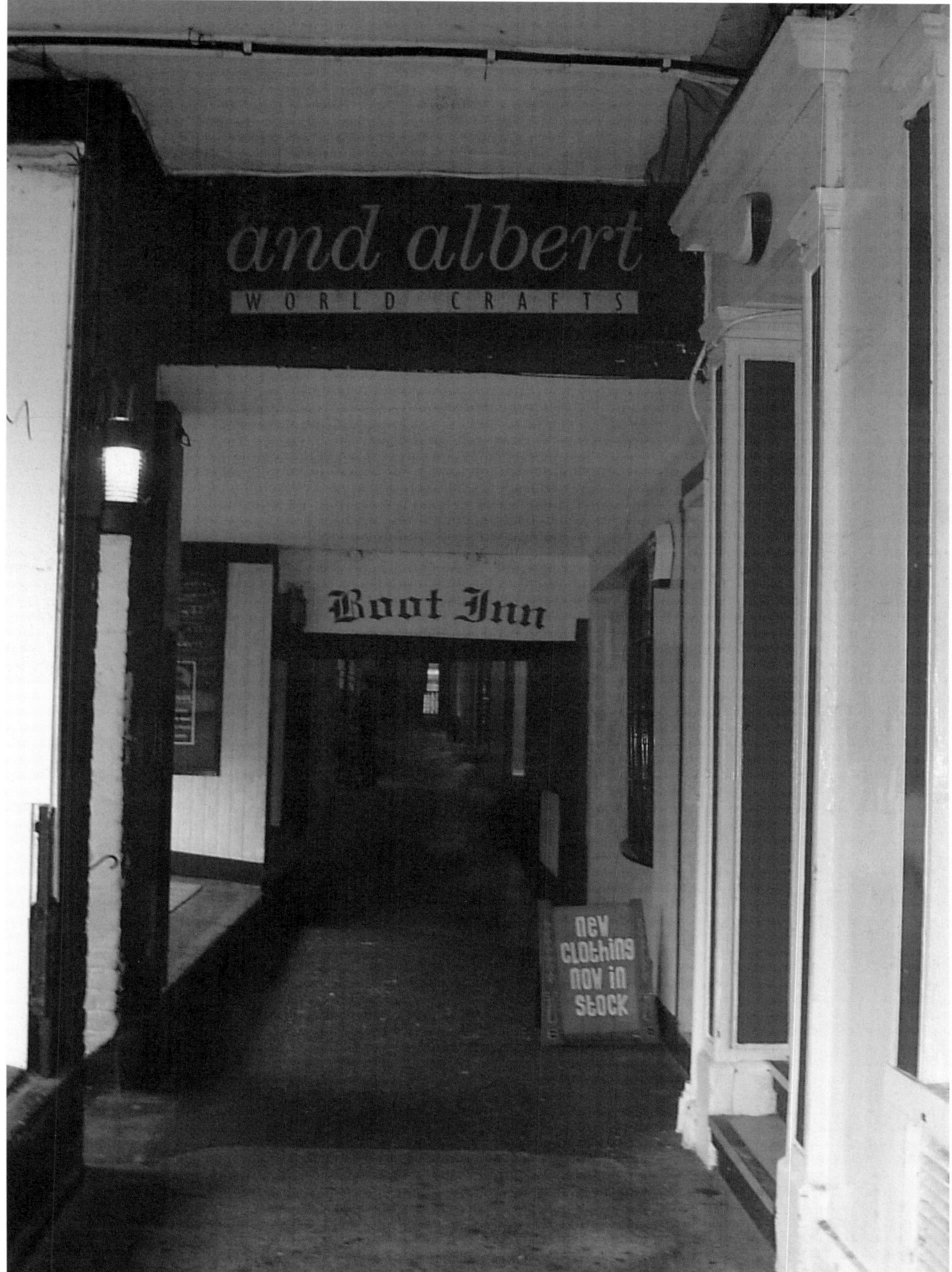

This elevated Row runs between Godstall Lane and Northgate Street and was possibly known as Dark Row.

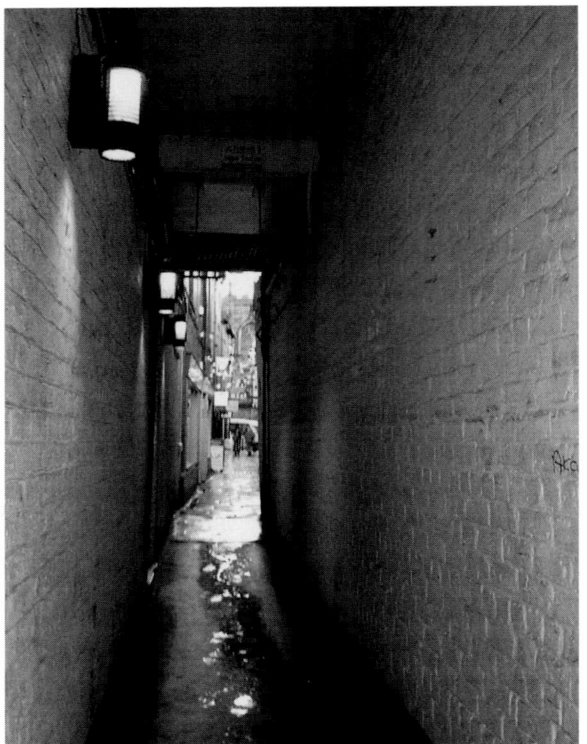

Thought to be named after a local hermit called 'Godescal', this passageway is reputed to have its foundations with the Roman builders of the city.

fairs. Not far away from the Boot Inn is Godstall Lane, said to be named after a Saxon hermit called Godescal who lived at the hermitage on the outskirts of the city. The passageway itself is reported to have originated centuries before and was thought to have been used and possibly built by the fortress's earlier Roman inhabitants.

The High Cross, as it does today, marked the junction between the four main thoroughfares within the city. As well as the markets held at Midsummer and Michaelmas, it was also said to be the site of the city's stocks where wrongdoers were punished for their misdeeds and offered as entertainment to the passing crowds. It was also thought to be the site where bear or bull-baiting occurred for public amusement. Behind the High Cross was the pentice building which housed the early assizes and the offices of the city officials, including the mayor, who it was said would watch the public spectacle of the bear and bull-bait from their balcony high above the event. The modern Linenhall Place in Chester was reported to have once been called Bearward Lane and reflected the historic route by which the bull or bear was led in and out of the city's centre.

It was also during the 13th and 14th centuries that a number of new churches and religious houses were founded within the city. Holy Trinity Church was erected on or near the western gate of the original Roman fortress, which suggests that this was no longer in place and had perhaps been demolished prior to that particular date. In the south-western area of the city St Martin's Church was built and Richard Lenginour (the engineer) was thought to have built the shrine to St Werburgh in the city's abbey church.

Another building of the time that was said to have been newly constructed was the 'anchorite' cell or 'hermitage' close to St John the Baptist's Church in the south-east quarter of the city. Legend has it that King Harold actually survived the battle at Hastings and after recovering from his wounds made his way to Chester and lived in this building as a blind hermit. Given the time difference of a few hundred years between the two historic events, the idea that the defeated monarch might have lived there is highly implausible. The building was almost certainly built simply to provide solitude and as a place of quiet contemplation for those people that wished to devote themselves entirely to God. The building in later years was known to have been used as a meeting place for the company of weavers in the city. John Spicer was reported to have established a hermitage close to the Old Dee Bridge in 1358 and an individual called John Benet was recorded as the occupant of St James's Hermitage in Handbridge during the 15th century, and who was later accused of running a brothel.

Richard Lenginour, who has been attributed with the title of 'engineer' when in reality he was a master mason, was said to have been employed by Edward I to help construct his castles at Flint and Rhuddlan around 1277 and was granted the rights to the city's Dee mills. He was thought to have held the office of mayor in 1305 and died in 1315. At the time of his death Richard had acquired substantial holdings at both Pulford and Eccleston and his lands at Eaton were said to have been settled on his daughter when she married. Richard's family were reported to have left Chester by 1321 and later relocated to Belgrave. Lenginour was also said to have built a mansion on the site of the chapel belonging to the ancient St Olave's Church which lies just off Lower Bridge Street in Chester. This building later became known as Pares or Paris Hall in memory of its later owner, Robert Pares (Paris).

In the hundred years marking the period between the 12th and 13th centuries there was a large rise in the numbers of religious devotees living within the city, either drawn by the existing communities or helping to establish new Christian orders. The first of these new communities to arrive was the Benedictine Convent of St Mary's which was said to have been established in 1150 with the permission of the fourth earl, Ranulph II, who granted them lands in the western part of the city, close to the developing Norman castle. A devotee called Helenwise was reported to have been the prioress of St Mary's Benedictine Nunnery in Chester during the 1350s, and was thought to be a member of one of Chester's leading families.

Around 1235 the Dominican Monks, or the Black Friars, arrived in Chester to establish their own community. They were followed some eight or nine years later by the Franciscans, or the Grey Friars, and finally there was the Carmelites, the White Friars, who arrived in 1290. All three of these orders were granted lands in the western sector of

A single remaining archway from St Mary's Convent which was swept away by Henry VIII's religious purges of the 16th century.

White Friars Street recollects the religious house of the Carmelite Order, who arrived in Chester around 1290.

the city and were aided by individual bequests from the earls of Chester as well as other wealthy patrons within the city.

It has been suggested that the arrival of these particular religious orders in Chester might in part account for the disappearance of some of the former Roman buildings and defences in the western part of the city, which may have been 'robbed out' to provide building materials for these new spiritual centres. By the end of the 13th century these four communities were known to have held lands which extended through the full length of the city's western flank, from the river to the northern defences. In the modern-day city, this would include all of the land to the west of the present-day Nicholas and Princess Streets and stretching from the later police headquarters northward to the city walls and the canal basin.

Despite the arrival of these new Christian communities in Chester the most important religious house in the city remained the Norman abbey. Roger Frend was recorded as holding the office of abbot from 1240 to 1249 and was thought to have been responsible for the completion of the chapter house and the cloisters. Roger was said to have died on 23 September 1249 and was later interred in the chapter house of the abbey.

Frend's successor, Simon de Whitchurch, was recorded as being the abbot of St Werburgh's from 1265 to 1291 and was thought to be responsible for the building of St Nicholas's chapel in around 1280. The chapel was initially built to replace the Church of St Oswald, which was said to have stood on the site of the abbey's south transept. Unfortunately, the new chapel was not easily accepted by the local parishioners and the building later became a court, then, later still, a theatre which hosted the likes of Charles Dickens when he visited the city. It was during Abbot Simon's tenure that the construction of the monastery was finally completed and the next project he initiated was the rebuilding of the abbey church, which included a separate lady chapel. Upon his death on 22 February 1291 Abbot Simon was reported to have been buried in the abbey's chapter house beneath a marble stone.

Thomas de Burchelle was the abbot of St Werburgh's from 1291 to 1323 and was said to have continued the various building projects which had been started by his predecessor, Simon De Whitchurch. Around 1310 Richard 'the Engineer' Lenginour was reported to have demolished the abbey's presbytery to make way for additional piers within the building. A shrine dedicated to St Werburgh was also built between the high altar and the lady chapel around 1310 but this was later severely damaged during the Reformation.

During Abbot Thomas's tenure Edward I was said to have given permission for the monks to construct a postern gate in the city's historic defensive wall, providing them with access to the monastery's cabbage patch which lay outside of the precincts. In order to fully maintain the fortress's security it was necessary for the monks to build a drawbridge to span the city's defensive ditch and they were held responsible for ensuring that the gate was secured every evening. This 'Kale Yard' gate still exists today and permits access from the cathedral through to the Frodsham Street area of the city. Sadly the vegetable garden of the monks no longer exists and is today covered by one of the city's many municipal car parks. The construction of the 'Kale Yard' gate ultimately proved to be a matter of some dispute between the abbot and the city authorities, which was only finally resolved during the reign of Edward II when the drawbridge was eventually constructed. Abbot Thomas died on 23 December 1323 and was said to have been interred in the main body of the church on the south side of the choir.

William de Bebington was recorded as being the abbot of the Norman abbey from 1324 to 1349 and was thought to have been responsible for the

Built by the brothers of Chester's Norman abbey, St Nicholas's Chapel has served as a place of worship, a civil court, a theatre, a picture house and, finally, as a retail store.

construction of a number of chapels and altars within the abbey's precincts. In 1349 the Black Death reached Chester and William was thought to have been one of its more notable victims, succumbing to the disease on 20 September 1349 and later interred on the south side of the choir.

Bebington's successor, Richard De Seynesbury (Sainsbury), was the abbot at Chester between 1349 and 1363 and was thought to have overseen the reconstruction of the south transept of the abbey. The south bay and southern wall of the western aisle were also reported to have been built during the same period. Sainsbury was said to have been attacked by members of his own community at a time when there was a highly troublesome and violent faction present within the abbey community and a number of the monks found themselves facing the courts on charges of robbery, arson and assault. So worrying were these troubles that, in 1362, Prince Edward ordered the abbot of St Alban's to visit Chester and resolve the disciplinary problems that were affecting the abbey. As a result Sainsbury was forced to resign his post and a number of the monks were removed to St Alban's to receive corrective training.

Thomas Erdeley, abbot of St Werburgh's from 1413 to 1434, had earlier been accused of breaking into Abbot Henry de Sutton's pay chest and stealing 20 marks and three gold rings. He was also thought to have stolen a chest and five marks belonging to Robert de Legh. It was during his tenure that a number of the abbey's monks were brought before the court for offences ranging from robbery to rape.

John Saughall was the abbot of St Werburgh's from 1435 to 1455 and was thought to have derived his name from the outlying area of Chester called Saughall, formerly called Salhare. He was said to have been a clerk at the Chester abbey who, along with a fellow monk Thomas Erdeley, displayed a level of violence and dishonesty that might easily have ended their religious careers, yet both men somehow went on to achieve the highest possible office within their community, that of abbot.

In 1349 the city had begun to see the effects of silting within the river, which in later centuries would completely suffocate Chester's international shipping trade and its commercial centres. The north-western water tower, which had been designed to guard the mediaeval harbour, was rebuilt as an extension to the much earlier Bonewaldesthorne's Tower in 1322 as the river began to recede further to the north and west. John de Helpeston was reported to have been a stonemason in the city who was responsible for the construction of the tower and charged £100 for its building, a high price for the time when most workmen were only paid one penny a day for their labour. A few years earlier

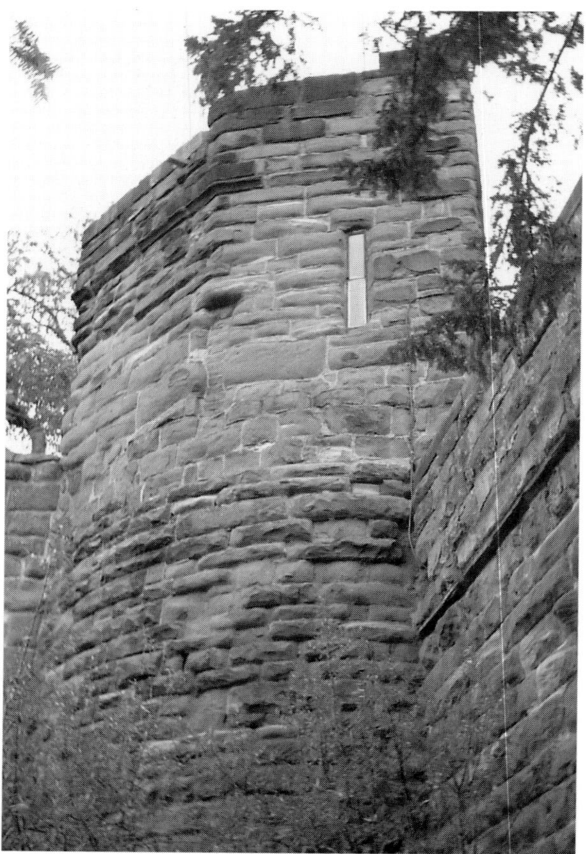

Bonewaldesthorne's Tower is thought to be named after an Anglo-Saxon nobleman who either financed or protected this ancient structure, which was built to monitor the city's early port and harbour.

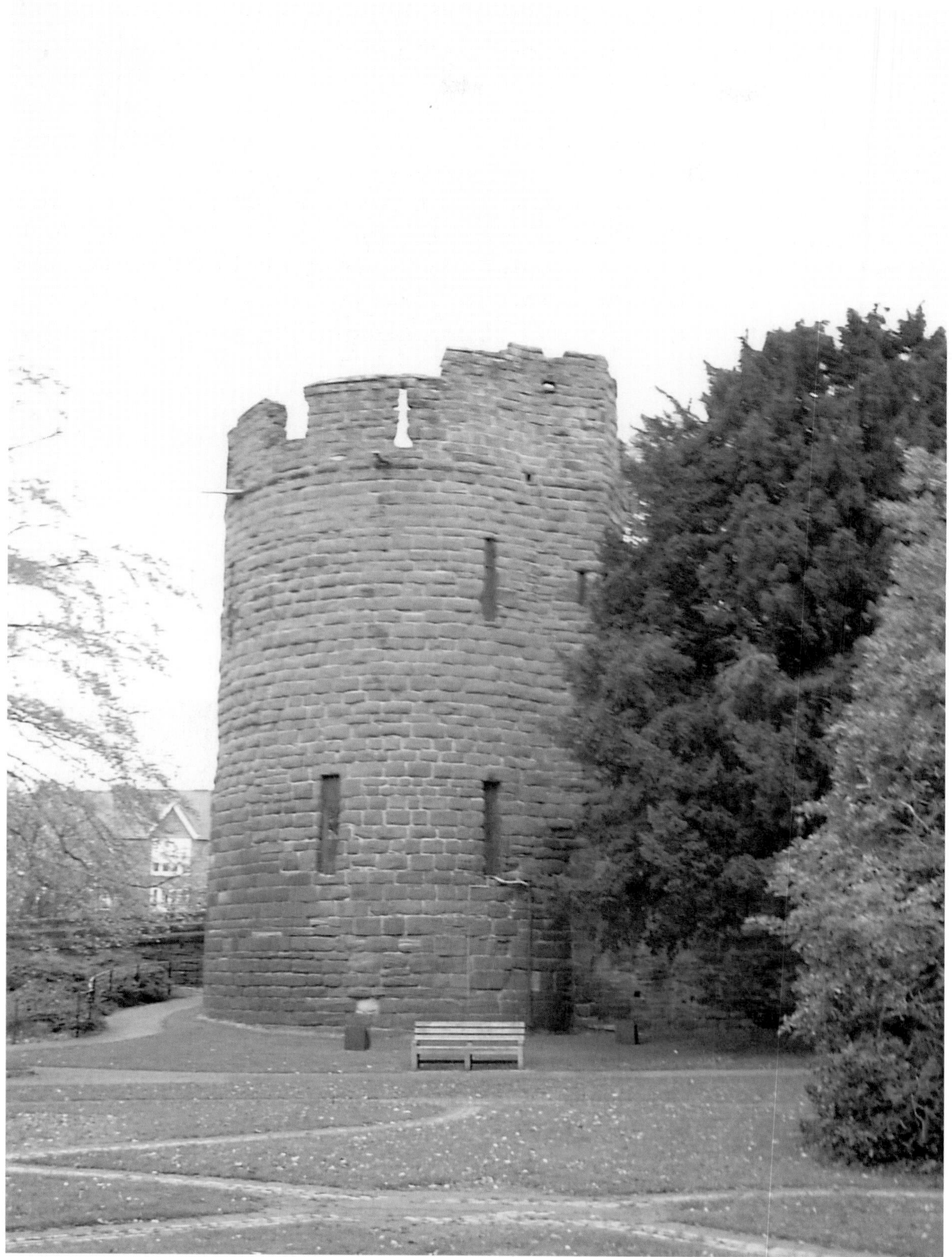

The Water Tower built *c.*1322 to protect Chester's vital harbour, but the redirecting of the river has now left it high and dry.

The 14th-century spur wall linking Bonewaldesthorne's Tower with the Water Tower built in 1322.

The archway associated with Bonewaldesthorne's Tower and the Water Tower.

A bridge crossing the River Dee was noted in the *Domesday Book* of 1086.

Pemberton's Parlour was built and was said to have been named after a local rope-maker, who was reported to have kept watch on his men from the tower while they worked below.

Further along the river the Old Dee Bridge that continues to stand today was said to have first been built during the middle years of the 14th century. References to its earlier predecessors have been found in a number of records including the *Domesday Book*. Stone guard towers which had originally stood at either end of the bridge were said to have been finally demolished in 1780 and the crossing itself was known to have been widened in 1826 as part of the city's modernisation program. These earlier guard towers were said to have stood as a defence against Welsh raiders who regularly attacked the city from the southern side of the river. The township of Handbridge, which stands on the opposite bank of the river to Chester, was commonly known as 'Treboeth' or 'Burnt Town' because it was so often destroyed by the raiders as they were attacking the city.

Chapter 9

A Monarch Deposed on the Road to Shrewsbury

Edward 'Longshanks' was succeeded by his son Edward in 1307, who, as King Edward II, was said to have visited Chester in 1312 to meet and welcome Piers de Gaveston who was returning home from Ireland. He in turn was later succeeded by his own son Edward III in 1327 who was blessed with five sons, all of whom were raised to the rank of duke. Sadly this would create a situation which would almost inevitably lead to years of deep division, mistrust and hostility between subsequent generations of the royal family.

King Edward's first son was Edward the Black Prince, born in 1330, and as the monarch's first born was made Prince of Wales, Duke of Cornwall and Earl of Chester. Following his death in 1376 while involved in a military campaign in Spain, the Black Prince's young seven-year-old son became the legitimate heir to the English throne and later succeeded to the crown as the ill-fated Richard II. During his minority the young prince should have been counselled by his uncle, John of Gaunt, but he was so despised by the English barons that an advisory council was appointed instead.

King Edward III's second son was Lionel of Antwerp who was born in 1338 and died in 1368, at the comparatively young age of 30. He was made the Duke of Clarence and during his brief life he was said to have married Elizabeth de Burgh, the daughter and heiress of the Earl of Ulster. Together they had one daughter, Philippa, who later married Edmund Mortimer, the Earl of March.

Edward's third son was the infamous John of Gaunt, who married Blanche Plantagenet and was made the Duke of Lancaster. Although he was a highly experienced soldier, Gaunt never commanded the level of respect offered to his father or his older brother Edward, a slight that seemed to follow Gaunt throughout his life. He was reported to have married three times. His second wife was Constance of Castille, whose younger sister, Isabella, had also married into the royal family. His third and final wife, Katherine Swinford, had initially been his mistress but later became his legally recognised spouse. Through his marriage with Blanche John had one son called Henry, who was made the Earl of Derby, and two daughters, Philippa who married John of Portugal and Elizabeth who married John, the Earl of Huntingdon.

With his mistress Katherine Swinford, John was recorded to have had three sons and one daughter who were all born out of wedlock and therefore deemed to be illegitimate. However, these children were later legitimised by an act of parliament and took the surname of Beaufort after the name of their father's castle in France. John Beaufort was made the Marquis of Somerset, Thomas Beaufort became the Duke of Essex and Henry Beaufort entered the church. His one and only daughter, Joan, was said to have married Ralph Neville, the Earl of Westmoreland.

Edward's fourth son was Edmund of Langley, who was made the Duke of York. He married Isabella of Castille, the younger sister of Constance who had been married to John of Gaunt. Edmund and his wife had two sons, the first of which was Edward who was made the Earl of Rutland. Their second son, Richard, was made the Earl of Cambridge and their daughter later married Thomas, the future Earl of Gloucester.

King Edward's youngest son was Thomas of Woodstock who was made the Duke of Gloucester. From his marriage he had a single daughter called Anne, who was married three times and was the foundation for the Stafford dukes of Buckingham and the Bourchier families. Thomas was said to have been appointed Justice of Chester in around 1393, but was so disliked by the local people that they rose up against him. His nephew, Richard II, having been made aware of this local antipathy towards Gloucester and having a regard for the local population, finally removed his uncle from office.

Legend suggests that Richard was invariably a mean-spirited and ruthless individual who was given to both erratic and violent mood swings. Despite the best efforts of his uncle, John of Gaunt, who tried to moderate the young king's behaviour, Richard seems to have been loathe to accept any sort of advice and was thought to have been responsible for the murder of his uncle, the Duke of Gloucester. The monarch was also said to have been liable for the murder of the Earl of Arundel and for the exile of the Dukes of Warwick and Norfolk.

Henry Bolingbroke was the eldest son of John of Gaunt and a grandson of the late Edward III, giving him a direct lineage and legitimacy to the throne of England. He was first made Earl of Derby and following his father's death was the rightful heir to the title of Duke of Lancaster. However, the family was deeply distrusted by Richard, who suspected that John of Gaunt and his sons were all conspiring to usurp him as the ruler of England and to seize the crown for their own.

Henry Bolingbroke, the Duke of Lancaster, came to Chester in 1399 to usurp his cousin, Richard II, from the throne of England, later ascending the throne himself as Henry IV.

Perhaps to forestall any attempt by the Dukes of Lancaster and their supporters to oust him, on the death of his uncle the suspicious Richard seized the lands and titles of his relatives and exiled his cousin Henry Bolingbroke from the country. The Earl of Derby had his period of exile extended from 10 years to life by the spiteful prince, who refused to allow Henry to succeed to his father's titles and estates. It was a malicious act that would ultimately have disastrous results for Richard and would lead him to lose both his kingdom and his life.

For his own part Richard appears to have been extremely fond of Chester and visited the city many times between 1398 and 1399. This fondness for the city and county is best represented in his decision to employ 2,000 Cheshire archers as part of his personal bodyguard. However, relations with the city were not always so cordial. It was reported that Richard ordered the constable of Chester to march against the Duke of Gloucester with a force of 5,000 local men. This force was subsequently beaten by Gloucester's army at Radcote with a large number of local men killed, forcing the king to pay the city 3,000 marks in compensation.

One of Richard's leading supporters, Baldwin de Radington, the controller of the royal household, was reported to have visited Chester in 1394 to procure accommodations and stores for the king. The royal agent was empowered to imprison any citizen or person that failed to comply with his requests and having reached the city he immediately presented himself at St Werburgh's. Whether or not the abbot refused his demands for accommodation and supplies is not entirely clear, but it was reported later that de Radington and his men attacked the

Benedictine house, occupied its precincts and helped themselves to large quantities of the abbey's wine stores.

A number of local men who had called to investigate the disturbance were then seized by de Radington's followers and held against their will. The city's mayor, along with his two sheriffs, then demanded to see the king's agent in order that he might explain himself and his actions. Believing the mayor to be in grave danger, someone sounded the alarm within the city which resulted in a large number of heavily armed citizens rushing to the rescue. Needless to say a riotous affray broke out in and around the abbey resulting in de Radington and his men having to flee the city by way of the 'Kale Yard' gate at the rear of the abbey and across the monks' vegetable gardens.

Furious at the treatment he had been handed down de Radington returned a few days later with a much larger force of men, determined to avenge his humiliation. Unfortunately for him, his approach had been witnessed by the local authorities and all of the city's defences were shut up against him and he was unable to exact any sort of retribution against those that he felt had wronged him.

As he was able to claim direct descent from King Edward III, by 1399 the exiled Bolingbroke had a large number of supporters within England and Richard's often brutal suppression of his political opponents or those that had a direct claim to his throne simply drove them closer to the exiled Henry's cause.

Confident that he had strong support within the country, Bolingbroke returned to England determined to reclaim his position and titles from the unpopular Richard. Having landed back in England the exiled duke made his way to London and enlisted the aid of a large number of the nobles within Richard's court.

Bolingbroke now had the military strength and popular will to confront Richard. Marching north, first to Shrewsbury and then on to Chester, Bolingbroke was later joined by a large military force in support of his cause. Richard was away in Ireland at the time and the rebel duke knew that the king would have to land in North Wales before he could hope to confront Lancaster's forces.

Bolingbroke knew that Richard's military support in the country was waning as his was increasing and it was perhaps in view of this that he chose to illustrate his resolve and lack of pity for Richard or his followers. A leading supporter of the king, Sir Piers Legh, who was seized at Chester, was executed on the orders of the Lancastrian leader and his decapitated head displayed for all to see. It was a stark reminder to those that might question their loyalty to him or were considering any possible support for his opponent.

It was possibly a sign of his confidence in his own military position that Bolingbroke does not appear to have marched into North Wales to meet the returning Richard. Instead it was reported that he sent a small party of nobles, headed by another cousin, Henry Percy, to meet and deliver the monarch to Flint Castle where the two feuding cousins might meet to finally resolve their dispute. It has been suggested that Lord Henry Percy had received an undertaking from Bolingbroke as he had no plans to seize the crown for himself, but was simply seeking to restore the family titles and lands.

Richard was said to have stayed overnight at Flint and the following day Bolingbroke arrived at the castle to speak directly with the monarch. The meeting between the two cousins was said to have been a fairly brief affair, both of them being aware of the situation and of the likely outcome, and little or nothing that was said was going to change their individual fortunes. Following this tense exchange Bolingbroke ordered that Richard and his companions be transported to Chester, where the prisoners were temporarily held in one of the gateway towers. A short time later the Lancastrian duke escorted the king to London and to his imprisonment at the tower prior to his deposition.

Henry Bolingbroke, Duke of Lancaster, subsequently ascended to the English throne as Henry IV.

Three years after the deposition of Richard II Chester hosted Henry 'Hotspur' Percy, a former sheriff of the city, within its ancient precincts, an event which would cause Henry IV to mistrust the city and its inhabitants in subsequent years. Percy and 200 of his local confederates along with their retainers led a revolt against the king that would culminate in the Battle of Shrewsbury and result in the rebels being defeated by the monarch's forces. One quarter of Henry Percy's dismembered body was later sent to Chester along with the severed heads of two of his allies so that they might be publicly displayed as a direct warning to any other potential rebels.

The son of the Duke of Northumberland and his wife Mary Plantagenet, a granddaughter of Edward III, Henry 'Hotspur' Percy was reported to have been the 'shining light' of his generation. At 11 years of age he was said to have been knighted by the then king, Richard II, and within a few years was being celebrated throughout England for his dashing good looks, his personal valour and chivalrous behaviour.

At the preposterously young age of 12 Percy was reported to have led the final charge in the relief of Berwick, which had been captured and occupied by Scottish forces who had crossed the border on one of their regular incursions in around 1376. Commanding his forces from the front, the young knight was said to have been surrounded by a large body of faithful Northumbrian troops who were dedicated to keeping their young lord safe from harm.

Having lost Berwick to the Northumbrians and the young Lord Percy, the Scots, under the command of the Earls of Montgomery and Douglas, once again invaded northern England with an army of some 50,000 men. As before they were to be faced by the Northumbrians and their charismatic young leader who, instead of confronting the Scottish army head on, allowed them to pass by his own force and only moved against them once he was sure that he had cut off any possible lines of retreat. Effectively trapped by the English, the Scottish leader Douglas challenged Percy to a bout of single combat, which the young knight perhaps foolishly accepted. Douglas was much more experienced than Percy and was thought to have easily unseated his young Northumbrian opponent.

Having been unseated by the Scottish knight, Percy might well have been captured by his enemies, had his comrades at Newcastle not rushed out to recover the temporarily incapacitated young lord from the dangerous situation. Later, Percy realised that he had not only lost his seat to Douglas but more importantly he had lost his lance to the Scottish leader, a disgrace he was honour bound to redress.

Douglas, too, recognised the importance of the captured lance to Percy and was reported to have publicly belittled 'Hotspur' regarding its loss. Having defeated the Northumbrian prince in single combat, the Scottish army besieged Newcastle and made several attempts to take the defences by force. With Percy now fully recovered, he and his brother Ralph were to be found in the vanguard of the defences and engaged in bitter hand-to-hand fighting. Time after time the Scots attacked the city, but each and every time they were repulsed by its valiant defenders. Realising that they were unable to capture the city, Douglas and Montgomery decided to lift the siege and withdraw back into Scotland. As they withdrew Douglas was thought to have taunted Henry Percy for a final time with his captured lance; it was an insult that Henry vowed to avenge.

As the Scots withdrew northward towards the safety of their borders Percy quickly gathered his forces and set off in pursuit of them. By the end of the day he was said to have caught up with the Scottish army and immediately engaged them in fierce hand-to-hand combat. The resulting Battle of Otterburn, which involved much bitter fighting between the two armies, saw Percy victorious and

Douglas defeated. True to his nature, though, 'Hotspur' then made the reckless decision to pursue the remnants of Douglas's army across the border and was subsequently captured by the Scots.

Although held captive for a period, 'Hotspur' was eventually freed, a ransom having been paid to guarantee his release. Following the bitter battle at Otterburne and the death of Douglas the border area between the two countries seems to have remained relatively settled.

In the same period when the Scottish border area was becoming settled and peaceful, the rest of England was beginning to fracture and divide as opposing factions within the country vied with one another for influence and power. Richard II had appointed a number of highly unpopular individuals to positions of power within the country and in doing so had alienated some of his previously loyal and most influential supporters. True to his highly erratic and unpredictable nature, the monarch rewarded and punished members of the nobility in an often arbitrary and casual manner, with his decisions frequently made on the basis of a perceived or unproven act.

For his part Henry Percy seems to have remained largely in Richard's favour and was reported to have been appointed as Justice of North Wales and Constable of the castles at Chester, Flint, Conway, Denbigh and Caernarvon by the king. He was also made a Knight of the Garter, Governor of Carlisle and Warden of the Western Marshes.

The Percy family's successes were generally regarded with great suspicion and jealously by their cousins, the Dukes of Lancaster, who saw them as potential rivals to the English throne. The death of John of Gaunt in 1399 marked a pivotal point in the fortunes of the family caused in part by the actions of the king himself.

Dismayed by the sovereign's actions, Hotspur later found himself under suspicion because he had dared to question Richard's unreasonable behaviour. It has been suggested that royal warrants were issued for the Percys' arrest, but the family were forewarned by their allies at court and left London for their estates in Northumbria. Fortunately for Hotspur and his family, troubles in Ireland seem to have distracted Richard and the warrants were never served on the family. These events, however, did illustrate to Hotspur the erratic and tenuous nature of the family's relations with the king and perhaps informed their future dealings with and attitudes towards Richard II.

While the sovereign was occupied in Ireland, his cousin Henry Bolingbroke had returned from France, having been persuaded by his supporters that the time was right to contest his claim against Richard. Two of the first nobles to meet with him on his return were Henry Percy along with his father, the Earl of Northumberland. They requested Bolingbroke to forego any claim against the Crown, but to instead simply settle for the return of his inheritance that had been unjustly taken from him by the king. Whether or not Bolingbroke was genuine about the undertaking he gave the Percys in respect of his claim to the Crown is unknown, but his later actions tend to suggest that he agreed the Percys' terms simply to reassure them and to gain their military support against the king.

Richard had returned from Ireland to find the majority of the country set against him and his army either disbanded or fragmented. As he arrived at Conway, instead of being met by a loyal army waiting to fight his cause he found messengers carrying news of his opponent's gains and military assets. With few options left open to him, Richard sent the Earl of Essex to meet with Bolingbroke at Chester, where the exiled duke was mustering his forces.

Having imprisoned Essex, Bolingbroke asked Percy and his father to meet with Richard, who was likely to be more trusting of his relatives than he would of a stranger. Riding westward along the North Wales coast, the earl and his son soon met up with the king who reluctantly accepted their guarantees for his safety and their offer of escort. Having issued arrest warrants against the Percys there was little reason for Richard to trust them, but given the situation he found himself in he had little if any choice. For their part, whether or not Hotspur and his father believed that Richard would remain safe was not an issue. They had received an oath from Bolingbroke that he would not pursue his claim to the throne and they were content that he would stand by that solemn undertaking.

The deposition of Richard meant that Bolingbroke had broken his sacred vow to the Percys not to pursue the Crown. He now sought to exclude Edmund Mortimer, the rightful heir to the throne who was in the care of the Percy family. Perhaps recognising that Henry Percy had the same rights and claims to the English throne as himself, Henry IV sought to reward the family's services to him. The Earl of Northumberland was said to have been made the Lord High Constable of England, while his son Hotspur was appointed as the Warden of the Eastern Marshes and named Governor of Berwick, Chester and Flint. The Percy family also gained possession of the Isle of Man and its dominions.

Despite the granting and receipt of lands and titles between the two parties, the relationship between the Percys and Henry IV continued to be cool and fractious. Charged with holding the troubled North Wales area for the king, Hotspur had to continually demand payment from the monarch to pay his troops and maintain the region's defences. Eventually the young knight became so exasperated by the task that he resigned his post, much to the displeasure of Henry IV.

Around 1402 a series of border skirmishes allowed Hotspur to distract himself from all the political intrigue and factional infighting that was circulating throughout the country. These incursions were only finally stopped when Percy met and defeated the Scottish raiders at the Battle of Nesbitt Moor. In response to this defeat the Scots once again launched a full-scale invasion of England with a force of over 10,000 men. Yet again Hotspur was called on to meet the military challenge and repeated his earlier strategy of allowing the invaders to pass by before blocking their retreat and then attacking them with his troops. Percy's force now included a large number of Cheshire Archers who devastated the lines of the Scots and led to a relatively easy victory.

Having captured a number of the Scottish leaders, Hotspur had planned to ransom them back to their families or exchange them for English prisoners. However, these plans were upset by the king who demanded that the Scottish leaders should be held as hostages in London to prevent further incursions from the north. Hotspur was not inclined to comply with the sovereign's orders and when he finally did obey the king's command he ensured that the main Scottish leader, the Earl of Douglas, was not among their number. Furious at Percy's refusal to hand over Douglas, Henry IV demanded that the young lord appear before him personally to explain his actions.

The sovereign refrained from punishing Hotspur, aware that the young lord could easily become a focal point for his enemies. Instead he granted Percy and his father the lands and titles of their prisoner, Douglas. It was a deliberate and planned act by the monarch who was relying on Hotspur and his father pacifying these new lands at no financial or military cost to the English Crown.

Henry IV already had it in mind to seize the Percy lands and estates at a point in time of his own choosing – an act deliberately designed to force the family into a military conflict with the crown. Given that the Percys' claim to the throne was equal to his own, the king had decided on a winner-takes-all strategy, which would either end or ensure his right to reign England unopposed.

The king's antipathy towards the Percy family may well have been strengthened by Hotspur's marriage to Elizabeth Mortimer and the later birth of a son to the couple. Elizabeth was an aunt of

Roger Mortimer, the Earl of March and the legitimate heir to the English throne. The young son born to Percy and his wife was also a threat to Henry IV's role as monarch and simply reinforced the Percy/Mortimer claim to the Crown.

Having been made aware of the king's plans, Hotspur decided to pre-empt the monarch by publicly proclaiming for the Earl of March and disputing the king's right to the Crown. Making sure that his wife and young son were safe, Percy rallied his forces and began his fateful journey southward towards Cheshire and North Wales. The Earl of Northumberland, Hotspur's father, did not immediately join his son, but remained in the north to gather allies that might support a rebellion against Henry IV.

Around July 1403 Percy was reported to have been in Chester where he was seeking men to support his cause on behalf of the Earl of March and to publicly denounce Henry IV for his treatment of the ousted king, Richard II. It was said that Percy announced that Richard was still alive and being held prisoner, but this is unlikely as Percy and most of the assembled men that were present must have known that Richard was dead and had been for some time.

Hotspur's other reason for being in the region was thought to have been to meet with Owain Glyndwr, the rebel Welsh leader who was an opponent of Henry IV and a potential military ally to Percy's cause. In earlier times Glyndwr had held Edmund Mortimer as a captive for his own ends, but following the Earl of March's marriage to Glyndwr's daughter had now become a supporter of the young Edmund's claim to the English throne.

From an early age Henry 'Hotspur' Percy was famous for his gallant and chivalrous behaviour and the treatment he accorded those under his care or in his custody. Despite having a distant claim to the English Crown himself, history suggests that he only ever sought to serve his monarch, regardless of the financial or physical cost to himself or his estates. It is not unsurprising, therefore, that following Henry IV's decision to renege on his earlier promises, Percy took the young Edmund Mortimer, the rightful heir to the throne, into his personal care.

Along with his assembled force Percy left the city of Chester and moved on to Sandiway where he was to be joined by his uncle, the Earl of Worcester, with his own armed retinue. After mustering their combined forces, Hotspur and his uncle moved towards Shrewsbury where they expected to finally confront their mutual enemy.

Prince Henry, later the famed warrior king Henry V, who had accompanied Percy on his earlier travels, was thought to have been stationed at Shrewsbury along with his own forces as the day of battle dawned. Some historians have suggested that the young prince actively participated in the later Battle of Shrewsbury against Percy, while others have stated that he deliberately withheld his force from the confrontation because he could not face having to oppose his former friend in combat.

Having arrived at the gates of Shrewsbury, the presence of Henry's standards in the town confirmed to Hotspur that his opponent was already in attendance and prepared to meet him. Moving his forces slightly north-west of the town Percy and his retinue were thought to have stayed at the nearby Berwick Grange on the eve of the battle. He was still hoping to be joined by the Welsh leader Owain Glyndwr, as well as the Earl of Northumberland, in his fight against the king and was confident that their combined forces would be more than a match for the king's army. Sadly, as it later transpired, both of these potential allies were more than a day's ride away and would afford Percy little aid in his subsequent battle with the king. Unknown to Percy, his father had been struck down by illness which had delayed his arrival from the north.

At the forthcoming battle Percy's forces would once again be supported by a large number of Cheshire Archers, considered to be some of the finest fighting men in the country. The following morning Percy and Worcester began to assemble their forces in a field a little over two miles outside of Shrewsbury in the parish of Albright Hussey and lying close to the main Whitchurch Road. Opposite them the army of Henry arrived from Shrewsbury and as both sides began to settle themselves into their military formations, the scene of battle was slowly beginning to be set.

In a final bid to try and prevent a bloody confrontation between the two parties, the king sent a messenger forward asking Percy and his uncle to come before him in order that they might resolve their differences in a peaceful manner. Unfortunately, by this time the monarch was so mistrusted by Percy and his uncle that they simply refused his invitation and an armed conflict became inevitable.

The Battle of Shrewsbury was thought to have been started by the king's army. His opening act was immediately met by a hail of arrows fired by Percy's Cheshire Archers who were in the vanguard of his force and were devastatingly effective. Having decimated the leading ranks of Henry's army, the fearless and headstrong Hotspur instinctively galloped forward to engage the enemy.

Fighting his way into the main body of the opposition forces, Percy caught sight of what he thought was the king and, pushing himself forward, fell upon Henry and cut him down. A shout went up that the king was dead, but then yet another figure appeared dressed in the royal attire. It soon became evident that the monarch had arranged for a number of knights to carry his colours in order to distract and confuse Hotspur and his men. The king himself was safe at the rear of his forces, having been escorted there by a number of his leading supporters.

In the heat of the battle and perhaps to try and clearly identify his enemy, Hotspur was thought to have lifted his visor, a mistake that would have fatal consequences. A stray crossbow bolt, fired by a member of the king's contingent, found its way through the young knight's defences and killed him instantly.

With their charismatic young leader dead, Hotspur's forces began to waver and in some areas began to flee the field, anxious to escape the inevitable fate of a defeated army. The battle now swung fully in the king's favour and within a short time there were few of Percy's men left alive and those that had survived soon faced Henry's inevitable revenge. For those that had fled the field in the hope of surviving the king's wrath it was a forlorn hope, as each one was hunted down by their enemy and forced to face royal retribution.

Following the end of the bloody battle, Henry ordered a search to be made for the body of Hotspur. The young knight's remains were reported to have been taken to a chapel near Whitchurch where prayers were said for his eternal rest. Initially Henry was said to have been distraught at his former ally's death, but shortly afterwards ordered Hotspur's body to be dismembered and one quarter displayed on the city gate at Chester as a deterrent to any other would-be rebels.

Because of the city's perceived support for Percy's cause, Henry IV deeply mistrusted the people of Chester as well as their Welsh neighbours. He ordered the city authorities to issue a series of local ordinances which restricted the rights and movements of Welsh citizens within the city limits, with severe penalties applied for any infraction of the new laws. All Welshmen were ordered to leave their arms at the city's gates and they were prohibited from meeting in groups of more than three people. They also had to leave the city precincts by the end of the day or risk the threat of execution. The city's fortunes did eventually improve in the coming years and later rulers would be far more generous to Chester and its citizens.

The fortunes of the River Dee would not improve however. When Henry VI visited Chester in 1454 it was reported that he could only get to within 12 miles of the city by sea, so extensive was the silting of the river. In order to reduce the hardship on the city the king agreed to reduce the royal levies that were due to him. Edward, the son of Henry VI, was crowned Earl of Chester in 1454 and it would be some 40 years before Henry VII would visit the city with his queen in 1494. By the time of his visit, it was said that large sea-going vessels could no longer reach Chester's ancient port and that only relatively small, shallow draught boats could gain access to the city's ancient harbour.

In response to these changes the city's traders and shipping merchants were compelled to construct new harbour facilities further west, along the northern bank of the river. Initially the new site was said to have been based at Blacon Point in Chester, where cargoes would be unloaded and transported into the city either by road or other smaller river craft. Sadly, this was only ever a temporary solution and as the silting worsened, so the port facilities were pushed further north and west to Shotwick, Parkgate, Hoylake and finally Meols at the tip of the Wirral Peninsula. Each and every one of these sites would be used in an effort to try and maintain the city's international trading routes, but all would ultimately prove to be unsuccessful.

Chapter 10

From the Stanley Family to the Tudor Dynasty

The Stanley family have played a sometimes pivotal role in Chester's history and are thought to have originated from the Audleys of Staffordshire, who had been landowners from the time of the conquest. During the reign of King John a member of this extensive family was said to have adopted the name 'de Standleigh', which was thought to reflect the name of their family estate in that county. As was common around that time this family surname was later contracted to 'Stanley' and its members were reported to be the predecessors of the Stanley family of Hooton, Latham, Knowsley and Alderley, who would later play a significant part in the development of north-west England. These early generations of the family were said to have amassed much of their family fortune and influence through strategic marriages or by their service to the various monarchs that were in power.

A William Stanley was reported to have married Jane, the daughter and heiress of Sir Philip Barnville of Storeton in Cheshire, which was thought to have marked the initial migration of the family into the north-western county. A later union of this same family line was said to have brought them lands and titles at Hooton on the Wirral, Knowsley in Lancashire and helped to establish the Baron Stanleys of Alderley.

Sir John Stanley was thought to be a direct descendant of the aforementioned William Stanley. Sir John was said to have been a faithful servant to the English monarchy, particularly to Richard II and as a result was reported to have greatly enhanced the family's influence, holdings and wealth throughout his lifetime. He was known to have married Isabel, the daughter and heiress of Sir Thomas de Latham, and as a result of this union acquired lands at both Knowsley and Latham. He was also said to have been appointed as Lord Deputy of Ireland by the erratic and often unpopular Richard II.

Following Richard's deposition, Sir John continued to retain his close links with the monarchy and was appointed as Lord Lieutenant of Ireland by the new King Henry IV. The aftermath of the rebellion led by Henry 'Hotspur' Percy and the resulting Battle of Shrewsbury in 1403 saw Stanley acquire the Isle of Man, which had been previously held by the defeated Percy family. The title to these lands granted Stanley almost sovereign-like powers within the island and in order to fully exploit these new concessions he was said to have built a new and impressive property in Liverpool, which fronted onto the River Mersey and allowed him easy sea-borne access to the island.

This grandiose town house was said to have survived largely intact through to the early 19th century, having served as the Stanley's town house, the city assembly rooms and finally as a city gaol. As for Sir John Stanley himself, he was reported to have died in around 1414.

His eldest son, a second John Stanley, was said to have spent much of his early life consolidating the fortune and titles amassed by his predecessor. He in turn was then succeeded by his own son, Thomas Stanley, who was appointed as Lord Lieutenant of Ireland and around 1456 was said to have been called to sit in parliament as the first Lord Stanley. Unfortunately for Thomas, he was thought to have only survived for a short period following his appointment. His successor, Sir Thomas Stanley, was born around 1435 and succeeded his father to the family estates as the second Lord Stanley, being made the first Earl of Derby by Henry VII in recognition of his service to the Crown. Sir Thomas has been credited with building the family's fortunes to undreamt-of levels, often by cleverly manipulating people or events that were happening about him. He was said to have married Eleanor, the daughter and heiress of Richard Neville, the Earl of Salisbury, and who was a sister to the Earl of Warwick – often regarded as the 'kingmaker' such was his power and influence. In 1459 a conflict erupted between Warwick and the Earl of Exeter, with both men trying to exert personal control over the luckless monarch, Henry VI. Ultimately, these political manoeuvrings ended in military conflict between the two sides which culminated in the Battle of Blore Heath. Stanley was said to have found his loyalties deeply divided, as the battle saw his father-in-law, Salisbury, in direct conflict with Lord Audley, the same family from which the Stanleys themselves were thought to have originally descended.

As a highly astute politician Stanley opted to remain neutral in any dispute between the two opposing forces and simply contented himself to offering moral support to both sides. When he was questioned by the king as to his regular absences from court Stanley simply excused himself by stating that he had been away or suffering from an illness. Perhaps surprisingly the king seems to have accepted his excuses and in 1460 ordered Stanley to bring the sons of the Earl of Salisbury before him. Sir John and Sir Thomas Neville had both been held at Chester's mediaeval castle following their defeat at the Battle of Blore Heath. Stanley's two brothers-in-law were accompanied on their journey by two of their comrades, Thomas and James Harrington, who were also ordered to be brought before the monarch. Thomas Harrington was the owner of Hornby Castle in Lancashire and James was his heir. Following their rebellion against the king their estates were later seized and subsequently ended up in the hands of the Stanley family.

Following Henry VI's deposition by the Yorkist claimant Edward IV, Stanley managed to retain his position as a friend of the monarch and was afterwards appointed as Justice of Chester. Some eight years later, the Earl of Warwick, the man who had effectively put Edward on the throne, changed his allegiance once again and now sought to restore Henry VI as king. In support of this cause the Earl of Warwick's forces, under Lord Wille, were comprehensively beaten by the king's forces at the Battle of Stamford in 1470. Having seen his army defeated Warwick then approached Stanley, his brother-in-law, for help in his quest to remove Edward from the throne. Typically, though, Lord Stanley was said to have refused Warwick's request for help and instead waited to see how events would develop before committing himself to any sort of pre-emptive action.

In spite of his refusal to Warwick, within a few months Edward had been ousted from the throne and his Lancastrian opponent, Henry VI, had been restored to the Crown. The 'kingmaker' Warwick was said to have been accompanied on his journey to London by his hesitant brother-in-law Stanley, who was now keen to actively support the cause of the reinstated monarch.

Some 18 months later the whole situation had been reversed yet again; Edward had returned and had defeated Henry's Lancastrian forces at the Battle of Barnet in April 1471. The most noted casualty was the Earl of Warwick, Stanley's brother-in-law, who had been at the root of all the political plotting and manoeuvring which had beset the country for a decade. The next month witnessed the Battle of Tewkesbury which finally and definitively settled the dispute between the two royal claimants and saw the Lancastrian cause finally consigned to history. When the former Henry VI died in mysterious circumstances while being held at the Tower of London, Edward IV was finally secured as the one and only king of England.

With the country relatively peaceful, Stanley was able to re-establish and secure his place at court, finally becoming Steward of the royal household to Edward. He accompanied Richard, the Duke of Gloucester, in his military campaigns against the Scots in 1482 and was reported to have led the force that liberated the town of Berwick-upon-Tweed, which has remained in English hands ever since.

During these turbulent years Stanley's first wife was reported to have died and around 1481 he was said to have remarried, this time to Margaret Beaufort who was a distant relative of John of Gaunt, the father of Henry IV. With a much disputed claim to the English Crown, at 14 years old Margaret had been married to Edmund, the Earl of Richmond, a half-brother to Henry VI, who had recently died in the tower. Edmund had died in around 1456 shortly after the birth of his one and only son, Henry, the Earl of Richmond, who would later become Henry VII. Margaret had then married Sir Henry Stafford, the son of Humphrey, the Duke of Buckingham, who subsequently died in around 1481.

Margaret's later marriage to Sir Thomas Stanley meant that he had inadvertently become the stepfather to a potential Lancastrian heir to the English throne. It was a fact not lost on a reigning monarch that had earlier been beset by counterclaims made by members of the same family. However, Stanley and his new wife had both developed keen political instincts that helped them to minimise any potential threat to the sovereign. Their devotion to one another and their service to the Crown no doubt attributed to the rise of the Tudor dynasty and their subsequent accession to the English throne.

During the reign of Edward IV there was only one candidate for the throne, the king's young son Edward. However, following the monarch's death in 1483 the matter became much more complicated with much of the country being divided into three separate camps, all of which supported their own particular candidate for the Crown.

Initially the line of succession had remained intact and the young Edward V had ascended the throne following his father's death. Although family ties might well have led Stanley to support his stepson Henry for the Crown, he was thought to have initially accepted Edward's right to rule England. However, events beyond his control conspired to see the young prince murdered and his uncle Richard, the Duke of Gloucester, seize the throne for himself. Stanley and his wife now needed all their political skills and wits to avoid becoming embroiled in a contest for the Crown which might well see their very own survival threatened.

As in earlier disputes, Stanley seems to have adopted a highly pragmatic view towards the whole situation and adapted easily to the new administration that ruled the country. Once again he was appointed as Steward of the royal household, the post he had previously held under Edward IV, and was also chosen as Constable of England which became a lifetime's posting.

Unfortunately for Lord Stanley, his new wife was not as discreet or forgiving towards the new monarch. A conspiracy to oust Richard in favour of Margaret's son Henry was discovered by the authorities, implicating both the Duke of Buckingham and Stanley's wife. Following the execution of Buckingham the king ordered an inquiry into the behaviour and involvement of Margaret with the plotters. Although she was subsequently found guilty of some connection with the scheme, it was only her own property and lands that were seized by the Crown and not those of her husband. As she was married to a great favourite of Richard III, Margaret escaped any serious punishment regarding her involvement with the affair; her fellow conspirators, however, did not.

In August 1485 Margaret's son Henry, the exiled Duke of Richmond, returned to England to settle his dispute with the usurper Richard III. On the 22 August the two forces met at the Battle of Bosworth, a confrontation which was ultimately decided by a member of the Stanley family.

The younger brother of Lord Thomas Stanley, William Stanley was reported to have used his forces against Richard as the battle raged and in doing so swayed the course of events. His older brother, Thomas, was said to have remained fairly inactive in the initial phase of the battle and only became involved as the tide began to go against the usurper Richard. With the battle finally won and Richard dead, legend has it that one of the Stanley's picked up the battered crown from the field and placed it on Henry Tudor's head. It was an act of recognition that the new Henry VII would not forget. Sir Thomas was subsequently made the first Earl of Derby by the new king in recognition of his service to the Crown. Sir William Stanley was appointed as Chancellor of the Exchequer and granted lands and titles by the new king. At the height of his power and influence he was reported to be the richest man in the country, until fate conspired to rob him of his lands, his influence and eventually his life.

Whether by accident or by design, William was reported to have become involved with a plot which centred around one Perkin Warbeck, a supposed pretender to the throne, who it was feared might threaten Henry Tudor's right to rule. The case against William seems to have rested on a single remark made about the pretender, which suggested Stanley's belief that Perkin Warbeck was indeed a genuine heir. When he was challenged about his remark, Sir William was said to have refused either to confirm or deny his beliefs in respect of the matter and in doing so inadvertently condemned himself. Sentenced to death by a council appointed by the king, Sir William Stanley was executed on 14 February 1485, with his lands and titles being sequestered by the Crown. Despite this Sir Thomas Stanley remained faithful to Henry Tudor and continued to consolidate and build on the family's notable achievements and good fortunes. When he died in 1504 he had survived the turbulent reigns of four different English monarchs including Edward IV, Edward V, Richard III and Henry VII. During his lifetime he had somehow managed to avoid the political pitfalls, seizures and executions that had befell many of his contemporaries. He was survived by two of his six sons, all by his first wife Eleanor. His eldest son George, Lord Strange, had died in 1497 and it was his son, Sir Thomas's grandson, that succeeded to the title of Lord Derby in 1504.

Around the same period that the fortunes and the fates of the Stanley family were being subjected to the peaks and troughs of nationally important events, the city of Chester and its citizens remained as a focus for simmering Welsh resentment, no doubt caused in part by the fortress's 500-year history as an English military stronghold and a place of Welsh suppression.

Robert Byrne was said to have been the Mayor of Chester who in around 1462 was seized by a local Welsh landowner while visiting a local fair being held at Mold. The landowner, Reginald ap Gruffydd, had had a number of disputes with the city and its authorities and was not well disposed towards them. Following a violent commotion between these Chester visitors and a group of local men, Gruffydd was reported to have seized Byrne and taken him back to his home where he strung the unfortunate man up from a metal fastener. On hearing that their mayor had been captured, a large number of Chester men hurriedly made their way to Mold and then on to Gruffydd's house where they believed that their kinsman was being held.

Having anticipated their actions Gruffydd was said to have hidden himself in some nearby woods and watched as the band of angry Englishmen broke into his property searching for their missing mayor. With the band inside his house the Welshman was reported to have rushed out from his hiding place and secured them inside the place. He then set fire to the building and watched as the flames consumed a good number of those that were inside. The remaining Englishmen, along with a small number that had somehow managed to escape the inferno, then found themselves being violently attacked by Gruffydd and his supporters. Outnumbered by the landowner and his men, the remaining Cestrians were forced to retreat in some disorder, with many of their number reported to have been drowned as they fell back across the River Dee.

Licensed since 1494, The Blue Bell Inn has been successively used as an inn, coaching office, shop and restaurant.

In July 1494 King Henry VII, along with his mother and his queen, was said to have come to Chester with a large retinue, and the royal party was later reported to have visited the nearby castle at Hawarden. It was thought to be during a later visit in 1506 that the king granted Chester its Great Charter, creating it a county town. The city's new corporation was reported to have included a mayor, 24 aldermen, 40 councillors, two sheriffs and two murengers, who were held to be responsible for maintaining Chester's historic city walls.

Two years after Chester had been granted its Great Charter, a new hospital was reported to have been founded within the city. St Ursula's was said to have been established in the Commonhall Street area of Chester in the town house of a former city sheriff, Roger Smith. In the same year Richard Goodman was elected Mayor of Chester and immediately issued a local ordinance demanding that lamps or lanterns should be hung in the doorways of all Chester men that had been either sheriff or mayor of the city. Local innkeepers were also said to have been required to keep a lantern above the door to their premises.

In later years Chester was required by Henry VIII to provide men for the protection of the Scottish borders in 1522 and 14 years later his first campaign of religious suppression was felt within the city. The three existing friaries, those of the Dominicans, Franciscans and Carmelites, were dissolved in 1536 by order of the king, with their properties seized and in some cases sold or destroyed. The Benedictine convent at Chester somehow managed to escape these earlier purges but was itself dissolved in the later round of closures initiated by Henry in 1540.

Although best known historically for his many wives, Henry's marital problems were generally thought to be matters of national interest, rather than regional. However, on at least one occasion the issue was known to have had dire consequences for one of Cheshire's leading families.

Sir William Brereton was said to have been a member of the historic Cheshire family whose name was thought to derive from the Manor of Bretune, which was first mentioned in the *Domesday Book*. Sir William was reported to have held the post of Chamberlain of Chester and according to a county legend was unfortunate enough to fall foul of Henry

The Old Queens Head displaying its 16th-century foundation date.

Each successive abbot helped to develop Chester's Norman abbey over a period of some 400 years.

VIII's infamous jealousy and political intrigues surrounding Anne Boleyn.

Along with Sir Henry Norris, Sir Francis Weston, Lord Rochford, who was Anne Boleyn's brother, and a young man called Mark Smeaton, Brereton was accused of adultery with the unfortunate queen, no doubt as part of the monarch's attempt to rid himself of his seemingly unproductive spouse. Found guilty by a jury chosen by the king, all were subsequently executed for their 'treason'. Even the entirely innocent Anne Boleyn did not escape the king's political machinations and was later beheaded at the Tower of London on 19 May 1536.

Following Henry VIII's official dissolution of the monasteries, St Werburgh's was said to have disposed of many of its possessions within 18 months of the proclamation and the church was later re-founded and re-dedicated as a cathedral to Christ and the Blessed Virgin. It was known to be only one of six former monastic houses that were granted cathedral status in all of England and became the centre of the newly formed Chester diocese. In 1543 Chester finally acquired parliamentary representation and was authorised to elect two new members for the national legislature based in Westminster.

Subjected to the religious purges of Henry VIII, Chester's ancient Norman abbey was later re-dedicated as a cathedral.

At the city's new cathedral John Bird, described by one source as a 'one-eyed rogue', was appointed as the first Bishop of Chester and held office from 1541 through to 1554. Bird had begun his religious career in Coventry as a member of the Carmelite community that existed in the city. During the reign of Henry VIII he was a member of the group that was involved in the arrangements for the king's marriage to Anne of Cleves. Later he was a staunch apologist for the monarch's marital disputes, a support which later gained Bird the Bishopric of Chester. Following Henry's death Bird was later dismissed from his post by the Catholic Queen Mary for being a married man. Despite his pleas that he had been tricked into the marriage and that he had now disowned his wife, his petitions were ignored by the queen.

An historic character in the city during Queen Mary's reign was Elizabeth Mottershead, the landlady of the Blue Posts Inn at Chester, located in the Bridge Street area of the city. During the reign of the staunchly Roman Catholic queen, the Protestant faithful in Ireland were mercilessly suppressed by the English monarch. In a bid to further reduce and undermine the influence of the Protestant church the queen ordered Dr Henry Cole, the Dean of St Paul's, to carry her new royal commission to her ruling council in Dublin detailing the fresh sanctions which were to be implemented against the Protestant faithful. Unfortunately for the queen, Cole stayed at the Blue Posts as he passed through Chester and loudly elaborated on his important mission to the city's mayor, a conversation which was said to have been overheard by Elizabeth Mottershead who had a Protestant brother living in Dublin. As Cole bid the mayor farewell, she was said to have stolen into his room and replaced the written commission with a deck of cards. Completely unaware of her actions, the dean then continued his journey to Dublin and called upon the Lord Lieutenant and his council to deliver the queen's new instructions. Needless to say Cole was shocked and outraged to discover that his royal commission had been 'magically' replaced by a pack of cards and was at a complete loss to explain the exchange. The bemused Lord Lieutenant was said to have ordered the dean to return to England for a new commission and in the meantime he and his council would amuse themselves with a game of cards. Before Cole could reach England however, Mary was dead and had been succeeded by the Protestant Elizabeth and the threat therefore removed. On hearing of the Chester landlady's actions the new queen was reported to have ordered that she be awarded a £40-a-year pension for life for her zeal and ingenuity.

George Cotes was recorded as the successor to John Bird and held the office of Bishop of Chester from 1554 to 1555. Cotes was said to be the man who finally and reluctantly condemned George Marsh to burn at the stake in Chester for his 'heretical' beliefs. Marsh was reported to have been a preacher from Lancashire who publicly criticised the Bishop of Chester for blasphemous idolatry, holy water casting, procession gadding, matins mumbling, mass hearing and other such heathenism's forbidden by God. The English Privy Council, on hearing of his preaching, instructed the Lord Lieutenant of Lancashire to take action against Marsh, but rather than seeing the issue as a secular one, he declared that Marsh's remarks were the concern of the church and passed the case to George Cotes, the newly appointed Bishop of Chester. Arrested and transported to Chester, Marsh was said to have been held for several months at the bishop's palace in the city, while the bishop, archdeacon and other learned men tried to reconcile with him. His constant refusal to recant his beliefs, however, almost inevitably forced the church to bring Marsh to trial on the charges being laid against him.

Brought to trial in the cathedral's lady chapel, Marsh appeared before a panel which included the bishop, the mayor of Chester and the chancellor, all of whom still hoped to persuade him of his errors. Unfortunately, the obstinate preacher could not be persuaded to recant his beliefs and left his judges with little option but to condemn him. Even as the bishop read out the judgement against him, the mayor and chancellor both tried to find a resolution that would help to release him, but Marsh was not to be moved from his view. Having finished reading the decision of the court, the bishop, in frustration, remarked 'Now I will no more pray for thee, than I would for a dog'. Having been tried and found guilty of heresy by the religious court Marsh was burnt at the stake the following year. Although he was offered a conditional pardon by the vice chancellor, a Mr Vawdrey, Marsh was said to have refused it simply remarking 'Not under these circumstances'. On the day of his execution John Cowper was reported to have been the city sheriff that tried to rescue Marsh from the stake but was prevented from doing so by the other city sheriff. Cowper himself was said to have been forced to flee the city and had his family's assets seized by the authorities.

Cuthbert Scott was reported to be the successor to George Cotes and held the office from 1556 to 1559. He was recorded as having been committed to the Tower of London for some offence or other, but was later released on bail. He was obviously not that certain about his future however, and while on bail took flight to France and was later reported to have died at Louvain in 1564.

George Lloyd was the Bishop of Chester between 1604 and 1615 and had previously been Bishop of the Sodor of Man in 1599. Reported to have been the owner of Bishop Lloyds Palace, which is located in modern-day Watergate Street, this particular building is thought to post-date his death so his ownership is highly unlikely. His brother David was said to have been Mayor of Chester from 1593–94 and his eldest daughter was married to Thomas Yale, a descendant of the American university's founder.

In spite of the major difficulties caused by the silting of the river, Chester continued to thrive as a centre for international trade and commerce throughout much of the 16th century. Its leather manufacturing industries had become one of the city's largest income generators and despite its ongoing decline the harbour remained the largest port in the whole of north-west England. Chester was a major national distribution centre for a number of basic products including wool, leather, cereal crops and livestock. Thomas Lyniall, said to have been a local merchant, was granted the lease on the Roodee in Chester during the reign of Elizabeth I and reportedly built an embankment on the site, extracting tolls from every ship and boat that berthed there.

The city was also said to have remained as a mustering and embarkation point for troops that were being shipped to Ireland, which continued to be turbulent throughout much of the period. It was recorded that Fulk Aldersey, a member of a wealthy local family, was Mayor of Chester three times and during his last term of office was disrupted by the large number of soldiers that gathered in Chester prior to their departure for Ireland. Reacting to their unruly behaviour, he arranged for a gibbet to be erected at the city's High Cross and imprisoned a number of soldiers. Fortunately for the miscreants, the intervention of their officers saved them from serious harm and they were quickly shipped out of the city.

Although she was said to have been far more tolerant to other faiths than her Catholic predecessor, Elizabeth was prepared to defend the Protestant faith at all costs and was merciless in her fight with the Catholic rebels in Ireland. Walter Devereaux, the Earl of Essex, was reported to have been in Chester on his way to Ireland when he was commissioned by the queen to suppress the Catholic unrest by whatever means necessary.

Lord Leicester, the Chamberlain of Chester during the reign of Elizabeth, was a keen advocate of the Protestant cause and campaigned tirelessly against the Church of Rome. By around 1578 most of the crosses in the city were said to have been removed, a task undertaken by a city sheriff called Mutton. These overtly religious symbols were known to have stood at the bars, the city's north gate and at the spital in Boughton.

At around the same time a royal decree was said to have been issued by the queen calling on Chester's civil authorities to fully investigate the comings and goings of Roman Catholics in the city. The local port was thought to have been used regularly by Catholic priests and converts to come in and out of England.

Towards the end of the century, around 1570, the city's governing body began to introduce a series of new measures which were designed to reduce the numbers of beggars, loafers and sickly people that were being attracted to Chester by the city's obvious wealth. A surgeon was appointed to ensure that any carriers of sickness and disease were held at the city limits and quarantined from the local community. A workhouse was built outside of the city's northern gate where the unemployed and indigent could be put to work in return for accommodation and food. A leading citizen of Chester, Henry Gee, is regarded by many as a reforming mayor who held the office in both 1533 and 1539. He was responsible for introducing the city's assembly book, creating a list of previous office holders within the city and recording details of the city limits and a list of custom duties and official fees. Gee was also reported to have enacted a raft of city ordinances, including legislation preventing unlawful gambling, excessive drinking and celebrations, and he introduced local standards regarding women's dress and behaviour. He was also said to have brought in local ordinances which required the unemployed and able-bodied people to present themselves for work.

During his second term of office in 1539 Gee was said to have issued additional local ordinances which forbade the owning or running of an ale house by a woman aged between 14 and 40 years of age, under threat of a £40 fine. He also introduced local statutes requiring all children over six years of age to attend school and forbidding single women from wearing white or coloured hats. All townswomen were forbidden from wearing hats, unless they were riding or 'abroad in the country'.

William Beswick was recorded as another Mayor of Chester who, in 1542, issued a number of ordinances that were designed to improve the morality and the behaviour of the citizens and included the suppression of the many brothels which existed within the city limits. Henry Hardware who was the Mayor of Chester between 1599 and 1600 was reported to have been fairly unpopular with the citizens of Chester because of his suppression of the city's traditional bull and bear-baiting contests and the annual fairs. He was also said to have ordered that the Midsummer Giants, a feature of the city's fairs, should be broken up.

John Radcliffe was mayor of Chester in 1602 and 1611, and was a Member of the Puritan congregation who attended services at St Peter's Church which were led by Nicholas Byfield. Radcliffe was said to have been elected as MP for Chester in 1661. During his first term as mayor he ordered the restoration of the city's Midsummer Giants which had been ordered to be destroyed by his predecessor, Henry Hardware.

A notable religious figure of the mid-16th century was the Protestant preacher Christopher Goodman. Although he was born in Chester in around 1520 Goodman was reported to have received much of his formal education in Oxford. A staunch Protestant, in order to escape the religious purges of the Catholic Queen Mary Goodman was said to have travelled to Germany and later accompanied John Knox to Switzerland. He was later appointed as pastor to the thriving English community in Geneva and both he and Knox chose to remain there, out of harms way, until Mary's death in 1558.

Goodman has been credited with helping Knox to compose *The Book of Common Order*, a directory for Protestant worship. He was also said to have maintained a correspondence with an old friend in England called Bartlett Green. Having received news that Mary had died, Goodman asked his old friend to confirm the news for him. Green had replied 'the Queen is not yet dead', but unfortunately for him the letter was intercepted by agents of the queen and Bartlett Green was later burnt at the stake for his beliefs.

Following Elizabeth's accession to the English throne Goodman returned to Scotland with Knox and preached there until around 1561 when he was appointed as the Minister of St Andrew's. Three years later he received an appointment as a minister in Edinburgh, but declined the post as he was keen to return home to England. Goodman then became personal chaplain to Sir Henry Sydney in his military campaigns against the Catholic rebels in Ireland around 1568. Fifteen years later Goodman was reported to be living in or around Chester, but it seems he was no longer a figure of national interest within the Protestant religion. He is said to have died in 1602, aged 83 and was thought to have been buried in St Werburgh's.

Francis Talbot, the Earl of Shrewsbury, was a member of the Talbot family reported to be the 'Sergeants' of Chester's ancient Bridge Gate. They were responsible for the bridge's protection and for collecting the taxes and tolls which were attached to that particular post. The family home in Chester was the 'Bear and Billet' in Lower Bridge Street. One of his ancestors, John Talbot, was said to have been created a peer by King Henry VI in 1442 thus

Built originally as the town house for the Talbot family, the Earls of Shrewsbury, who as sergeants of the city's mediaeval Bridgegate were responsible for collecting tolls and protecting the ancient entrance from attack.

becoming the first Earl of Shrewsbury. Francis was the fifth earl and survived the reigns of Henry VIII, Edward VI, Mary I and Elizabeth I. He had succeeded to the title following the death of his father in 1538 and before his own death in 1560 had risen to become one of the most powerful and wealthy men in England.

Richard Dutton was a member of another of Cheshire's leading families and was recorded as holding the office of mayor in 1627. One of his many properties in the city was said to have included the former church of St Thomas Becket, which stood at the junction of the modern-day Liverpool Road and Parkgate Road. Formerly known as 'Jolley's Hall', the house was later said to have been owned by John Fletcher who published one of the city's leading newspapers. The building is now used as a public house called the 'George and Dragon'.

The wealth and importance of Chester continued to grow throughout the period and that was reflected in the scale and fashion of the new buildings that were erected for a number of its leading citizens. Stanley Palace, which has also been known as Derby House, was constructed in about 1591 for one of the city's leading families. It was built as the town house for the Stanleys of Alderley who were the sergeants of the Watergate and were

The city home of the Earls of Derby who became the sergeants of Chester's Watergate. Built at the beginning of the 17th century, it has been home to a number of notable builders in the city.

An original Chester black and white building in Watergate Street, possibly 17/18th century.

responsible for exacting tolls and levies on all goods brought into the city from the harbour area and from elsewhere.

Edward Stanley, the Lord Monteagle, was the son of Sir Thomas Stanley, the first Earl of Derby, who married the daughter of Sir John Harrington and through this union became the owner of Hornby Castle in Lancashire. He was reported to have escorted Princess Margaret, the daughter of Henry VII, to Scotland when she was married to King James IV of Scotland, a move designed to cement relations between the two countries. Unfortunately, the union between the two nations was ultimately unsuccessful and Stanley was later involved in the Battle of Flodden. He was reported to have played a pivotal role by coming to the rescue of the English commander, the Earl of Surrey. By way of thanks for his actions he was awarded a peerage and given the title of Lord Monteagle, a title held by the family for many years. Edward was reported to have been appointed as Chamberlain of Chester in 1563.

James Stanley was the youngest son of Sir Thomas Stanley and was destined for a career in the church which he later achieved with the support of his stepmother, Margaret of Richmond, and her son Henry VII. He eventually rose to the dizzy heights of the bishopric of Ely and lived to see his illegitimate son, Sir James Stanley of Harford, attend the Battle of Flodden.

Ferdinando, the Lord Strange, was said to have been elected as a city alderman at Chester in 1586. Later, as the Earl of Derby, he was thought to have been approached by an agent called Hesketh in 1593 acting on behalf of Philip of Spain. They reportedly offered Ferdinando the crown of England in return for his support in helping to depose Elizabeth but instead he arrested Hesketh and transported him to London, where he was tried, convicted and executed for his treachery.

In 1608 the ancient Wolfe Gate was rebuilt just inside the south-east corner of the former Roman fortress. Thought to have been part of the extended city defences undertaken by Aethelflaeda, the gate itself had become part of the Chester's legendary past. It was said to be at the Wolfe Gate in 1573 that a local alderman's daughter eloped with her young suitor.

Ralph Aldersey was a member of the influential Aldersey family who had held the office of sheriff in Chester around 1541. While serving as a city alderman in 1573 his daughter, Ellen, was alleged to have eloped with a draper called Ralph Jaman without the permission of her family. The young couple was thought to have escaped the city by way of the Wolfe Gate, now known as the Newgate, and in response her father persuaded the council to have the gate closed at night times in order that such an event could not reoccur. Two local men, Hugh Rogerson, an alderman, and Richard Wright, a draper in the city, were both charged with being

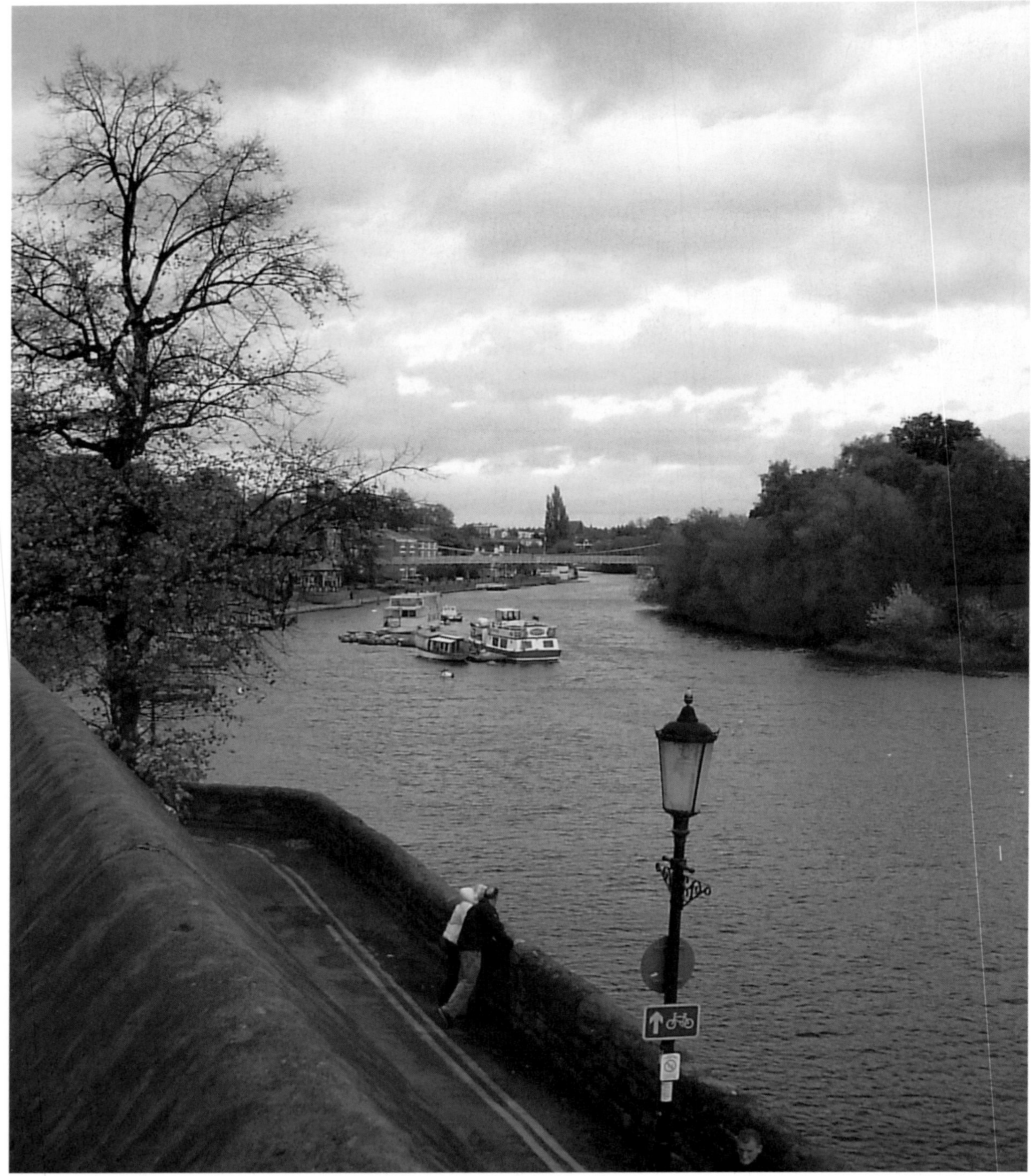

Sir James Stanley was reported to have built his home along the banks of the River Dee.

accomplices to the event. For his part Rogerson was reported to have been fined 10 shillings and Wright had his business premises in the city closed. However, father and daughter were later reconciled with one another and the gate was said to have been reopened in 1574.

The Wolfe Gate has also been commonly known as the Pepper Gate, which might suggest a link to local spice traders who were thought to have been situated in the nearby streets. Just outside the Wolfe Gate are the remains of the south-east angle tower of the original Roman wall's foundations, still visible to this day.

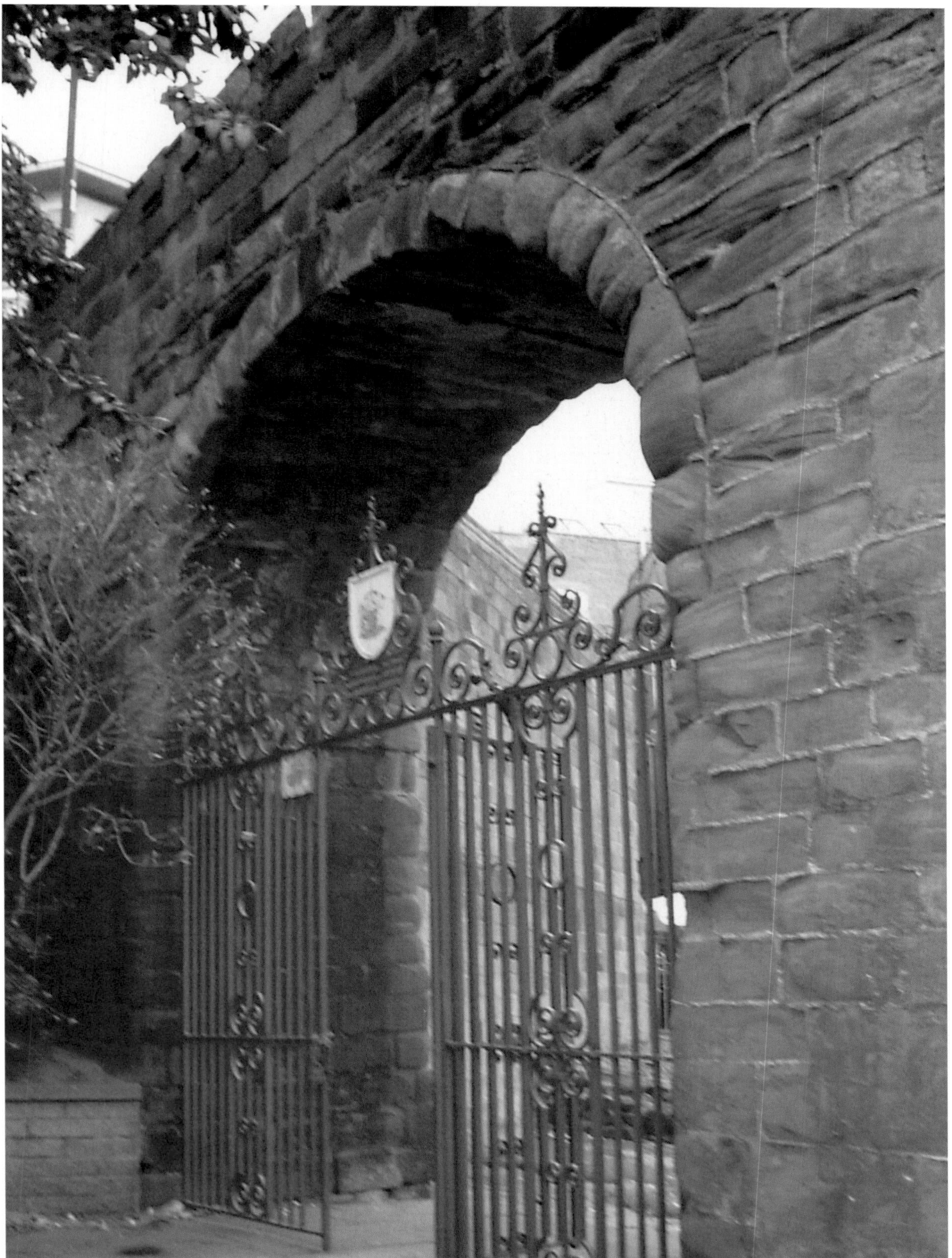

The ancient Wolfe Gate has existed in the city for well over 1,000 years and has been associated with the Hiberno-Norse community, who lived in this part of the Anglo-Saxon settlement.

Foregate Street location *c*.1650.

Another notable individual of the age was William Prynne, who was reported to have been infamous for publishing pamphlets that were critical of King Charles I and his queen. Around 1633 he was said to have been fined and imprisoned for his scurrilous accusations, as well as having part of his ears removed.

Some three years later he was thought to have repeated the offence and was once again imprisoned at Chester's historic castle, supposedly for life and with the remainder of his ears being taken off. He was also said to have been physically branded as a seditious libeller and his supporters in the city were heavily fined by the authorities and forced to recant their support for him. Portraits of Prynne were also reported to have been burnt at Chester's High Cross by royalist supporters in the city who were outraged by his claims and pronouncements against the royal family.

Following the rise of the parliamentary cause, Prynne was said to have been released from prison and paid reparations for the misfortunes that he had suffered at the hands of the monarchists. By 1648 he had been elected as a member of parliament, but perhaps surprisingly rejected the call for Charles I to be executed and was subsequently excluded from the House of Commons during Pride's Purge.

He was also thought to have been a vocal opponent of Cromwell's Commonwealth and was imprisoned for his views between 1650 and 1653. Later he was a supporter of moves to restore Charles II and as a reward for his stance was appointed as the record keeper at the Tower of London in 1660.

Yet another notable figure of the age was Edward Whitby, MP for Chester, a former recorder of the city during the 1640s and the final owner of the original Bache Hall, which was demolished during the siege of Chester. Whitby had owned the hall from 1606 and the building which currently stands on the site today is much later and thought to date from around 1829. As recorder of Chester Whitby gave a speech before the king when he visited the city in 1617 and at the same event the city's mayor, Charles Fitton, was said to have presented the monarch with a silver gilt cup filled with 100 Jacobins of gold. William Stanley, the Earl of Derby, was also reported to have been in attendance in his role as chamberlain of the county.

This particular William Stanley was thought to have been the sixth earl of Derby and was reported to have built a house and gardens on wasteland which lay close to the River Dee, near to where the modern-day Groves and Grosvenor Park exist today. Following the death of his wife in 1627 Sir William was reported to have retired to the property and lived there until his death in 1642.

These closing years of Chester's late mediaeval period saw the city, its citizens and its future prosperity in a generally optimistic mood. In a little more than 500 years, from the time of the conquest to the end of the Elizabethan period, Chester had continued to develop and consolidate its position within the north-west region of Britain. It had grown to become one of the most important logistical and commercial centres in the whole of England and despite occasional antipathy to individual holders of the Crown the city was generally loyal to the English monarchy.

Some 25 years later however, this civic loyalty to a king of England would result in the city being besieged by its fellow countrymen and would lead to the loss of some of its most important citizens and buildings. The start of the 17th century would also mark the beginning of the end for the city's prosperity, which had been built almost entirely on its busy mediaeval port and the international trade that it had previously generated.

Chapter 11

The City's Siege, Surrender and Suffocation

The opening years of the 17th century did not start well for the city. With two major outbreaks of bubonic plague in 1603 and 1605 the local population was decimated and the city's ability to trade and transport effectively limited. Many of its wealthier citizens were able to remove themselves and their households from the city but the poor and working class were compelled to stay and take their chances. Edward Dutton, a member of one of Chester's leading landed families, was recorded as mayor of Chester in 1604 but his wealth and position failed to protect him or his family from misfortune and it was reported that he lost a number of his children to an outbreak of plague.

At around the same time, another of the city's leading figures, John Tyrer, was said to have constructed a water tower in the south of the city close to the old Bridge Gate. It was designed to distribute fresh water throughout the city via a series of lead pipes which were laid beneath its main streets. Tyrer was reported to have been a lay clerk at Chester Cathedral who, in 1622, built a waterworks on the site of the natural springs just outside the city at Boughton. This new building was located on the site which a thousand years before had been used by the Roman legionaries to supply water to the fortress for their bathhouses His water tower was finally demolished in 1780, having been seriously damaged during the siege of Chester in the mid 1640s. He reportedly laid the floor in the nave of Chester Cathedral and was thought to have died around 1634.

By 1608 Chester had substantially recovered from the earlier outbreaks of disease and its population was slowly beginning to be restored, as was its important trading and distributive industries. Both the social and economic diversification of the city was continuing to be developed and by 1609 the first annual St George's Day race meeting was said to have been held on the Roodee racecourse. Its fairs and markets remained vitally important to the city's prosperity and continued to attract traders and merchants from all over England, as well as from Ireland.

In 1609 Robert Amerye was reported to have been a sheriff of Chester who presented three silver bells to the first three horses home in a five-circuit race of the Roodee. Initially staged on St George's Day, these races later became known as the St George's Bells and later still the Chester Plate.

Queen Elizabeth's successor James I was reported to have visited Chester in 1617 to attend the annual race meeting and was said to have visited a number of the events and plays that were taking place throughout the city. Despite the obvious wealth within the city, reflected in the size and fashion of its private houses, the Crown properties within Chester had not fared so well in the previous decades. A survey undertaken by the city's assembly in 1624 found that the Great Shire Hall was in an extremely dilapidated condition and that the castle's chapel was also in a fairly ruinous state. A great number of the buildings at the castle were known to have been rebuilt around 1570, so their perilous condition only 50 years later tends to suggest that either poor workmanship or materials were responsible for their later predicament. It is not entirely clear if remedial work was undertaken by the assembly at this time, but it has to be assumed that some degree of restoration was undertaken if only to make the buildings safe. Within the city itself the main streets and alleyways were so filthy that the assembly urgently introduced an ordinance to compel the local population to clean up the mess. The local householders could be fined if they did

This particular section of city walls was heavily attacked during the civil war siege of Chester.

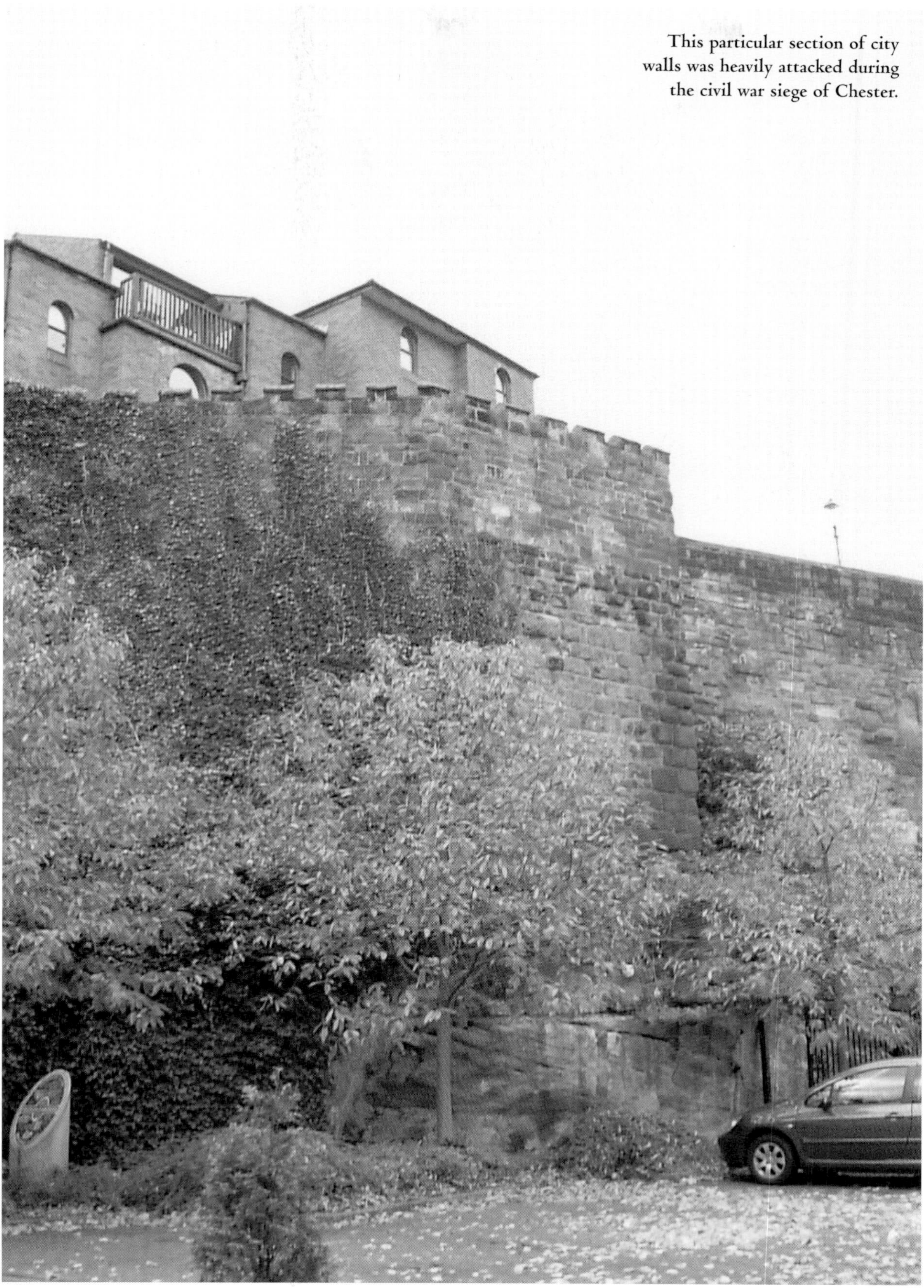

Although Chester built its early history and wealth through the River Dee, today it simply serves to host pleasure craft rather than working vessels.

not clean up their properties and the surrounding areas and maintain them in a proper condition.

In 1636 the Mayor of Chester, William Edwards, ordered that all the dirt in the city's streets should be collected together to make a bank that would both enlarge and protect the Roodee, but still allow ships into the city's port. A second order issued by Edwards instructed all householders in the Eastgate area of the city to clear the streets in front of their doors. Those that failed to obey the instruction within a month were reported to have faced a fine of 10 shillings.

In 1625 James I died and was succeeded to the throne by Charles I. Regarded by most as a devoutly religious and fair-minded king, Charles was generally very tolerant of his subjects' right to practice their own religions without undue interference from the Crown or state. Sometimes a stubborn and insensitive man, Charles's main failing seems to have been his insistence on believing that God should be worshipped in a highly public and materialistic fashion, a view that would ultimately lead him into conflict with other faiths. In 1639 Charles initiated a dispute with the Scottish churches which would later be known as the Bishops War, following his insistence that Anglican religious reforms should be introduced into Scotland as well as England. In pursuing his demands Charles sent his military forces into Scotland but due to a lack of finances and faith within his army was forced to withdraw them without ever having engaged the opposition.

In 1640 Charles was compelled to recall parliament in order to raise funds to pursue his campaign against the Scottish churches. However, many MPs saw this as an opportunity to extract additional concessions from the king and there were

Dating from 1622, the Old Kings Head was thought to be the home of the Randle Holmes, generations of heralds and historians.

those that were very strongly opposed to any sort of military action against the church under any circumstances. Realising that he would not get his finances, Charles dismissed this 'short' session of parliament and went ahead with his campaign against the Scottish churches anyway, being subsequently beaten by their forces.

Following this defeat in November 1640 Charles was forced to recall parliament yet again and this 'long' session of the legislature was notable for the mutual antipathy and suspicion shown by both parties. In January 1642 he attempted to arrest five MPs and sent troops into the parliament building to seize them, but the individuals had been forewarned and were able to escape. The king left London shortly afterwards, but following his actions against these elected representatives both sides began to stockpile weapons and the countdown to war had begun. It is thought that the English Civil War officially began in August 1642 with Charles I raising his standard at Nottingham and parliament appointing Robert Devereaux, the third Earl of Essex, as their military commander.

At the beginning of the English Civil War, Cheshire as a region remained relatively quiet and the only disputes caused by the conflict was the political in-fighting among the city's assembly. Chester itself was seen as a royalist island surrounded by a parliamentarian sea represented by the county itself. North Wales, on the other hand, was staunchly royalist; it had been and remained an ideal recruiting ground for the king and his forces. In addition Chester was a main point of access to the English troops that were then serving in Ireland and who were loyal to the king himself. Royalists knew that in order to gain access to this considerable force in support of their cause, they would need to hold the city's port.

Within the city assembly itself, there were great divisions, with both royalist and parliamentary sympathisers battling for control of the highly defended castle, walls and armaments that were held within the city's armoury. The arrival of large numbers of Protestants fleeing the troubles in Ireland significantly ratcheted up the level of tension between the two parties and there were reported to be increasingly violent brawls between the supporters of both rival parties.

The question regarding the city's stance in the dispute seems to have been finally resolved in September 1642 when the king himself visited Chester. Royalist supporters were quick to exploit the opportunity and were said to have used the occasion to undermine their parliamentarian opponents in the assembly and forced them to abandon the city in fear for their lives. One of those that was forced to flee the city was the leading parliamentarian supporter Sir William Brereton, who was known to have served on the local assembly and owned substantial assets within the city.

Born on the 13 September 1604, Brereton was thought to have been the eldest son of William Brereton of Handforth in Cheshire and became heir to his father's estates following his death in 1610.

Sir William Brereton was a Chester landowner, but became parliamentary Commander of Cheshire during the English Civil War.

The family was reported to have owned large amounts of land and buildings in the western part of the city, particularly those lands formerly owned by the religious houses which had been dissolved by Henry VIII in around 1540.

Sir William was educated at Brasenose College, Oxford, and later at Grays Inn, and in the following years he became a notable and energetic magistrate in the county. Brereton was made a baronet in 1627 and was a staunch puritan, who called for root and branch reform of the Anglican church. He was a keen writer and military student who travelled widely and was known to have visited Holland and France, as well as travelling throughout much of England, Scotland and Ireland. He was said to have been elected to parliament in 1628 where he represented Cheshire, his seat being at Handforth Hall in the county. Re-elected in 1640 he was a vocal opponent of the king, Charles I, and his misuse of parliament, and as such he became a fervent supporter of the parliamentary cause. By 1641 Brereton had been appointed by the House of Commons to supervise the shipments of men and materials from Chester to Ireland in order to suppress a rebellion that had broken out in the province.

As a leading citizen in the city of Chester itself and having been elected as MP for the county on two occasions, he was involved in a long standing dispute with the city authorities regarding his liability for a local tax called 'ship money'. On 8 August 1642 Brereton, along with a small number of supporters armed with a drum, were reported to have staged a demonstration at the city's High Cross calling on the citizens of Chester to support the parliamentary cause.

The Mayor of Chester, Thomas Cowper, arrived on the scene accompanied by a number of city constables intent on arresting the ringleaders and putting an end to the demonstration. The group was said to have resisted his authority and Cowper was so outraged at his office being treated so disrespectfully that he stepped forward to seize one of the demonstrators and handed him over to the constables. He then reportedly took up a sword and cut the offending drum to pieces, arrested the drummer and a number of the others demonstrators and the disturbance was quelled.

For his part in the disturbance Brereton was said to have been brought before the city's magistrates to explain his actions. Attempting to raise the issue of the offending 'ship money' once again, the court refused to acknowledge his defence but Brereton was discharged by the magistrates nonetheless. However, the matter had created intense reactions on the part of some royalist supporters within the city and Brereton was advised to leave the city for his own safety late in August 1642.

When Charles I visited Chester at the beginning of the Civil War, he ordered the mayor of Chester to search Brereton's home for illegal arms and ammunition. The houses of aldermen William Edwards and Thomas Aldersey were also thought to have been searched, along with the Red Lion and Golden Lion Inns in the city.

Such was the antipathy felt towards Brereton by some members of the city's royalist garrison that his family home in Chester, the former Benedictine convent of St Mary's called Nuns Hall, was subsequently attacked and severely damaged by bands of royalist soldiers.

Sir Nicholas Byron was said to have been appointed as Military Governor of Chester by the king himself, prior to his Edgehill campaign and his subsequent march on London. Byron was aided in his defence of Chester by a professional soldier called Colonel Robert Ellis from the king's army, who had gained extensive military experience in modern warfare and defences. He had spent a great deal of time in Europe and had studied the techniques being used by various European forces. Given this expertise Ellis was asked to strengthen Chester's defences in order to prepare the city for the forthcoming conflict.

The whole length of the walls were said to have been reinforced by mounds of rubble and earth piled against the inside face of the ancient sandstone defences, which, it was hoped, would make the walls strong enough to resist cannon and mortar fire. The three remaining city gates were strengthened and their mediaeval drawbridges were brought back into service, providing an additional barrier to those forces that might attack the city.

Following his appointment as Parliamentary Commander of Cheshire in January 1643, Brereton had immediately begun to recruit supporters to his cause and developed a network of spies and agents throughout the region. Shortly after taking command of the parliamentary forces in the county in March 1643 Brereton defeated a royalist force at Middlewich which helped to consolidate parliamentary dominance in Cheshire. In the same month he defeated the royalist forces under the command of Sir Thomas Aston who were holding Nantwich, which, having been taken, was then refortified and remained as Brereton's military headquarters throughout the first civil war.

Brereton would later become both the scourge and saviour of the city of Chester. On Friday 13 July 1643, at the head of a large parliamentary force, Brereton made the first of many attacks on the city's defences but was easily beaten back by the royalist garrison. Having failed to capture the city, Brereton then led his forces across the River Dee at Farndon, which was done in the face of fierce opposition from the royalist forces stationed at nearby Holt Castle. Having crossed the river, Brereton's men captured the town of Wrexham in November 1643 and then moved north-west towards the Norman castle at nearby Hawarden.

Brereton's forces easily captured the town and castle at Hawarden which allowed him to sever the royalist supply lines from both Ireland and North Wales. He then sent a summons to the city of Chester demanding their surrender, which was ignored. Unfortunately for Brereton, the position at Hawarden left his men exposed to a counter-attack by royalist forces and he hastily withdrew the parliamentary garrison to the English side of the Dee. The withdrawal by Brereton then allowed royalist forces from Ireland to land at Mostyn in Flintshire and march through to the isolated city. This relaxation of the siege was also thought to have allowed the royalist forces to re-supply their stores.

In December 1643 Charles I was reported to have appointed Lord Byron as Royalist Commander in Cheshire, Lancashire and North Wales. He conducted a series of successful raids and military strikes against Brereton's forces throughout December 1643, including the capture of Beeston Castle to the east of the city. The parliamentary commander of the former Norman fortress was reported to have been subsequently executed for cowardice following the loss of their position. The royalists then managed to score a second notable victory over the parliamentarians when Brereton's forces were beaten at a second battle at Middlewich and were forced to retreat north to Manchester.

Brereton's troops were eventually pushed back to his military headquarters at Nantwich and were later besieged by the royalist forces under Lord Byron. Parliament then ordered Sir Thomas Fairfax to march to Brereton's aid so with a force of 2,000 men, he joined Brereton at Manchester and together they set out to relieve their besieged garrison in Cheshire.

Formerly known as 'The Moon' this public house has been licensed since 1643 but was heavily rebuilt during the 18th century.

Byron was aware that a relief force was approaching Nantwich but was undone by pure bad luck and the poor judgement shown by one of his subordinate officers. Extremely bad weather and heavy rain had compelled Byron to reposition his artillery and while in the process of doing so he inadvertently split his force at completely the wrong time. While Byron was trying to replace his artillery the remainder of his force, consisting mainly of infantry and under the control of a Colonel Gibson, had been deployed to intercept the relief force of Fairfax and Brereton.

This unexpected division of the royalist force would ultimately have dire results for Byron's troops. Detached as he was from his infantry, Byron had little or no immediate control over their movements or deployment. Two regiments of parliamentary troops were tasked with holding Byron's cavalry at bay while the remainder of Fairfax's forces confronted the royalists commanded by Gibson. At a pivotal moment in the engagement the parliamentary troops from the Nantwich garrison were said to have moved out from the town, adding their numbers to Fairfax's forces and causing the royalist infantry to fall back and disperse.

Having witnessed the defeat and surrender of his infantry units, Lord Byron then retreated to Chester taking with him the remnants of his cavalry force and soldiers who had avoided capture by Fairfax. With the Nantwich garrison relieved and replenished Brereton was then able to consolidate his forces and immediately made plans to recover the ground lost in the previous months. From around November 1644 onwards Brereton was reported to have begun establishing a ring of parliamentary garrisons around the besieged city of Chester.

Back in the city itself, the overcrowding from the sudden influx of large numbers of Irish soldiers had begun to tell on the patience and resources of the local inhabitants. Their resentment had been further fuelled with the arrival in the city of the Dutch Prince Rupert in March 1644. His review of the city's defences seems to have led to the wholesale destruction of large swathes of suburban buildings, which it was believed might offer shelter to the parliamentary forces that were seeking to capture the city. As many of these buildings were privately owned the decision to simply demolish them was met with a storm of protest from the individual householders and landlords. On the south bank of the river, the settlement at Handbridge was said to have been completely razed by the city's defenders in order to prevent the township from falling into enemy hands.

With the city's defences once again reorganised Rupert was reported to have left Chester shortly afterwards and, along with the troops that accompanied him, set off to raise the siege at Newark which he was said to have achieved a short time later. Between April and June 1644 Rupert campaigned throughout the whole of Cheshire and south Lancashire and then turned his attention to York, where the city was being besieged by a joint Scottish and parliamentary army. On the 2 July 1644 the two opposing forces met on Marston Moor, just outside of York, and in the ensuing battle the royalist army was crushed by their adversaries. The city of York itself then fell to the parliamentary forces, with Prince Rupert and what remained of his force retiring to Chester in order to regroup. In the following month Rupert was said to have taken his forces out of the city and moved them further south.

By November of the same year tensions within the city were said to have remained high, as the presence of large numbers of Irish troops and the shortages that this caused to the civilian population continued. The incessant demand for funds to support their campaigns fell directly on the local citizens through the introduction of additional levies and taxes which they were forced to pay. There was no outright display of the local population's anger or frustration towards their royalist leaders, but it was said to be significant that aldermen with the greatest royalist sympathies attracted less support than their more politically neutral colleagues when local elections were called in the city's wards.

Brereton was not thought to have immediately reinstated his siege of Chester following the royalist defeats at Nantwich and York, but had instead recovered lost ground and substantially strengthened his military forces. By the end of November 1644 however, he was ready to apply direct pressure to the city once again and set about establishing a ring of garrisons around the outskirts of Chester. The closest of these was said to have been sited at Christleton and they were regarded so seriously by the royalist supporters that a relief force under Prince Rupert's brother, Maurice, was sent to lift the siege on the city which he managed to achieve in February 1645. Once again the immediate defences were thought to have been rearranged and large parts of Chester's northern suburbs demolished by the city's defenders.

Prince Maurice was then thought to have left the city and took with him some of the most experienced troops that were stationed there, leaving behind only Welsh troops and a number of poorly trained civilian militia. The parliamentarians under Brereton resumed their siege of the city soon afterwards and were said to have sent troops into North Wales to once again try and capture the strategically important Hawarden Castle. Aware that his forces could be isolated if Charles's army arrived in Cheshire, Brereton again withdrew his men from the Welsh side of the border and rejoined his forces outside of Chester. The city was by now the only royalist centre in the whole of north-west England and as such was vitally important to both sides in the conflict.

King Charles and his army had indeed been on their way to Chester but having heard that Brereton had raised the siege on the city again he withdrew his forces to the south-east. In June 1645 the king's royalist army were said to have finally met the New Model Army of Oliver Cromwell at the Battle of Naseby and was subsequently destroyed by the new professional force that was set against him.

Brereton had to temporarily give up command of his military forces under the terms of the Self Denying Ordinance of November 1645, which prevented elected members of parliament from holding military commands. During his enforced absence Brereton's place was taken by a council of junior officers that dictated military policy and planning. They decided not to reinstate the siege at Chester, thereby allowing its defenders to re-supply their stores and to add to their defensive positions. It was during this period that a royalist fort was constructed on the southern bank of the river at Handbridge. However, Brereton along with Oliver Cromwell and Sir Thomas Middleton were eventually exempted from this particular piece of legislation and were allowed to return to their military posts.

Direct military operations against the city were said to have resumed in September of 1645 following criticism of the apparent inactivity on the part of the parliamentarian forces. On the night of the 20 September their forces were reported to have overrun the royalist defences in the eastern suburbs of the city, simply by using the gardens of adjoining houses. The areas including St John's Church and Foregate Street were now firmly in parliamentary hands and large artillery pieces were thought to have been brought in to bombard the city's walls. James Lothian was a major in the parliamentary force which was besieging the city and he was reported to have been part of the Roundhead forces that finally overran the royalist's eastern earthworks and actually brought the siege to the city's gates. A notable local individual, Randle Richardson, who was a sheriff of Chester during the siege of the city, was reportedly killed in 1645 by a bullet fired by a parliamentary sniper located at the nearby St John's Church, which had been recently captured by Brereton's forces.

Despite this close siege of the city, Charles I managed to enter Chester in September 1645 accompanied by a small cavalry force with which he

Thought to stand on the foundations of a much earlier Roman corner tower, it has also been known as King Charles's and the 'Newton' Tower throughout its life.

hoped to raise the siege on the city. On the 24 September this force commanded by Sir Marmaduke Langdale was decisively beaten by the parliamentarians under General Lambert at Rowton Moor, an area of meadow which lay just outside of the city's limits. Legend states that the king watched the battle from the Phoenix Tower which is located along the eastern wall of the city's defences and now bears the name King Charles's Tower.

Yet another legend relates that as he watched the battle at Rowton from the top of the city's cathedral a royalist captain that was accompanying the king was hit by a musket ball fired from the nearby St John's Church and was killed on the spot. The king accompanied by Sir Francis Gamull, who would later lose much of his fortune for the sake of his monarch, left the city the following day. On his departure Charles left orders with Lord Byron that he could surrender the city if he did not receive any relief within 10 days. Despite these instructions however, the city continued to hold out for a further 20 weeks, from the 25 September through to the 3 February 1646. During those tortuous weeks the population would eventually be driven to eating the cavalrymen's horses, as well as cats and dogs, rather than surrender Chester to the parliamentary forces who lay outside the city.

Thomas Gamull was the son of Edmund Gamull, four times Mayor of Chester and the father of Sir Francis Gamull who was a leading royalist supporter during the English Civil War and the siege of Chester. Along with his wife, Thomas was laid to rest in the church of St Mary-on-the-hill, close to the city's historic mediaeval castle. Their family altar tomb is said to be located in St Catherine's Chapel within the church.

St Mary-on-the-hill has a strong connection with Chester Castle and is the final resting place for a number of the city's most notable figures.

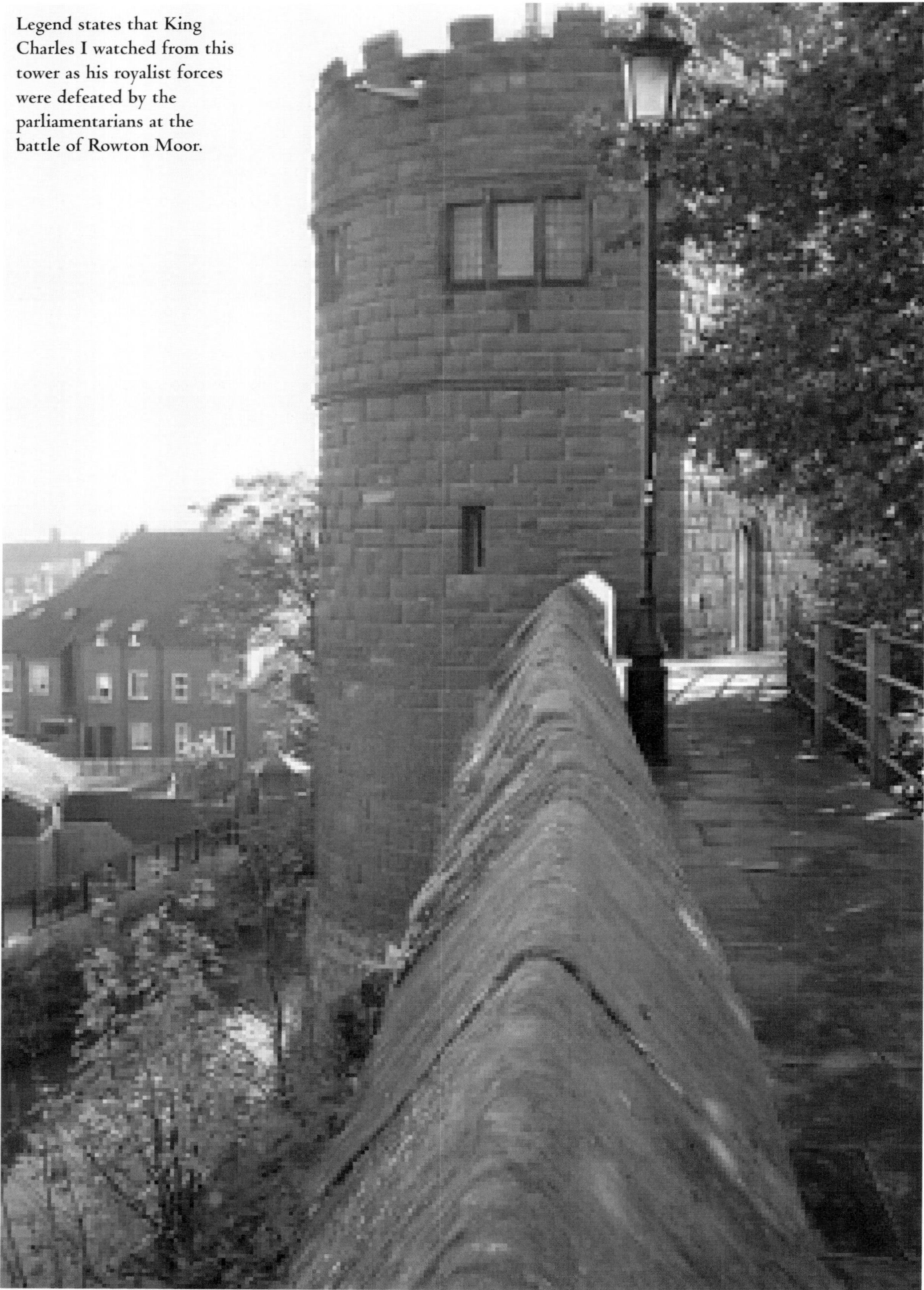

Legend states that King Charles I watched from this tower as his royalist forces were defeated by the parliamentarians at the battle of Rowton Moor.

Thomas's son, Sir Francis Gamull, was a notable member of this leading Chester family. He had been elected Mayor of Chester from 1634 to 1635 and during the civil war and subsequent siege of Chester he was said to have been appointed as Commander of the city's local defence force. King Charles was reported to have stayed at Gamull's Chester town house during his many visits to the city and to have been attended by Francis as he watched the battle at Rowton Moor, where his royalist troops were lost to the opposing parliamentary forces. The family's home in the city, Gamull House, which is located in the Lower Bridge Street area of the city, later became a rundown tenement building, but was substantially renovated during the 20th century and remains to this day as a number of separate living spaces.

In around 1601 Francis was reported to have gone into partnership with John Tyrer, the man responsible for building a water tower above the city's ancient Bridge Gate. His royalist sympathies and support for King Charles I would cost him dearly following the English Civil War, with much of his family wealth and estates being sequestrated by the parliamentary authorities.

For their part, following the royalist defeat at Rowton and their overrunning of the eastern suburbs, the parliamentarians now sought to strengthen their grip on the city. The northern suburbs of Chester soon fell to their forces and large siege cannons and mortars were brought in to attack the city's massive stone defences from both the east and the north. Cannons placed at St John's Church and in Foregate Street in the eastern suburbs were used to target and destroy royalist gun emplacements and to breach the city's walls. Tyrer's water tower and the Dee mills, both of which stood

A tower at St John's was used as a cannon position during the civil war siege of Chester.

The eastern wall and cathedral seen from the Kaleyards, formerly used by Roman legionaries as a parade ground.

The eastern wall of the city was heavily attacked by the parliamentarians during the siege of Chester.

in the southern section of the city close to the river, were said to have been severely damaged by cannons which were located at the nearby St John's Church.

Despite these measures the royalist defenders continued to hold the city and the defensive fort located at Handbridge on the southern bank of the river. From these positions they could continue to control military movement from the south and suppress the parliamentarians within the immediate area of the fort. In order to deal with this threat the parliamentary forces were said to have established a gun emplacement on the southern bank of the river which was joined to the opposite northern bank by a bridge made up of individual boats. Nowadays, the location of this gun emplacement is said to be close to the area of the modern-day meadows, directly opposite the city's Dee Lane which itself lies on the northern bank of the river.

On 8 October 1645 the parliamentarians were once again thought to have called for the city's defenders to surrender, but once again this was rejected by its royalist leaders. Following a heavy bombardment of Chester's defences by their cannons and mortars the city walls were said to have been breached and the parliamentary forces attempted to storm their way through the resulting

Remainder of the tower base wall in the Kaleyards area of Chester, possibly destroyed during the civil war siege of Chester.

A more modern way of accessing the city's ancient defensive walls.

gap. After much heavy hand-to-hand fighting however, the royalist defenders apparently managed to repulse the attackers, but with many casualties suffered on both sides. Numerous attempts were made to scale the city's eastern walls, between the modern-day East Gate and Saddlers Tower which used to stand in the area of the present-day 'Kale Yard' gate, but all proved to be unsuccessful as the city's defences were so resolute.

The beleaguered royalist commanders were unable to prevent the constant bombarding and sniping of the city by the besieging parliamentarians and were only too aware of the falling morale among the local people and the military garrison. A plot was thought to have been hatched by the royalist commanders to destroy the bridge of boats which linked the parliamentary gun emplacement on the south bank of the river with their forces on the opposite bank. Fire boats filled with gun powder were said to have been floated down the river towards the boat bridge but reportedly drifted off course and exploded harmlessly or else failed to explode at all.

During the winter months of 1645 morale within the city was said to be at its lowest since the start of the conflict. The lack of food and fuel, the constant bombardment from the parliamentary siege guns and the coldest winter for decades all led to a deepening of the divisions which had been smouldering for months. Outside of the city Brereton was not slow to exploit these opportunities and appealed to the townspeople directly to bring an end to the dispute. Whether or not there were those within the city that would have helped bring an end to the siege is not clear but there was said to have been no direct reply to his advances. It was reported that as the city's food stores slowly disappeared throughout the winter, the inhabitants of Chester finally resorted to eating the horses, cats and dogs that roamed throughout the city. It is also to be supposed that fuel for heating and cooking was widely supplemented by the use of materials taken from the city's historic structures, particularly those that had been damaged or destroyed by enemy fire.

By the middle of January 1646 however, the situation was so dire that even the mayor of the city was thought to be calling for direct negotiations between the two warring sides. By the end of the month terms were said to have finally been reached that were mutually acceptable to both parties. In return for the safe delivery of both the city and castle into Brereton's hands, royalist soldiers were permitted to leave the city with their arms, horses and valuables. Other forces were allowed to leave but without their arms and mounts, Welsh-born soldiers were allowed to return home, but Irish forces were to be imprisoned at the castle. Brereton also undertook to protect the local population's properties and goods and to ensure that no damage was done to the city's churches. The official surrender of the city was said to have taken place within the Great Shire Hall which adjoined the castle and which, 20 years earlier, had been reported as being totally dilapidated.

On the 3 February 1646 the royalist forces under their military commander Lord Byron evacuated the city and shortly afterwards Sir William Brereton headed the parliamentary soldiers that moved in to take possession of Chester. Colonel Michael Jones was immediately appointed as military governor of the city but, despite the guarantees offered by Brereton, some areas of the city were subject to occasional vandalism and looting by parliamentary troops. During the siege itself there were hundreds of deaths in the city, both military and civilian, and a large proportion of the city's buildings were completely burnt down or severely damaged. It was thought that Cromwell himself had ordered that all royalist castles should be destroyed so that they could not be used against his forces in the future. However, this was not the case at Chester and it has been suggested that both Cromwell and Brereton were mindful of its logistical importance and possible military use in the future.

Sir William Brereton was said to have played a pivotal role in the final battle of the first civil war, which occurred at Stow-on-the-Wold, where he accepted the surrender of Sir Jacob Astley, the royalist commander in March 1646. Following parliament's total victory over the royalist cause, Brereton was richly rewarded for his services and was granted Eccleshall Castle in Staffordshire as well as Croydon Palace, the former home of the Archbishop of Canterbury.

Following the war however, Brereton effectively retired from public life and played no part in the trial of Charles I, the second civil war or the Protectorate of Oliver Cromwell. Following the restoration of Charles II to the English throne, Croydon Palace was said to have been returned to its rightful owners, but Brereton was permitted to live there as a tenant until his death in 1661.

A renowned family in Chester throughout the whole of the English Civil War period was the Holme family, who were heraldic painters and historians in the city. Randle Holme I was said to have been born around 1571 and to be the founding member of a line of antiquaries and heralds who all shared the same name and were all natives of the city. Their family home was reported to have been the modern-day Ye Olde Kings Head which is located in the Lower Bridge Street area of Chester, close to Gamull House. Around 1587 he was said to have been apprenticed to Thomas Chaloner who was a herald and had been Ulster king-at-arms. Following his master's death in 1598 however, Holme was thought to have inherited Chaloner's papers as well as marrying the dead man's widow. It has also been reported that Holme may have succeeded Chaloner as deputy of the Heralds College in Chester around 1600. He served as a city sheriff in 1615 and was elected Mayor of Chester between 1633 and 1634. Upon his death he was reported to have been interred at the church of St Mary's on-the-hill, close to the city's mediaeval castle in 1655.

Randle Holme II was thought to have been a key royalist supporter during the first English Civil War and the subsequent siege of Chester. He was elected Mayor of Chester in 1643 and 1644, but did not live much beyond his own father's death and was said to have also been interred at the church of St Mary's in around 1659.

Randle Holme III was said to have been born around 1627. He has been called 'The Great Randle' and was known to have co-authored a book entitled *The Academy of Armour*, which was published in an unfinished form in 1688. The book remained incomplete due to Randle's lack of funds, which might suggest a failing business or poor trading conditions in Chester generally. The manuscript is now held by the British Museum and forms part of their library. Randle was also thought to have written a series of articles and memoirs detailing the city's role in the English Civil War and the subsequent siege of Chester.

It was also this particular Randle that was thought to have owned the 'Old Lamb's Row', which was known to have stood close to the 'Falcon Inn' in the city. Unhappily for the family's heirs, the building was reported to have fallen into such a state of disrepair that it simply collapsed around 1821. Although the family no doubt despaired, other locals were said to have celebrated its demise as it had blocked easy access along the street for well over 150

The Falcon Inn was the former home of the Grosvenor family in the city, which was restored by Douglas around 1894.

years. Married three times, Randle Holme III was reported to have died in 1699 and upon his death was interred at the church of St Mary-on-the-hill, along with his father and grandfather.

Randle Holme IV was thought to be the final member of the family to bear the name. He was a member of the stationers company and deputy to Norroy, king-of-arms, but does not appear to have been as successful or as notable as his predecessors.

Earlier generations of the Holme family were said to have been prolific collectors of historic materials that were particularly relevant to Chester and these three earlier generations managed to amass thousands of pages of information on the subject. It was reputedly Randle Holme IV that sold the family collection to Robert Harley, the Earl of Oxford, because he was greatly impoverished and needed to raise funds. Fortunately for the history of the Holme family these archives were later donated to the British Museum and now form part of the *Harleian Manuscript*. In around 1711 it was recorded that Holme had then sold his heraldic painting business to a Mr Bassano and on his death was interred at the church of St Mary-on-the-hill, along with his father, grandfather and great-grandfather.

Chapter 12

Royalist Rebellions and the Restoration

The international and regional trade that was so vital to the city's economy and future prosperity had been so badly affected during the civil war that the assembly was forced to sell the city's treasures in order to meet the fines and levies imposed by the new parliamentary regime. Every source of civic revenue was exploited and exhausted in an effort to settle the debts that were laid at the city's door and it was usually the less fortunate that paid the highest price. Financial provisions for the poor and the sick within the city were diverted away by the authorities to pay for the settlement of these accumulated liabilities, leaving the city's worst off in an even worse condition.

By the end of February 1646 the city was once again utilised by the new government as a mustering and provisioning point for its forces that were destined for Ireland. With the city streets still filled with filth and a shortage of both food and clean drinking water, the city also had to find supplies to satisfy the thousands of troops that were regularly gathering in Chester. The assembly was forced to introduce regulations which would help to guarantee the price and availability of stores so that the troops could be fully provisioned and any profiteering by unscrupulous traders fully eliminated

In June 1646 matters were brought to a head when another round of plague broke out in the city and its already limited resources were stretched to breaking point. Thought to have been introduced by a number of the soldiers that passed through the city on their way to the port at Parkgate, the disease decimated the local population. In a little over 12 months the death toll was said to have exceeded over 2,000 people, with a majority of the fatalities being from the poor and working classes within the city.

By the middle of the following year the city was finally beginning to turn a corner with many of the wealthier people that had fled Chester to escape the illness starting to return, and slowly but surely the local economy beginning to grow again. Trade had changed though and the regulations that had been introduced to help control the price and supply of critical food stores were just the beginning. Many of the merchants and traders that now conducted business in and around Chester were not local businessmen, but merely agents for outside merchants or simply visitors to the city. In many cases the profits that were made from buying and selling did not remain in the city, but instead went to the home towns of the visiting traders.

Damage caused to the historic corn-grinding mills on the Dee and the general slow down in trade with Ireland, no doubt in response to the continuing military activity there, were both instrumental in suppressing trade within the city. Over time the cereal trade and wine importation from the continent did begin to recover, but the livestock trade upon which Chester's leather industries relied continued to be slow with a corresponding slow down in production.

This reduction in the city's wealth continued to have a directly negative effect on the very poorest within the community and during the period from 1644 through to 1648 there was little if any assistance for the city's beggars or the unemployed. The workhouse which had existed outside of the northern defences had been demolished during the city's siege and the food and shelter that it had afforded its former residents had disappeared almost overnight. The public and private monies that in usual times would have supported such charitable organisations had either been diverted to the defence of the city or else had left the city with its rich benefactors.

Substantial damage to the very fabric of Chester had been extensive, both during and after the siege

Excavations in this area have discovered its former involvement in the city's mediaeval tanning and leather industries.

itself. Tyrer's water tower, the city's walls, the Dee mills and St John's Church were just a small number of the vitally important and historic buildings that had suffered as a direct result of the city's bombardment. Several of the Chester's finest churches had been systematically vandalised by gangs of parliamentary soldiers who took exception to their fine stained glass, crosses, fonts and altars and regarded them as nothing more than 'papist' accessories that had no place in a house of God. The city's High Cross, which had been used as a rallying point for Chester's citizenry for hundreds of years, was torn down by these same parliamentarian forces and was only finally restored to its rightful place some 300 years later.

Throughout the length of the city's defensive walls there were sections that had been both battered and breached and yet despite their harsh treatment had remained largely intact. Six years earlier in 1641 a report for the assembly had noted that the walls were in an extremely poor state and in some places had actually fallen down. It is a testament to the skills of the men that rebuilt these ruinous sections that a short time later these same walls would survive relatively intact, having been subjected to the best that modern siege guns could throw at them.

Following the surrender of the city Chester retained a relatively small military presence, no doubt to ensure that it remained in parliamentary hands and also because of the large numbers of troops that were mustering in the city prior to leaving for Ireland. Though Chester itself had been subdued there were still occasional outbreaks of fighting and civil unrest throughout the country right through to 1651. In December 1647 Charles was reported to have fled to Scotland and, in return for his promise to reform the legislation that he had enacted against the Scottish churches, was given forces that might help him defeat the New Model Army. In July of the following year Charles was said to have led this army into England, but was met and defeated yet again by the new parliamentarian forces.

At the time, and despite his decision to employ foreign forces against the English people, parliament had still hoped to return Charles to the throne after having agreed new constitutional changes with the monarch. There were extremist elements within the army, however, that believed the king was no longer worthy to rule the country and these set in motion a series of events that would end the rule of Charles I forever. An army officer, Sir Thomas Pride, was said to have arrested a number of MPs and prevented 146 others from attending a session of parliament that would call for the king to be tried for treason. The 75 MPs that were permitted to attend this 'Rump' Parliament were far more sympathetic to the army's wish for an end to Charles and so with little or no opposition to their debate a call for the king to be tried for treason was passed.

Despite Charles's assertion that he ruled by divine right and that therefore the court did not have the authority to try him, events had progressed too far for them to be undone. The court, not surprisingly, found the king guilty of treason against the people and imposed the only possible sentence. On the 13 January 1649 Charles I, the annointed King of England, was taken out and beheaded as a traitor to both his country and to his people.

History would later record that it was a Cheshire-born man that played an unplanned yet pivotal role in the temporary abolition of the English monarchy and the rise of the parliamentary system. John Bradshaw was said to have been born at Wibbersley Hall in Malpas, Cheshire, in December 1602, although some records suggest that his actual birthplace was 'Peace Farm' in Stockport, Cheshire. He was reported to have been the youngest son of one Henry Bradshaw, a member of a minor county family, and his wife Catherine Winnington, daughter of Ralph Winnington.

John's early education was thought to have been undertaken at the local grammar schools at Bunbury and later at Macclesfield. He was then said to have

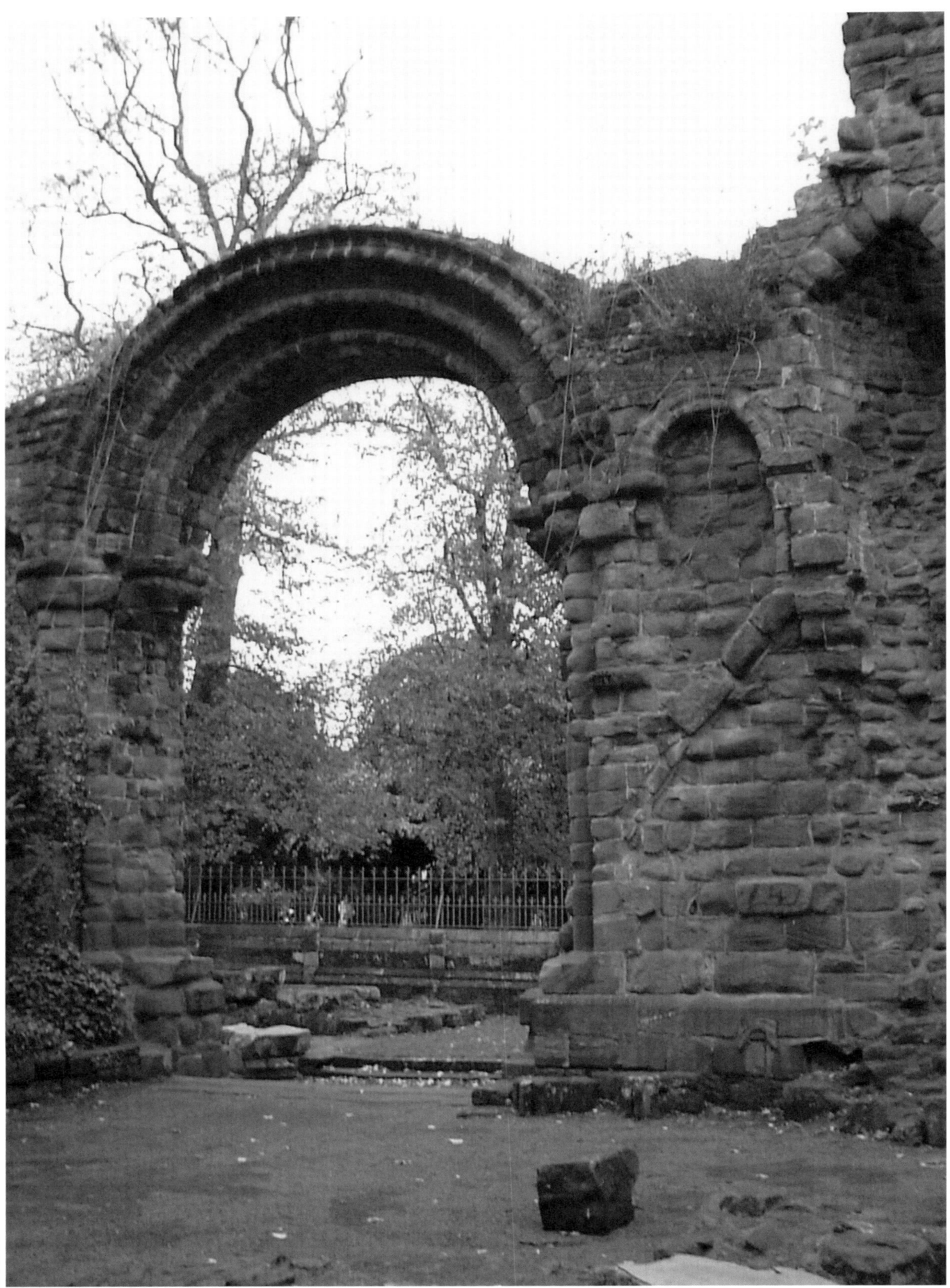

Many landmark buildings in Chester were damaged as a result of the civil war siege.

studied under a local attorney in Congleton, having developed an interest in the legal profession. Bradshaw later studied at Grays Inn from 1622 and was thought to have been called to the Bar in 1627 at the age of 25. He was known to have practised as a fairly successful lawyer for a decade or so before being appointed as Attorney General for Cheshire and Flintshire in 1637, the same year he was elected mayor of Congleton in Cheshire. Three years later he was said to have moved to London and been appointed as a judge in the sheriff's court at the city's guildhall. It was around this time that a number of high-profile legal cases brought him public recognition. He acted for the prosecution against the Irish rebel lords, McGuire and McMahon, which led to their executions in 1644. He was then said to have acted as the defence barrister for John Lilburne in his appeal against the sentence which had been imposed on him by the Star Chamber eight years earlier.

In 1645 he was reported to have been appointed as junior counsel for parliament and the following year was nominated as the Commissioner of the Great Seal, although this nomination was later blocked by his political opponents. Shortly afterwards Bradshaw was appointed as Chief Justice of Cheshire and Flintshire in 1647. The same year he was involved in the prosecution of Judge Jenkins who was tried by parliament for high treason.

During the first English Civil War Bradshaw himself was not directly involved in the military conflict, but was said to have carried on with his legal duties. In 1648 he was appointed as Sergeant at Law by the Rump Parliament that had made the decision to try Charles I for high treason.

In 1649 Bradshaw was offered the post of President of the High Court of Justice, which many of his contemporaries had chosen to refuse. Despite his best efforts to avoid the appointment he reluctantly accepted the post, determined that justice should be done regardless of the accused person's status or role.

Inevitably he was required to preside over the parliamentary commission that would try Charles I and which would consider the evidence that was brought against the monarch. It was a task that Bradshaw undertook in a diligent and thoughtful manner. When the commission finally reached its almost pre-determined decision it fell to Bradshaw to publicly announce its verdict: that the king had been found guilty of treason and that the sentence was death. His final onerous task in respect of the monarch was to sign the death warrant and he was thought to be the first member of the commission to do so.

Following the king's execution Bradshaw was rewarded with the first presidency of the Council of State in 1649 and was appointed Chancellor of the Duchy of Cornwall. He was also re-appointed as Chief Justice of Cheshire and was granted large sums by parliament to support and manage his great public offices. It was also Bradshaw's fate to preside over the trials of the royalist leaders of the second civil war which saw him judge and condemn to death Hamilton, Capel and Holland.

Seemingly a highly principled individual later in his career, he came into direct conflict with Oliver Cromwell, particularly with the protector's decision to close parliament by force of arms which Bradshaw publicly condemned. His public admonishment of Cromwell was never forgiven by his former ally and in later years Bradshaw found his position constantly undermined by the protector and his supporters. Despite Cromwell's opposition to him Bradshaw was elected to parliament as Member for Cheshire and sat in the protectorate parliaments throughout the 1650s.

In Cheshire itself Bradshaw's religious and political radicalism was said to have made him extremely unpopular with a number of the county's leading families and was thought to have been a contributing factor in George Booth's uprising in 1659. It was only Bradshaw's failing health at the beginning of 1659 that finally forced him to surrender many of his heavy and onerous duties. As his life drew to a close he was unrepentant regarding the role he had played in the late monarch's death. He also remained scathing about Cromwell and his decision to suppress parliament and to initiate his singular, seemingly unopposed rule of the country.

Bradshaw died in October 1659 aged 57 and was reported to have been interred at Westminster Abbey. However, following the later restoration of Charles II his remains, along with those of Cromwell and Ireton, were reported to have been hung in chains on the gibbet at Tyburn. In an act of political spite their heads were also removed and publicly displayed as 'regicides' in Westminster Hall, supposedly for a period of more than 20 years. The rest of their remains were thought to have been burned, with the ashes buried beneath the gallows.

In the same year that his father had been executed Charles II was said to have been crowned in Scotland and immediately set about trying to recover the English throne. At the head of a large Scottish army he invaded England in 1650 but was met in the September by Oliver Cromwell and his new professional army, who quickly overcame the invading forces. Despite this defeat, Charles II along with the remainder of his force continued to push forward into England and it was only at Worcester on 3 September 1651 that they were finally stopped by Cromwell. Following this final defeat and the near total destruction of his army the new king and his surviving retinue were compelled to flee the country and to seek sanctuary on the European continent.

The English Parliament now held total control of the country. With the royalist cause temporarily stifled there were hopes that the country could be reconciled and the people's hopes and expectations fulfilled. However, parliament was still divided by competing groups who sought to exploit its power and authority for their own advantage, which would achieve no real benefits for the people that they

The Bluecoat School occupies the site of St John the Baptist Hospital, which was founded by Earl Ranulph Blundeville.

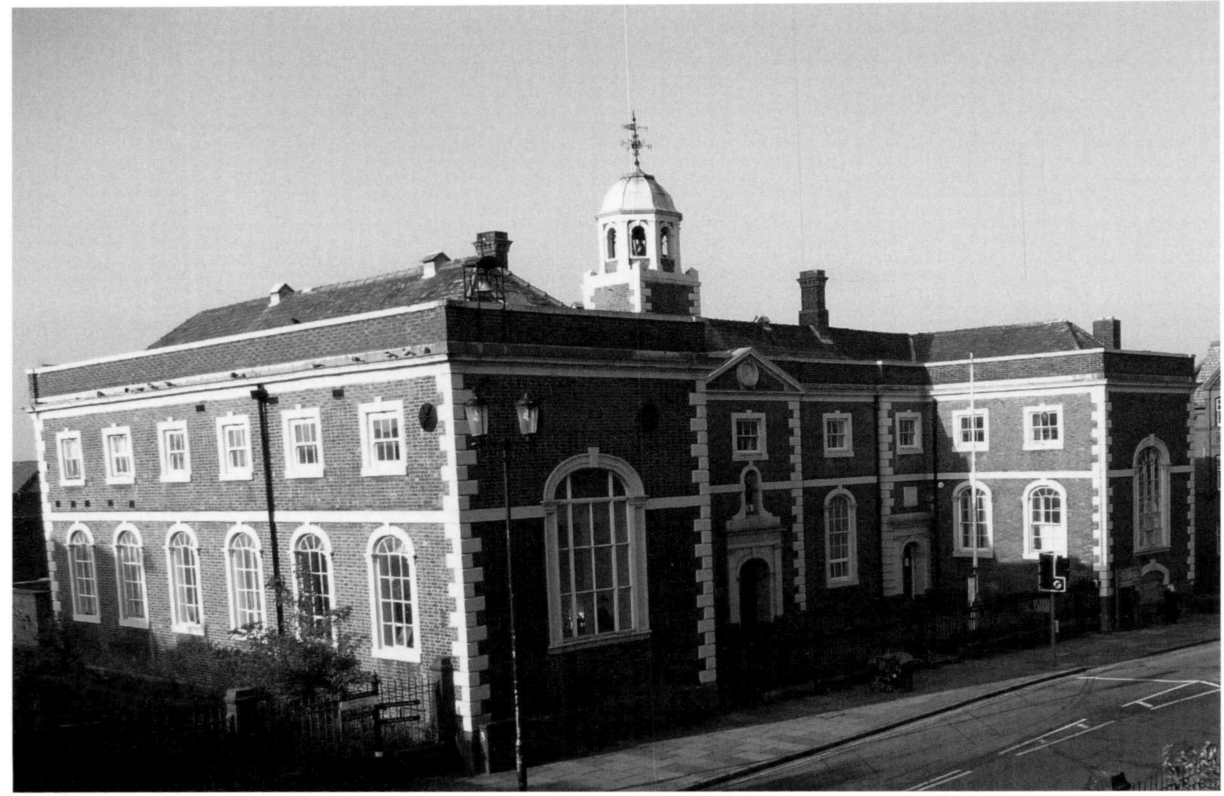

governed. Because of this stalemate within the legislature and the blatant misrule of the country, elements of the army under the control of Oliver Cromwell were reported to have marched on Westminster to dissolve the parliament. Having been appointed as Lord Protector, Cromwell ultimately introduced new laws, suppressed rebellion in the country and helped establish the foundations for the English Commonwealth system which remains with us today.

Following its eventual capture by the parliamentarians and in spite of its national importance as a major logistical centre which handled the passage of thousands of troops going to Ireland, Chester did not seem to warrant any special consideration in terms of its continued security from the national authorities. Given the relatively small military presence in the city at the time it is perhaps not surprising that this particular situation would be exploited at some time by one of the many royalist factions that still existed in the country.

Roger Whitley was said to have served as a royalist colonel during the English Civil War and was reported to have married Charlotte, the sister of Charles, Lord Gerrard, later the Earl of Macclesfield. Along with his brother-in-law, Whitley was thought to have served under Prince Rupert during the national conflict and in the later siege at Chester. Charlotte was reported to have died in 1662, but had borne Whitley three daughters and two sons. His daughter Elizabeth was thought to have married into the wealthy and influential Mainwaring family, marrying Sir John Mainwaring in 1656. His other two daughters were Henrietta Maria and Charlotte. His two sons were Thomas, who lived at the family home at Aston Hall in Hawarden, and Roger, who was reported to be constantly in debt and thought to have spent much of his time trying to avoid his creditors.

Whitley was said to have attended Charles II while he was exiled in France and played a part in George Booth's unsuccessful uprising which was defeated at Winnington Bridge. Following the restoration of the king in 1660 he was handsomely rewarded for his services to the monarch including being appointed as deputy postmaster, an important post that would subsequently bring him into conflict with both the king and parliament. He was also known to have been appointed as the warden of the hospital of St John the Baptist in Chester and it was during his tenure that the building was largely rebuilt. A highly active politician both locally and at a national level, Whitley served in parliament throughout the 1680s, as well as in 1695, and was accused of being involved in Monmouth's rebellion of 1683 which he always vigorously denied.

Whitley came under suspicion by both the king and parliament following the Rye House plot in 1683 and his home was searched for contraband. Later in the same year he and his sons, along with the Earl of Macclesfield and Lord Brandon, were forced to provide security for their future conduct. These undertakings were made in front of Sir George Jeffreys, Chief Justice of Chester, who would later be remembered for his 'Bloody Assizes'. Brandon was later charged with treason and the Earl of Macclesfield fled the country rather than face the authorities.

Despite his occasional misfortunes Whitley was elected to parliament once again in 1689 and was said to have been appointed as a 'Gentleman of the Privy Chamber' by the monarch William of Orange in around 1690. William III had replaced King James II in a bloodless coup, having landed at Torbay in 1688 and found that the English army and parliament supported his claim to the throne. For his part James II had met with William shortly after he had landed and by December 1689 was on his way to exile in France.

In June 1690 the new English king, William of Orange, was reported to have stayed at Whitley's Cheshire home, Peele Hall, while on his way to Ireland and the famous Battle of the Boyne, a victory still celebrated by Irish Protestants some 300 years later.

The gun platform was first introduced to house defensive cannons during the 18th century, when the city was thought to be a target for rebels.

Whitley was finally elected Mayor of Chester in 1693 and served subsequent terms until 1696, when he decided to retire from public office. Before leaving office however, Whitley was reported to have made a large contribution to the cost of Chester's new Exchange Building, the predecessor to today's town hall. Whitley was said to have died in 1697, just a year after retiring from the post of mayor and 12 months before the new exchange building was completed.

In common with most of Cheshire's leading families, Sir James Stanley, the seventh Earl of Derby, was a faithful subject of Charles I at the time of the civil war and following the monarch's later execution actively supported and campaigned for his son's claim to the English throne. This particular member of the family is often referred to as the 'Great Stanley' and was thought to have succeeded Sir William Stanley, who died at Chester in 1642.

It was reported that around 1651 Sir James, along with a force of 300 supporters, had left the Isle of Man to meet with the exiled Charles II at Worcester. Along the way he was said to have recruited additional men from both the counties of Cheshire and Lancashire and with this force attacked the town of Wigan. There he was met by a large force of parliamentary dragoons and battle ensued between the two forces. Despite being hit several times by enemy fire and having his mount shot from underneath him Stanley was reported to have still managed to escape the field as his force was defeated by their enemy. Together with his remaining forces Stanley was then said to have made his way back into Cheshire where they were unexpectedly intercepted by another parliamentary force and subsequently forced to surrender.

Tried by a parliamentary court for treason, Lord Stanley and a number of his supporters were found guilty of their crime and condemned to die. While being held at Chester's mediaeval castle however, the earl almost succeeded in escaping his fate after supporters managed to get a rope into the prison with which he might escape. Having successfully scaled the walls of the castle and reached the river where a boat was waiting to spirit him away, his escape was said to have been discovered and following a brief search he was soon recaptured and taken back into custody.

Rather than risk any further attempts to free Stanley the parliamentary authorities decided to move him to his home town of Bolton the following day. A short time later, Sir James Stanley, the Earl of Derby, was said to have been beheaded by the royal executioner in the marketplace in Bolton. It was a similar fate to that which befell his ally Sir Timothy Featherstonehaugh, who was said to have been executed at Chester's marketplace outside of the abbey's gateway a day or so earlier.

Charles Stanley was the former Lord Strange who succeeded to the title of Earl of Derby following the death of his father, James, who was executed at Bolton in 1651. Born in 1627 Charles was said to have accompanied his late father to the mustering of King Charles I's royalist forces at Preston in 1642 when he was only 15 years old. Around 1650 he was reported to have married Dorothea Helena who was the maid of honour to the queen of Bohemia. This marriage was undertaken without his father's permission and it was said to have been a cause of continued conflict between the two men.

In spite of his father's active participation in the first English Civil War, Charles himself appears to have taken very little part in the struggle and was thought to have remained relatively neutral throughout. Following his father's execution the new earl and his countess had chosen to remain at Bidston Hall in Cheshire, the house which had been built by his grandfather, William Stanley, the sixth Earl of Derby.

Regardless of his own relative inactivity during earlier royalist campaigns Stanley was said to have been an active participant in the uprising led by Sir George Booth in 1659. Booth seized Chester during the rebellion against parliamentary rule but was subsequently defeated at Winnington Bridge by General Lambert. William was reported to have raised a large body of men in Lancashire to support Booth's rebellion, but these were defeated at the same time. Following their defeat by Lambert, Booth and Stanley were both arrested and held prisoner but the later restoration of Charles II saw both men released and restored to their earlier positions.

In around 1659 George Booth was said to have been commissioned by the still-exiled Charles II to take military control of Cheshire as well as the city of Chester. In collusion with a number of the city's corporation who were all opposed to the parliamentary regime, he managed to gain access to the city at the head of an armed force of some 3,000 men and take control of its inner precincts. The military governor, Colonel Thomas Croxton, was thought to have been forced to withdraw to the castles defences and await the arrival of a relief force.

As a child Booth was reported to have been orphaned fairly early in life and was brought up by his grandparents instead. Shortly after reaching his majority the young Booth was said to have taken up arms in support of parliament during the first English Civil War and was elected as MP for Cheshire in 1645.

Nine years later he was reported to have been appointed as a commissioner during the rule of the Major Generals and was known to be a highly critical opponent of the system, which was introduced by the national authorities. He was also vocal in his opposition to the religious and political radicalism of John Bradshaw, a fellow MP and the president of the Council of State.

In 1659, having become totally disillusioned with the parliamentary cause, Booth was said to have become involved with royalist factions that were seeking to restore the monarchy to England. Booth himself led the local rebellion against parliamentary rule in Cheshire, a part of which involved his seizing Chester for the cause. His fellow conspirators within the city were thought to have included the Mayor Gerard Jones, the Sheriff William Heywood and the City Recorder John Ratcliffe. It was said to have been Heywood that arranged for the city's gates to be left open in order that Booth's forces could enter Chester unopposed.

Having taken control of the city and isolated the small military contingent within the castle, Booth then set about recruiting Chester's inhabitants to his cause and along with his confederates within the corporation was said to have managed to raise three companies of foot soldiers to support him. They reportedly held control of the city for about three weeks, until Booth and his irregular forces were met and defeated by the parliamentarians under General Lambert at Winnington Bridge on the 16 August 1659. Booth himself was reported to have escaped the field in disguise but was later taken at Newport Pagnall and sent to the Tower of London. Colonel Croxton and his defenders in the castle were thought to have finally been relieved by Colonel John Lambert shortly afterwards and the rebellion within the city was said to have collapsed almost immediately afterwards.

As punishment for their part in the rebellion the city corporation was ordered to be dissolved and its status as a county town revoked by the parliamentarians. These penalties were never applied however, as the parliamentary authorities did not stay in power long enough to enforce the sanctions.

Fortunately for Booth and his companions the tide of political and puritanical radicalism which had earlier swept the country was itself beginning to wane and it was calmer voices that prevailed in England. Released on bail Booth was shortly afterwards elected to the Convention Parliament and was chosen as one of its representatives to invite the exiled Charles II to return to England as its king. Richly rewarded by the restored monarchy for his services to the Crown, Booth was later created Lord Delamere at the coronation of King Charles II in April 1661.

The following year saw yet another reoccurrence of the dreaded plague within the city and the historic Michaelmas fair was said to have been cancelled in order to prevent visitors spreading the disease to the wider region. As with the earlier outbreaks, the city's poorer inhabitants seem to have taken the full force of the epidemic and the city's economy was once again hit by the restrictions that were imposed to prevent further outbreaks. Overseas trade was now being depressed by a number of continental conflicts and piracy on the high seas was thought to be increasing. Chester was having to rely more heavily on coastal trading within England itself, but fortunately for the city the trade in lead and ore from North Wales remained relatively stable.

In common with much of the city, the Cathedral of Christ and the Blessed Virgin was said to have been in a seriously poor condition at the beginning of the 1660s. The lack of investment in its maintenance and repair was added to by the deterioration of the soft red sandstone that formed the bulk of its structure. In 1664 the house of the earls of Shrewsbury which lay in the southern part of the city close to the Bridgegate had to be rebuilt and immediately afterwards became an inn which stands today as the Bear and Billet. In the same year Charles II was said to have awarded Chester its new Royal Charter and once again confirmed its status as a county town. The 1660s were said to have ended with the dismantling of the great spire which stood atop St Peter's Church at the city's High Cross. This ancient church, which could trace its foundation back to the time of the Saxon kings, was thought to be so badly neglected that its steeple was regarded as a danger to the inhabitants of the city that it had served for so long.

For the next 20-odd years or so Chester was reported to be busy rebuilding its shattered infrastructure and allowing many of its historic buildings to decay even further. It was only with the arrival of James II in 1687 that the city once again became an important logistical centre for the Crown and it was thought that the cathedral had been improved sufficiently for the king to attend services there during his visit. It was also notable that his presence in Chester was marked by a decision to build a new armoury at Chester Castle and enhance its fighting capabilities. In the following year the city once again played host to English troops, only this time they were returning to the mainland in order to support an unstable monarchy. Troops serving in Ireland were said to have been recalled by James II to join soldiers from Lancashire, which he intended to use to reinforce his claim to the throne of England.

The counterclaimant for the English Crown was the Dutch monarch William of Orange, who disputed James's right to rule and it was clear that their differences would ultimately have to be resolved by force of arms. James was not that confident of victory, however, and towards the end of 1688 was said to have fled the country and in doing so handed the crown to his adversary. Chester's governor and its leading citizens on the corporation were not slow to endorse the new foreign monarch and all immediately proclaimed their allegiance to the new king.

Lord Delamere, the son of Sir George Booth, was an active supporter of William of Orange in his claim for the English throne and was said to have marched his forces to meet the new king as he came ashore in Britain. The city of Chester itself was seized by Lord Molineux and Lord Aston, but following James's flight out of the country it proved to be an unnecessary precaution. Despite the relatively bloodless exchange of monarch the country continued to be a restless and turbulent place, with any number of occasional rebellions and uprisings taking place throughout the period.

The native peoples of both Ireland and Scotland were thought to have shared a common grievance against the English monarchy, the feudal system that it supported and the Crown's continuing oppression and dispossession of their lands. A relatively small number of titled English landowners were known to have held great swathes of land in both countries gifted to them or their ancestors by the Crown as rewards for their service or loyalty. When these English families took possession of the Irish or Scottish estates they simply expelled the native peoples who had lived there for generations and in doing so planted the seed of insurrection in their souls.

The Scottish people had a second reason to fight the new monarch that had succeeded to the English Crown. James was first and foremost a Scot and as such his sympathies were very much with his native people. The usurping of his throne by William of Orange, a foreign king, was as good a reason for them to oppose English rule whenever and however they possibly could.

In 1689 the Irish people were reported to have rebelled against the English forces that remained in their lands and the Crown was once again compelled to send additional troops to reinforce their overstretched military garrisons. As before, Chester became a central mustering and provisioning point for these forces prior to their embarkation from the Dee ports. The sick and wounded troops from the conflict were said to have been returned to the city and treated at a temporary hospital that was established there in 1691. A number of prisoners of war and alleged spies were also known to have been held at Chester Castle during the period of the emergency.

A number of those involved in a Lancashire-based Jacobite plot were also said to have been held at the castle during 1694 and 20 years later these same cells were used once again to house some of the ringleaders of the 1715 Jacobite uprising. The conditions within the castle's gaol were said to be so severe that most of the ringleaders did not survive long enough to stand trial, but succumbed to the cold and fever that were prevalent at the time. Most of those that did survive the rigours of Chester's gaol were later reported to have been sentenced to transportation to the British colonies, never to see their homeland again.

These three separate Jacobite rebellions were also thought to be a direct result of the divisions and hatred which existed between the Catholic, Protestant and Presbyterian faiths that each particular party represented.

James II of England had come to the throne in 1685 following the death of his brother, Charles II, and was almost immediately involved in a dispute for the crown with James Scott, the Duke of Monmouth. He was the illegitimate son of the late King Charles and believed that he, rather than James, was the legal heir to the throne. In any event the uprising led by Monmouth and his supporters was quickly quelled by James but the incident left its mark on him. Eager to fully secure his authority and position, the new monarch set about appointing Roman Catholic supporters to key positions and effectively isolating the Protestant faithful, only serving to cause even greater resentment towards the Crown.

James's later introduction of the 'Declaration of Indulgence' which permitted all religious groups apart from the Protestants to worship their God without intervention further compounded the sense of injustice which was felt by the Protestant faithful and effectively handed their allegiance to his counterclaimant, the Protestant William of Orange. In 1688 James was reported to have made an allegiance with the Catholic king of France and as part of this agreement had arranged for a number of leading clergymen to be arrested. He was then said to have converted from Anglicanism to Catholicism, and when his second wife produced a male heir the largely Protestant English Parliament were faced with the prospect of a Roman Catholic sitting on the English throne, a situation they judged to be intolerable.

William of Orange was Europe's leading Protestant monarch and throughout his reign had dedicated himself to reducing the influence of the predominantly Roman Catholic kings of France and Spain. He was married to James's daughter Mary and his mother was Mary Stuart, a daughter of Charles I, so William was directly related to his rival for the English throne both by marriage and by blood. The English Parliament was said to have approached

William directly and pleaded with him to rescue England from the prospect of a Catholic monarch.

In November 1688 William was said to have arrived in England with his highly professional European army to pursue his claim and found that the majority of the British military and citizenry were already sympathetic to his cause. James was thought to have retreated from England with a guarantee of safe conduct from his son-in-law and made his way to France and to permanent exile. In what has often been referred to as the 'Glorious Revolution', William had managed to claim the throne of England without any real blood having been spilt.

Following the successful ousting of James II the English Parliament then hoped to adopt William's wife Mary as the new English monarch, with her husband being appointed as prince consort. However, Mary was always subject to her husband and so a compromise had to be found which would satisfy each party's requirements. An equitable arrangement was reached which saw William and Mary succeed to the throne as co-rulers and to be known as King William III and Queen Mary II, or more commonly as simply William and Mary. The English Parliament was to get its wish by default as William was soon back on the continent fighting the Protestant cause, leaving Mary to reign as the monarch in her home country.

Large parts of Scotland were known to be Roman Catholic and generally supported the ousted king, James II, but the Scottish Parliament itself was said to have been controlled by influential supporters of the Protestant and Presbyterian faiths. They managed to arrange for the legislature to officially condemn James II for his behaviour and his 'papist' legacy. The two continental countries that supported James's right to the English throne were France and Spain, both of which were sworn enemies of Britain. Having such allies was unlikely to help James endear himself to the highly sceptical and religiously orthodox population that inhabited Britain.

The first of the 'Jacobite' rebellions was said to have been led by John Graham, the Viscount Dundee. In April 1689 Graham proclaimed for James and was immediately supported by a number of the Scottish highland clans who joined his campaign. A little over two months later Graham's army met and defeated a government force that had been sent to meet them. Unfortunately for the 'Jacobite' cause, Graham himself was killed during the battle and, lacking his leadership, his army dispersed quickly afterwards. In the same year the 'Bill of Rights' was enacted by the English Parliament which finally eliminated the 'royal prerogative' which had allowed earlier monarchs to determine and implement any policy that they chose to employ. The new bill prevented a monarch from maintaining an army without parliamentary consent, granted the Crown an annual income for the maintenance of the office and established the Bank of England to deal with the country's finances.

In 1690 the ousted James II was said to have landed in Ireland to attack William's forces and rapidly assembled a force of some 20,000 men to face his enemy. On the banks of the River Boyne, James's army was then met by over 30,000 of William's supporters and after having been defeated by this army James was forced to retreat to France.

In 1701 James II was reported to have died in France and was then succeeded by his son James III, who was then proclaimed by Louis XIV of France, despite his having been exiled from England.

In order to finally resolve the issue over the rights of succession, the English Parliament passed the 'Act of Settlement' in 1701 which restricted any accession to the English throne to the House of Hanover or to the heirs of the Protestant Queen Anne, the last of the Stuarts. It also established parliamentary supremacy over both the country and the monarchy and forbade the declaration of war without the approval of parliament.

The act also prevented non-indigenous people from holding public office, subjected ministerial appointments to parliamentary approval and removed judges from royal punishment, so that in future years they had to be formally impeached by parliament. The people's representatives also gained the right to name the successor to the English and Scottish thrones, thus ensuring that a Roman Catholic would never again reign as the English or Scottish sovereign. In 1707 the 'Act of Union', which tied the monarchies of the two countries together, was orchestrated by members of the Protestant and Presbyterian faiths and effectively ended any hopes of a Catholic Stuart ascending to the throne of either country.

In 1708 James III led a brief invasion of Scotland but was compelled to retire to France after coming under threat from government forces. Five years later England and France signed the Treaty of Utrecht, part of which prohibited the harbouring of James III and forcing the exiled monarch to move to Spain. In 1714 Queen Anne died and was succeeded to the English throne by George I, a foreign king from the House of Hanover, who could not speak a word of English.

A Scottish Lord, the Earl of Mar, who was opposed to the new foreign king, raised the colours of the exiled James III. He was said to have rallied the highland clans to his cause and sent word to the banished monarch informing him of the new attempt to restore him to the throne. Mar and his forces moved on Perth and soon captured the city, later using it as their military headquarters. Meanwhile a second 'Jacobite' force was being assembled in the south of the country which, instead of reinforcing the northern rebels, turned south and invaded Lancashire where they were soon defeated by a government army at Preston.

The Earl of Mar was said to have mustered a force of about 12,000 men to his cause and on 13 November 1715 saw his supporters beaten by a government army led by the Duke of Argyle. The remaining rebel forces were thought to have been defeated and in full retreat even before their king, James III, had set foot on Scottish soil. When he finally did arrive in December 1715 there was little he could do but avoid capture and a few weeks later was forced to retire back to the continent. A Scottish nobleman, Lord Charles Murray, and a number of his accomplices were held at Chester's mediaeval castle following their unsuccessful uprising and once again many were reported to have died because of the terrible conditions within the gaol. The English government, in response to these rebellions and in an effort to stamp out any further uprisings, introduced the 'Disarming Act' in 1716 which forbade all highlanders from owning or indeed carrying weapons.

There was yet another short-lived attempt at rebellion in 1719 led by supporters of James III, but this too was doomed to failure and ultimately resulted in even greater repression of the highlands by the English army. Under Major General George Wade military communications were reported to have been improved and extensive military bases constructed at both Fort Augustus and Fort William in order to help suppress any further Scottish rebellions.

In 1720 James's wife delivered a son called Charles and five years later a second son who was called Henry. Twenty-five years after his birth the king's first son Charles would lead the final and most disastrous rebellion against the English Crown. In 1745 he would see his highland forces decimated by the English at the Battle of Culloden and he would forever be known as Bonny Prince Charlie. As with the uprising of some 30 years earlier, a number of those that survived the slaughter at Culloden were later taken and held at Chester's historic castle prior to being tried for their act of rebellion.

The end of the 17th century was a turning point in English history, marking as it did an end to the many royal and military disputes that had continued to wrack the country for hundreds of years. For its part, the city of Chester was busy trying to identify new sources of income and a new way of life for its citizens as the country began to prepare for the unknown times that lay ahead.

Chapter 13

THE NEW CUT, CANALS AND CIVIC CONSTRUCTION

By the middle of the 18th century Chester was beginning to see and feel the full effects of its dwindling sea-based economy; Liverpool was now emerging as the international maritime centre which would ultimately take its place. Although its annual markets and fairs remained economically important to the city, these too would suffer the effects of a lack of investment and poor communications. The salt trade, which in the past had been distributed via Chester, was by the 1720s being transported by the new canal systems that had been constructed. The emerging coal industry that had sprung up in North Wales was being serviced by new ports that had been specifically established to meet their needs. A lack of both foresight and civic ambition meant that Chester was isolated from these new industries and as a result was unable to benefit from them.

These often missed opportunities meant that the city inevitably began to see a marked decline in the traditional industries that had existed in Chester for centuries. The maritime trades that centred on the ancient harbour began to disappear, as well as the associated distribution and leather manufacturing industries that had grown up alongside it. The leather industries had been restricted by new regulations introduced in the 1680s which prevented live imports of cattle and only permitted

Canal cutting beneath the city's northern wall, marking the line of the Roman defensive ditch or fosse.

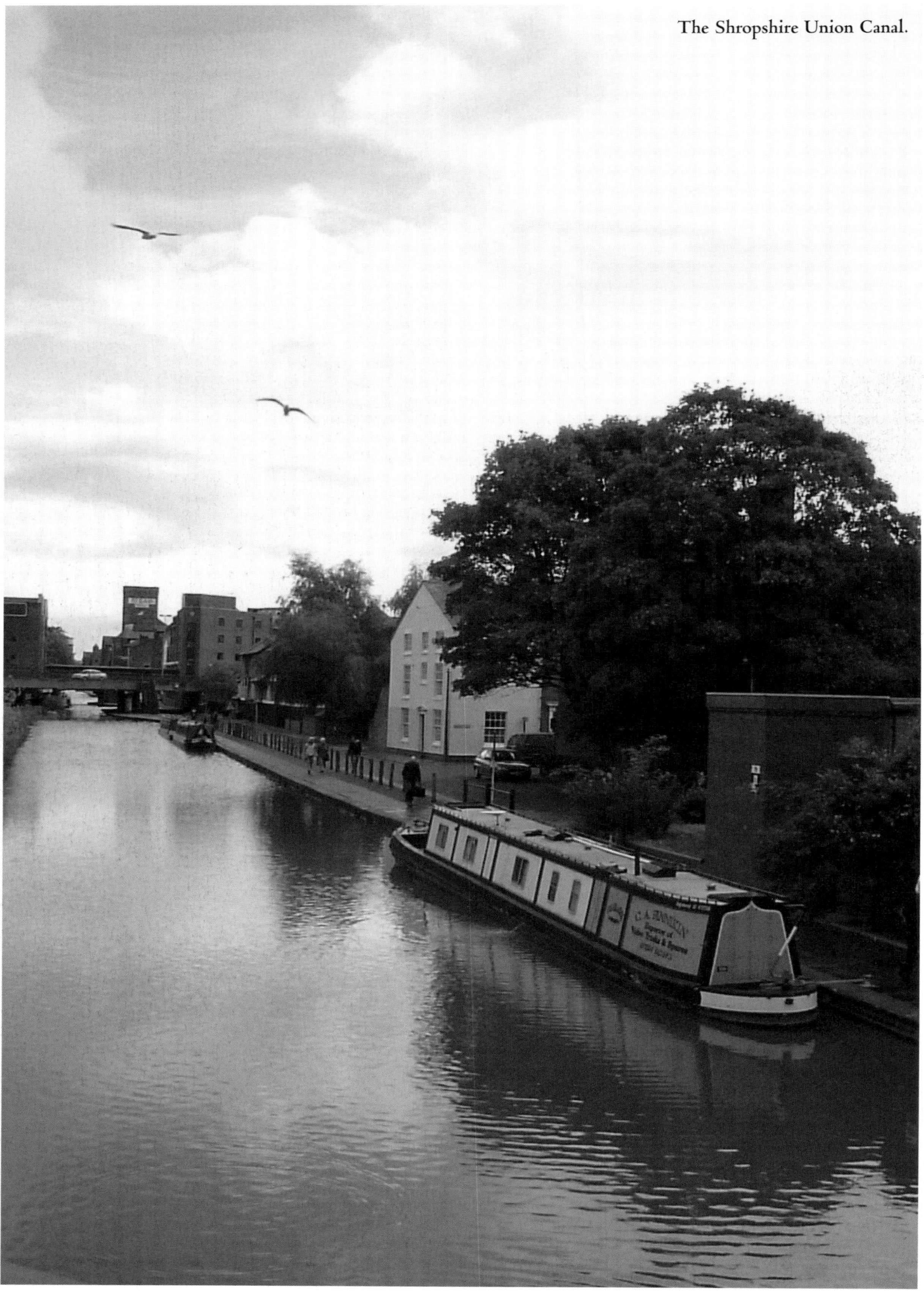

The Shropshire Union Canal.

A modern flight of steps accessing the city's ancient eastern wall.

the importation of cow hides from Ireland. At Chester's old port the annual tonnage continued to fall as merchants and traders moved their businesses northward to the new port of Liverpool and its much larger, brand new dock facilities which could handle the more modern larger ships and their cargoes.

By 1707 Chester's corporation were said to have repaired the city's defensive walls and flagged the guard walks that ran along their length. Within a few years the Groves area adjoining the river had been developed into public walks where both citizens and visitors alike could promenade along the banks of the Dee. The area known as the Roodee, which was thought to have been created in part by the progressive silting of the river, was now protected from regular flooding following the construction of the 'Kop' at Crane Bank in 1710.

A noted resident of Chester at the beginning of the 18th century was Sir Peter Denis, who was born in the city around 1712 and educated at the nearby King's School. Having left school he joined the royal navy in the 1720s and served as a lieutenant under Anson during his voyage around the world in 1740. He later commanded the 'Centurion' at the Battle of Finisterre and was a member of the court martial that tried and condemned Admiral Byng, who was executed by firing squad. Denis was reported to have led the naval attack on Belle Island and was singled out by his commander Sir Edward Hawke for a special mention regarding his actions. He was said to have been trusted by King George to escort Queen Charlotte to England. He was later made a baronet in 1767 and was given command of the royal navy's mediterranean squadron in 1771. Later, as admiral, Sir Peter Denis was reported to have died in 1778.

Another noted local man was Matthew Henry, a non-conformist religious leader and preacher who was said to have written a book called *Commentary on the Holy Scriptures*, a book that he would never finish. Born at Isycoed, Flintshire, in 1662, he had initially trained to become a lawyer but later changed his mind and gave up his studies to become a dissenting minister. By 1687 he was reported to have been appointed as a pastor in Chester and in 1700 friends of the preacher built a chapel in Trinity Street, adjoining the modern-day guildhall, where his

Linenhall Place was the site of Chester's linen industries, constructed in 1778.

message could be heard. Henry was thought to have died at Nantwich in Cheshire but his body was interred at Holy Trinity Church in the city on 22 June 1714.

Within the city itself large numbers of new coaching inns and public houses were being constructed to cater for the ever-increasing numbers of travellers that were visiting Chester or just passing through to other destinations. As today, travellers to Ireland embarked from the north-west region and Chester was a regular stopping point on the coach journey to and from the major cities of England and Ireland. Between 1720 and 1740 the number of public houses and coaching inns is thought to have actually doubled, reflecting the increased levels of human traffic that was flowing through Chester. The period also marked the beginning of large-scale retail and residential development within the city centre itself, much of which still exists to the present day. The great and the good of the city, including those whose wealth had come from Chester's former life as an international port, had started to establish their elegant residences in and around the city streets. Throughout the 1740s Northgate Street, King Street, Castle Street and Newgate Street were all filled with fine multi-storey Georgian town houses that fully exhibited both the prosperity and social standing of their occupants for all to see.

It also represented a return for the provision of public and private charitable institutions that would help cater for the large numbers of homeless and indigent people that still lived within Chester. In 1759 a new corporation workhouse was established by the city's leaders where the poor and needy were housed and fed in return for their labour. This new

King Street, formerly Barn Lane.

building was located in Paradise Row on the western fringes of Chester and was built as a replacement for the small number of individual parish poorhouses that had previously existed within the city. Later the following year new housing for the working classes of the city was built at Crane Street, close to the wharves, timber yards and small ship-building businesses that had by then established themselves by the newly 'canalized' river. Within a matter of some 50 or 60 years however, many of these properties were little more than slums which would only finally be demolished in the late 1950s. At the market square a new business exchange was built, where the city's government could be conducted by the local aldermen and councillors and where its traders could meet to discuss the future commerce of the city.

The latter part of the 18th century was the period that marked the clear division between ancient Chester which had its roots in the Saxon and Norman periods and the move towards the modern city that is with us today. Local ordinances were introduced by the corporation which saw the streets being cleaned and policed and the local buildings being protected by a dedicated fire service. In 1761 the Chester infirmary was built in the city, located on ground that 1,500 years earlier had been used by the Roman garrison as a cemetery for their fallen comrades. A physician at the new infirmary, John Haygarth, was said to have gained some note within the city and in the wider region for his unique approach to combating contagious diseases by isolating patients in clean and well-ventilated wards.

As with other towns and cities of the time, Chester was divided into wards and city constables were appointed by the mayor for each individual area. Initially the men who were appointed to the post were craftsmen, merchants or other respected members of the local community. It was a highly unpopular and onerous duty, as it was often unpaid and involved keeping watch when most honest people were fast asleep in their beds.

The common expression 'hue and cry' is thought to find its origins in the country's mediaeval past when the 'neighbourhood watches' were generally undertaken by the city's sergeants, watchmen or constables. As the name suggests, putting up the hue and cry alerted people to the fact that an unwarranted event had taken place within the area, bringing citizens out of their houses to help pursue the wrongdoer. It was not uncommon for a villain to be chased from ward to ward, area to area and district to district, all the time being harried and hounded by the cries and shouts of his pursuers.

Curfews could often be imposed in order to control the night-time movements of both visitor and resident. At Chester, curfews typically ran from eight or nine o'clock in the evening through to daybreak during the lighter months, but were even longer during the winter months. Watches were posted to safeguard the city from strangers or

Local legend suggests that if you can run up and down these steps on one breath of air, your wish will come true. The steps themselves are a relatively modern part of these ancient defences, dating from around 1785.

Chester Royal Infirmary was built on land that 1,500 years earlier had been used to bury the soldiers of Rome who died at their fortress.

disasters and were usually posted at each of the city's ancient gates. This duty was the responsibility of the 'Sergeants': the well-heeled families who extracted tolls and taxes from traders and merchants visiting Chester to sell their wares. Due to their status however, these watch duties were generally undertaken by a retainer within their household or by a paid substitute, rather than by the actual post-holder themselves.

By the late-17th century the handing over of the city's keys was a ceremony in itself. The mayor, aldermen, councillors and city sheriffs would parade through the city, before the mayor would solemnly pass the keys to the city gates to the appointed watchmen.

The advent of the city constables also marked the beginning of criminal reporting by the enforcement authorities within the city, allowing records to be kept on the county's criminals and the sentences handed down to them. History suggests that although the law has continually developed and 'progressed' over the centuries it was perhaps at its most severe in the later 18th, 19th and early 20th centuries.

The transportation of criminals was thought to have begun in 1597, with those found guilty of breaking the law often finding themselves being transported to the Americas and helping to colonise that new, harsh and unforgiving land. Given the length and manner of their transport to this New World, many did not survive the arduous journey and the possibility of returning to England was almost non-existent. For those that did manage to survive their sentence, which was often served on the newly emerging American plantations, the remainder of their lives would often be spent settling in this new continent.

Following the loss of the American provinces to its immigrant people who no longer wished to bow to the English monarchy, the penal system in Britain needed a new destination for the increasing numbers of people who were being sentenced to transportation. By the beginning of the 18th century Chester's courts were reported to be sending those prisoners sentenced to transportation to Liverpool or Bristol where they might be held for months, often in the most onerous conditions. From around 1776 however, the new southern lands of Australia were chosen as the final destination for those that had transgressed the English law. As with their counterparts who had been shipped to the Americas, those transported to the other side of the world for often the most minor of offences would very often never see their family, friends or their homeland again.

Within the city those convicted of relatively minor offences could just as easily be sentenced to a term of imprisonment in the bridewell, which was thought to have been a local house of corrections more like a workhouse rather than a prison. Inmates at the local bridewell were thought to have actually been paid for the work that they undertook while incarcerated. The house of corrections at Chester was reported to have stood opposite the modern-day Bluecoat building, later being used as a bakery and today as retail units or office space.

The period between 1769 and 1833 saw wholesale changes being made throughout the city as some of its ancient landmarks were gradually swept away and substituted with many of the structures that continue through to the modern day. From 1769 to 1810 all four mediaeval gates were demolished and replaced by their modern counterparts. The first was the Eastgate which was built in 1769 with financial help from the Grosvenor family. In 1782 the Bridgegate was erected and at the same time Tyrer's water tower, which had supplied fresh water to the city, but which had been badly damaged during the civil war siege, was finally demolished. The architect of the Bridgegate, Joseph Turner, would also be instrumental in the design and construction of the new Watergate which was built in 1789. Four years later one of his most overlooked commissions was completed. The 'Bridge of Sighs', which spanned the

The Bridge of Sighs was designed by local architect Joseph Turner *c.*1793 and served to carry condemned prisoners from the infamous Northgate gaol to the chapel, where they would receive their final sacraments.

new canal gorge outside of the Northgate, was built by Turner to provide a walkway for condemned prisoners from the infamous city gaol to the chapel where they would receive their last rites. This narrow walkway is said to have derived its name from the habit of condemned prisoners to sigh heavily as they crossed its length. Whether this was through sheer relief or total resignation is not entirely clear, but given the intolerable conditions within the gaol itself either sentiment might be true. Thought to originate from before the Norman conquests the conditions within the gaol itself were said to be tortuous and offered little if any comfort to its inmates. Cut deep into the natural rock, two of the rooms, the 'Dead Mans' cell and the 'Little Ease', were both claustrophobic and oppressive. As they were constructed below ground level and with no natural ventilation, the only air supply was provided by pipes which ran from the surface down to the cells. The Northgate gaol was finally closed in around 1808 in preparation for the replacement of the mediaeval gateway two years later.

The Liverpool Arms lies close to the site of the city's infamous Northgate Gaol.

Architect Thomas Harrison's castle portico, which was first raised during the redevelopment of the Chester Norman castle site between 1788 and 1829.

The last of the four mediaeval city gates to be replaced was the Northgate itself which was demolished and rebuilt in 1810, with the later gate being designed by local architect Thomas Harrison who is now synonymous with the city of Chester. In 1785 the corporation had run a competition to find a suitable replacement for the gaol which was housed within the precincts of the mediaeval castle and offered a prize of 50 guineas to the winner. Prison reformer John Howard had likened it to 'the black hole of Calcutta' and called for the city authorities to do away with the prison. From the entries that they received the city chose the plans of a relatively obscure 40-year-old architect called Thomas Harrison, who did not even live in Chester. Although unaware of it at the time, the adoption of his proposals would mark the start of a lifetime's work for the Yorkshire-born designer that would only end with his death in 1829.

As a young man Harrison had showed an early talent for both mathematics and mechanics and it was not long before his abilities attracted the attention of a local benefactor, keen to develop the young man's talents. He arranged for the young Harrison to receive an extensive education including the Grand Tour, which allowed him to study the great architectural buildings of Europe. It was during this trip that he began to develop the architectural skills that he would later employ in future commissions. In Rome his services were said to have been appreciated by the Pope who rewarded the young architect with a gold and silver medal.

Almost immediately Harrison's proposals for the gaol at Chester were extended to include the entire castle complex and the replacement of the ancient castle itself, the great shire hall and other mediaeval structures that had degraded over the previous years. Beginning in 1785 these ancient buildings were systematically deconstructed and swept away to be replaced with the modern castle development which inhabits the site today. Harrison's new castle would include a magnificent shire hall, crown court, armoury, prison and military barracks, all of which would take him the next 35 years to complete.

By 1792 the new gaol had been completed, its dirty disease-ridden communal chambers replaced by new individual cells for the prisoners that offered light and space to those that were incarcerated. Inmates that were being held for minor civil offences like debt were now kept separate from the more serious felons. At the time of its completion this new gaol was regarded by most as a real step forward in penal reform and yet it was later demolished to make way for the new county hall which stands on the site today.

Between 1791 and 1801 the centrepiece of the new castle complex was constructed, the magnificently colonnaded portico incorporating the county's shire hall and judicial courts. To the east and west of this central building, new wings were added which would subsequently accommodate the armoury and military barracks. Now extending well beyond the limits of the mediaeval walls, Harrison designed a new gateway for the castle in the form of a *propylaeum* built on large stone columns. Although the problem was not obvious during Harrison's time, the decision to build the shire hall and its courts directly above the former mediaeval castle's moat would later prove to be a costly decision. In the 1920s large cracks began to appear in the court buildings which were

Napier House, a later military building erected within the mediaeval castle's inner bailey.

attributed to the inadequate foundations that lay below them. Remedial work was undertaken almost immediately and by 1922 the building and its supporting columns had been fully restored. To this day Chester Crown Court regularly hears a number of high-profile criminal cases, but is most commonly linked with the 1960s trial of Myra Hindley and Ian Brady who were tried and found guilty of the infamous Moors Murders.

Harrison was also said to have undertaken a partial restoration of the city's historic cathedral, which had suffered much over the previous centuries. Visitors and commentators alike had been moved to highlight the dreadfully poor condition of

Adjoining Agricola's Tower, the archway is likely to originate from the rebuilding of the castle during the 18th century.

its magnificent stonework and to call for action to save the historic structure. Between 1818 and 1820 extensive renovations were undertaken to preserve the building's inner and outer fabric and to ensure that it would survive intact in the coming decades.

Harrison was also responsible for the design of Chester's second river crossing, the Grosvenor Bridge, but sadly did not live to see its completion as he died in 1829 aged 85. Opened by the then 13-year-old Princess Victoria in 1833 the bridge project was reported to have been completed by William Cole, a pupil of Harrison's. Up until 1864 the Grosvenor Bridge was thought to be the world's greatest single span stone bridge, standing 200 feet wide and 60 feet high.

Before his death Harrison was also said to have rebuilt the ancient St Bridget's Church in around 1825 after it had been demolished to make way for Grosvenor Road, relocating it close to the castle complex. Sadly the rebuilt church failed to survive later city developments and finally disappeared forever during the 20th century, along with many other of the city's historic buildings

Foliot House in Northgate Street was another Harrison building that has managed to last the test of time, but was later hidden by the odeon cinema and has now been converted into offices. Chester's northern gate was also designed by Harrison and was erected between 1808 and 1810. He was also the architect of the city's Commercial building and News Room which was situated on Northgate Street.

While Thomas Harrison was building his new complex at the castle, Chester was trying to build new means of communications with the wider region. Sadly for the city the most economically vital scheme, that of the Chester canal system, was hampered by a lack of both vision and money within the corporation. One proposal which had promised a restoration of the River Dee's navigation for trading ships was also hit by a level of scepticism within the community and an apparent lack of intent on the part of its builders which would finally put an end to any future hopes for its now marooned historic port.

In 1737 work was started which would see the course of the River Dee diverted five miles to the south of its original position. This 'new cut' required the river to be redirected through an artificially built channel which was 10 miles long and ran from Connahs Quay through to the city itself. This new 'canal' allowed large tracts of land to be reclaimed from the river course and which today are represented by the present-day Sealand area. The scheme was said to have worked for an extensive period but the River Dee project was never likely to be a real long-term success, simply because of the lack of intervention on the part of the River Dee Company themselves and the constant re-silting of the channel through the natural action of the river. The year 1771 was reported to have been the most productive for the port at Chester with large

Chester's Crown Courts have hosted some notable trials, including that of the Moors Murderers Myra Hindley and Ian Brady.

numbers of ships going in and out of the ancient harbour. In the course of the next 50 years or so the city enjoyed a short-term resurgence in its trade, but the inevitable silting of the channel would finally dispel any hopes of prolonged prosperity and would lead to accusations of wrongdoing against those involved with the scheme.

The lands on the northern bank of the river which had been reclaimed as a result of the new channel were said to have belonged to the speculators that had invested in the new venture and were thought by some to be the real reason for diverting the River Dee so far off its early course. The northern bank of the Dee estuary, including the former historic ports at Burton and Parkgate, have more recently become strangled with marshland. Its effect has been augmented by the introduction of hard grasses which were planted by the John Summers Steel Works in 1895 in an effort to stabilize the ground which adjoined their industrial complex and which was then allowed to spread unchecked along the length of the estuary.

There is a new suggestion that the River Dee was always doomed to fail and that man's use and interference has only hastened what was an inevitable end. The theory goes that the river's estuary was formed by ice sheets moving south-east from the Irish Sea and not by the scouring action of the water itself. Once the ice had retreated the resulting estuary was too shallow and wide to support a great body of water, which in normal circumstances would have carved its own deep river channels and cleared obstructions through the force of its currents. This lack of natural power in the river prevented the clearing away of sand and soil deposits which over the centuries accumulated to the point where they inhibited successful navigation of the river's course.

Some 20 years after the start of the River Dee's 'new cut' scheme had been started, a number of local business leaders within Chester proposed the building of a canal system from the city to Middlewich. It was hoped that this new waterway might help the city to compete with the new trading and shipping port of Liverpool that was beginning to dominate the whole of the north-west region. Following complaints from the competing Trent and Mersey canal company however, plans for the new system were amended so that the new canal would run from Chester to Nantwich and a link to Middlewich would be constructed at a later date.

In April 1772 the Mayor of Chester, Joseph Taylor, performed the official opening ceremony for the new Chester canal system which promised so much for the city's future prosperity. As it turned out though, the waterway proved to be an unmitigated disaster for everyone involved. Having cost over £70,000, the lack of the final link to Middlewich and its vital access to the regional system meant that Chester's canal was of little use to the manufacturers and traders that were supposed to use it. With no finances left to develop this final link and nobody using the stretches of canal that did exist, within a few years the system was deserted and large parts of it had become derelict.

In 1791 at Ellesmere in Shropshire another group of businessmen came together to launch a proposal for a canal network of their own, one that would help to link the three major rivers within the region: the Dee, the Severn and the Mersey. By 1796 the first part of the system had been completed by William Jessup who was aided in its construction by a then relatively unknown junior engineer called Thomas Telford. The northern terminus of this canal was located at Netherpool and ran across West Cheshire, through the townships of Caughall, Backford and Mollington before reaching its southern limit at the city of Chester. Such was the success of this first 'Ellesmere' canal that Netherpool was renamed Ellesmere Port and it was used to carry passengers along this 'Wirral' line from Chester to the ports on the River Mersey.

Plans to develop the canal system southward were far more problematic and it would be some years before the Ellesmere and Chester canals could finally link to the waterways that were being constructed in Wales. The Pontsycyllte aqueduct which was a pivotal link in the amalgamation of the two watercourses proved to be an extremely expensive and time-consuming feat of engineering. Until such a time that it was completed there was a 17-mile gap between the two systems which prevented the easy and economic transport of goods from one region to another. The southern end of the Ellesmere canal was fed by the River Dee as it flowed through Llangollen and was located close to the troublesome Pontsycyllte aqueduct. By linking the two waterways at this point the whole system was opened up for the manufacturing businesses of both regions and within a short time this stretch of water was reported to be one of the busiest in the country.

In 1804 the Ellesmere canal company tried to buy the Chester canal from its shareholders, but the offer was refused as the Chester company still hoped to build the vital link to Middlewich and gain access to both the regional and national canal networks. In spite of the unsuccessful takeover the two companies still retained good working relations and the Shropshire company settled for re-routing their canal to Hurleston, which was to the north of Nantwich and where they could finally link up to the Chester waterway. In 1805 the much delayed Pontsycyllte aqueduct was officially opened and a permanent link between the north-west of England and Wales was established. This year also marked the true beginnings of the economic value of the system as the first commercial cargoes began to be transported by the new canal network.

Eight years later the two canal companies finally decided to merge and became the Ellesmere and Chester Canal Company. Although still detached from the regional and national waterways because of the missing link at Middlewich, the new company began to flourish. In 1821 the network was further extended and enriched by the opening of the Montgomeryshire canal which ran northward from Newtown in mid-Wales and meant substantially more boats and barges using the system on a day-to-day basis.

In 1824 new plans were put in place to develop the Ellesmere and Chester canal system even further by building a brand new link from Nantwich through to the village of Autherley which was on the outskirts of Wolverhampton. From here commercial traffic could then join the Staffordshire and Worcestershire canals and begin to reach the wider regions that had evaded them for so long. At the same time the Ellesmere and Chester Canal Company put forward plans to build a short link from Barbridge through to Middlewich and the wider network. First proposed in 1770 this vital link was finally achieved in 1833 under the control of its engineer Thomas Telford. Some 60 years after it had first been suggested, the essential element that had been missing for so long was finally a reality.

In 1825 the construction of the Birmingham to Liverpool canal system which linked two of the new economic powerhouses that were emerging within the country was completed. As this waterway passed Nantwich it offered the Ellesmere and Chester Canal Company a golden opportunity to extend its transport links to the south and north of the country. Ten years later a new canal was built, linking the waterways in the south with those in the north and enabling freight to be carried anywhere in the country.

By 1840 these new canal systems were beginning to be seen as crucial to the economic development of the hundreds of towns and cities that they united. At Chester regular steamboat services were carrying passengers to and from the River Mersey to meet up with the continental and transatlantic ships that were operating from Liverpool. By 1845 the railways were beginning to make serious inroads into the passenger transport services and the Ellesmere and Chester Canal Company merged with the Birmingham and Liverpool Junction Canal Company to become the Shropshire Union Railways and Canals Company.

Constructed for the convenience of Roger Comberbach, Recorder of the city who lived nearby, the Recorder's Steps were built in 1700.

Originally the 'Recorder's House' in Chester, it was rebuilt in both the mid-17th and 18th centuries to become The Bull, a well-known Coaching House.

As in most developed countries the lifespan of the canals and inland waterways as commercial highways was a relatively short-lived affair. The emergence of the railways as passenger transports and commercial vehicles soon surpassed barges and boats in terms of both time and cost. Any hopes that the city of Chester might have had in limiting the economic importance of Liverpool, or of competing against this major port, were seemingly undermined by a lack of both vision and finances. The potential for Chester to benefit from the rapid development and spread of the new canal systems was lost forever during the 60 years that it took to build a vital link to the outside world. The city did gain new business from these inland waterways – the steam and corn mills were in operation by 1819 and the lead works had been built earlier than that – but no new large-scale industries had settled in the city as a direct result of the canal's presence. By the middle of the 19th century the two biggest employers in Chester were the lead works and the Dee mills and one of them had already been in the city for the best part of 900 years.

In the city itself the pace of modernisation continued under the guidance of the architect Thomas Harrison and Chester's corporation. Around 1778 a new Linen Hall was erected to serve the city's cloth fairs with individual stalls and shops congregating around a new central courtyard where business was conducted. On the south-eastern flanks of the city's walls close to the river, the Recorder's Steps were built reportedly at the request of Roger Comberbach, the Recorder of Chester between 1700 and 1719, whose house was located nearby. Beyond these lay a series of six small flights of steps which are often referred to as the Wishing Steps, built in 1785. Legend has it that if a person could run up and down these flights of steps on one breath of air then their wish would come true. In 1800 the public stocks and pillory post which had stood for hundreds of years and which had acted as both public entertainment and deterrent were finally removed. Three years later the inner pentice which had sat next to St Peter's Church near the High Cross was finally demolished. It had served as a meeting place for the mayor and his corporation and had hosted the city's petty sessions, but with the construction of the new exchange building on the market square had eventually become obsolete.

In 1807 a new county gaol was built between the infirmary and the Watergate, close to the modern-day Queen's School which lies along City Walls Road. The ancient Northgate gaol, with its miserably damp and airless cells, was finally consigned to history, reflecting a far more humane approach to crime and punishment.

In the market square area of the city new buildings were constructed to accommodate the growing ranks of

The main crossroads in Chester is the High Cross, much of which was designed by Thomas Meakin Lockwood and completed around 1888.

The Queen's School occupies the site of Chester's former county prison which replaced the city's infamous Northgate gaol. The Queen's School building was designed by local architect Edward Ould and dates from *c.*1880.

entrepreneurs and traders that made their livings from the local population. The new exchange building which was the forerunner of the modern-day town hall housed the administrative and commercial heart of the city and provided a central point for the various parades, markets and marches that took place within Chester. At the northern end of the square, private residences built by the likes of the Massey family were constructed and would later be the site of the Shropshire Arms. Where the Odeon cinema stands today was the home of local artist James Hunter, who gave his name to Hunter Street. That house would itself be replaced in the 1820s by Northgate House, which would later become the lodging house for judges that sat at Chester assizes held in the city's exchange.

As the Georgian period came to an end the city was slowly becoming the tourist attraction and retail centre that it remains to this day. Many of the innovative projects and strikingly handsome buildings that emerged during these years are immediately recognisable today and that is a true testament to the likes of Harrison and Turner who did much to change the fabric and direction of this ancient city.

Within a short period it would become renowned for its historic fortifications, its covered shopping rows and the density of both its churches and pubs. The dawn of the Victorian age would see this traditional view of the city consolidated and developed in the years that lay ahead.

Chapter 14

Chester's History on Crime and Punishment

Thought to have derived many of its origins from the Roman period of British history, the English legal system is known to have been constantly adapted and developed throughout the subsequent centuries to include the laws and traditions of the later Saxon and Norman peoples, as well as the dictates of the emerging Christian church. Possibly because of that and perhaps even in spite of it, nearly 2,000 years after it was first introduced our legal system is still generally regarded by many as one of the most equitable and transparent judicial organisations in the world today.

It is perhaps surprising to note that even from the earliest times the application of capital punishment by the state was thought to have been a fairly rare event and was only ever employed in the most serious of cases. Early courts were said to have made use of financial penalties as punishment against a wrongdoer. It was known to be fairly common for a murderer to be ordered to financially compensate the family of a victim, rather than lose his own life as a consequence of his illegal actions.

The first and possibly oldest gaol in Chester is thought to have been one that formed part of the early castle complex which had been constructed by the first Norman earls of the city. Given that the entire county was reported to have been ruled in an almost sovereign-like way by these early lords and that their judicial courts were based at the castle, it seems entirely likely that most offenders would have been held there to face Norman justice. It was only in later times, when a clear division was made between the Crown and local authorities, that the castle's gaol was used almost exclusively to hold those who had transgressed either against the monarch or the elected parliament. Even these prisoners, though, were generally handed over to the civil authorities of Chester for their sentence to be carried out and it was only in exceptional cases where they would face justice away from the city.

Chester's infamous Northgate gaol is thought to have been originally constructed during the city's early mediaeval period. It may well have been built specifically to hold those accused or convicted of local or civil wrongdoing and which would be commonly dealt with by the city's Pentice Court or Chester's regularly held criminal assizes. The fortress's early Roman gates were said to have included a pair of stone-built guard rooms which flanked the entrance and it might well be the case that the later mediaeval portal was constructed in a similar fashion or as additions to these early features. In addition to the main structure there were known to be at least two rock-cut cells lying below ground level where condemned prisoners were thought to have been held prior to their execution.

Following the abandonment of the public gallows at Boughton and prior to the construction of the later county gaol in City Walls Road, the Northgate gaol was thought to have been used for the execution of prisoners in Chester. Despite the change in venue however, such events continued to remain a public spectacle and large crowds would gather to see the guilty parties get their just rewards.

The later construction of the new county gaol which was built towards the end of the 18th century saw the end of the mediaeval Northgate and around the beginning of the 19th century the historic prison was finally demolished and its underground dungeons done away with forever. For the next 60 years or so public executions were said to have continued at the new county gaol in the city, often in a completely different fashion to that which had taken place at the Spital in Boughton.

The new gaol building on City Walls Road was said to have included a platform above its main entrance where condemned prisoners were effectively 'launched' into eternity at the end of a strong rope. On at least one notable occasion however, this new method of dispatching the guilty was reported to have failed miserably as the rope snapped and the condemned man plummeted to the ground. Sadly for the prisoner in question this failure in the equipment was soon resolved and having replaced the rope he was subsequently executed once again, this time successfully. In around 1866 the last public execution was reported to have taken place at Chester's county gaol and perhaps reflected a much wider change in public attitudes to such punishments. Sometime later it was said that all condemned prisoners from Cheshire were sent to regional prisons in Liverpool and Manchester for such sentences to be carried out away from the public gaze.

Justice often had to be seen to be done in order that people could understand its purpose and witness the basic right of society to publicly punish wrongdoers in a fair and adequate fashion. In order to fully demonstrate society's unwillingness to accept any sort of criminal or anti-social behaviour a number of punishments and associated devices were introduced into common use.

The ducking stool was a device which was thought to have been in regular use between the 11th and 15th centuries and was designed to punish local gossips or women that constantly nagged their husbands. The offender was said to have been publicly displayed on the stool before being immersed in a pond or pool.

The Chester 'branks' was said to have been a metal frame which was fitted over the offender's head, not dissimilar to a modern medical frame which is designed to protect or support the skull. The most important part of the brank was said to have been a rough rasp that fitted into the offender's mouth and kept their tongue from moving. It was typically used as a deterrent for gossips and scolds and was an alternative to the ducking stool. These instruments were reported to have been used in Chester right through to the 19th century.

The gibbet was a construction designed to display the dead bodies of executed villains or wrongdoers, so that those who passed by could witness justice and be warned as their own conduct. A gibbet was thought to have stood at each of Chester's ancient gates, as well as the High Cross and on several of the main routes leading in and out of the city. It was not uncommon for the body of a prisoner that had been hung on the city's gallows to be tarred and placed in the gibbet cage, simply to rot away or to be predated upon by scavenging birds and insects.

The pillory was said to have existed in the city from the time of the Romans and was reported to have been a version of the stocks, where wrongdoers could be publicly flogged, humiliated and displayed to the local people. Miscreants often had notices and signs which advertised their crime hung around their necks in order that other local townspeople could know their shame.

A variation on the theme was the practice of 'flogging' a wrongdoer through the streets of the city. The unfortunate individual was said to have been tied to the back of a cart and their back laid bare to the waist. As the cart made its way through the streets of the city the victim was constantly flogged by one of the city's law officers. The beating would only stop once the cart had reached one of the city's gates, where the guilty party would then be expelled from the city's precincts.

The cucking stool was reported to have been a version of the ducking stool and was generally used for women who were guilty of some local transgression or crime. It was thought that those sentenced to be placed on the cucking stool were displayed in such a way as to be completely humiliated before their friends and neighbours.

Branding was, as the name suggests, where wrongdoers were branded with letters relating to their particular crime. SL, for instance, was thought to reflect a person who had been found guilty of seditious libelling, as in the case of William Prynne who was branded during the 17th century.

As time passed and our laws 'progressed' the legal penalties for even minor infringements became far more severe, no doubt supported and justified by the increasing influence of the Christian church whose teachings were constantly interpreted and adopted into the system. This is best reflected with the cases of George Marsh and John Plessington, both of whom were executed for 'religious' crimes rather than any sort of civil or criminal wrongdoing that we would recognise today.

John Plessington was a practising Catholic priest who was accused of involvement in a Jesuit plot to assassinate James II. Despite his vehement denials regarding his involvement, he was found guilty by the court and was subsequently sentenced to be hung, drawn and quartered on Gallows Hill in Boughton on 19 July 1679. In 1980, nearly 300 years after his death, Plessington's name was finally added to the memorial dedicated to another of the city's religious martyrs, George Marsh, who had been burnt at the stake for heresy in 1556.

Richard Sale was reported to have been a Quaker preacher in the city around 1656 that fell foul of this same religious prejudice that was prevalent in Chester at the time. He was arrested twice by the local authorities, firstly for speaking to a priest in the street and in the second instance for preaching in the street. A man of large stature, Sale was incarcerated at the city's ancient Northgate gaol and forced into a cell called the 'Little Ease', which was totally unsuitable for a man of his size. Said to have been only four feet six inches high and some 17 inches wide, it was reported to have taken four men

Chester's North Gate, built in 1810.

to squeeze him into the cell. The cramped dungeon ultimately proved to be extremely hazardous to Sale's health and he was said to have died within two months of his imprisonment.

Richard Hickock was another of the leading Quakers within the city that conducted a campaign of civil disobedience and disturbance which included haranguing citizens, disrupting church services and deliberately ignoring the city authorities. A number of these Quaker leaders were subsequently arrested and then fined or jailed. Hickock himself was accused of preaching in a 'Steeple House' and was imprisoned in the Northgate's notorious 'Dead Mans Room', a rock-cut cell which lay below the gaol. He was only finally released when an officer in Cromwell's army heard of his plight and had Hickock brought before a judge with a writ of *habeas corpus*. The judge found his imprisonment to be illegal and the preacher was subsequently released.

Although it is not entirely clear that the Malpas-born John Bradshaw was the actual judge, it seems likely that as Chief Justice of Cheshire he may well have presided at a number of 'witchcraft' trials which took place in the county during the middle of the 17th century.

Anne Osboston was a native of Rainow, near Macclesfield, Cheshire, who was accused of employing witchcraft between 1651 and 1655. She was charged with bringing about the deaths of John Steenson, Barbara Potts, her husband John and a fourth person called Anthony Booth. Found guilty by the court, Osboston was hung at Boughton in Chester along with Ellen Beech and Anne Thornton, two other local women that had been found guilty of similar charges. The remains of all three women were said to have been buried at St Mary's on-the-hill, close to the old castle's ditch.

Elizabeth Powell was a local widow who was charged by Thomas Annion, a local blacksmith, with using witchcraft against him. It was thought that the charges brought by Annion were entirely spurious and were a result of a property dispute between the two parties. Powell was held at Chester's infamous Northgate gaol in terrible conditions and was reported to have succumbed to the dire conditions in 1669, before ever being brought before the courts.

Proving whether or not an accused person was a witch was a gruesome affair and it often entailed the employment of professional 'prickers', who earned relatively high fees and would go to extreme lengths to find a prisoner's 'mark of guilt' or 'Devils mark'. The process of 'pricking' involved sticking a needle into the accused person's body, often right down to the bone itself. The investigators were trying to find a particular spot that was insensitive to pain, or would not bleed and was said to be the 'Devils mark'. The process of pricking the victim until they managed to find such a spot could be repeated indefinitely until they managed to find what they were looking for.

As society developed beyond the ill-informed mediaeval, Tudor and Jacobean periods, so too did the national instruments of civic, legal and religious control. Instead of the courts being controlled by local authorities who had some form of control or discretion, crime and punishment within England tended to come under the absolute control of centralised government who sought to impose recognised standards and sentences throughout Britain. As the population grew and certain areas became richer the law itself became far more severe to those that transgressed society's rules, regardless of whether their actions were driven entirely by choice or by basic need. The thief that stole to feed his family was treated in equal fashion to the thief that stole purely for gain and English courts were often loathe to make any distinction between the two entirely different situations.

As the county town of Cheshire, the city of Chester continued to retain its position as the administrative and judicial centre of the region, entitling it to host the main courts and prisons that were fundamental to and symptomatic of the age.

Joshua Horton, a resident of Watergate Street, was found guilty of forgery.

Consequently, criminals from all over the county found themselves being brought to the city and held in its dismal gaols before finally being brought before its courts and assizes.

Chester's mediaeval castle was the site of a mint established in 1696 to help in the re-coining of England's currency that was undertaken at the time. Coins were regularly defaced by people 'clipping' them, thereby paying for their goods and services with a piece of the coin rather than the entire thing. As a result of this practice much of the precious metal was lost or wasted and was a major concern to the government. The man who was put in charge at the Chester mint was Edmund Halley, who was appointed to oversee the production of the new coinage and who would later identify the comet that would forever bear his name. Sometimes the practice of 'clipping' coins was regarded so seriously that the courts would hand down the ultimate penalty to those found guilty of the crime. It has been suggested that at least one man who was tried and convicted was sentenced to be hung, drawn and quartered for the offence. His quarters were then displayed on the city gates as a warning to any other felon that might be tempted to repeat the offence.

The sentence of being hung, drawn and quartered was a particularly brutal one, even for the period. The guilty party was effectively strangled to the point of unconsciousness, then taken down and revived. Their stomach and chest were then cut open while they were awake and their intestines and vital organs were removed in front of them. Fortunately for the prisoner, the shock and loss of blood would have killed them long before their body was then cut into quarters and publicly displayed on the gates or towers of the city.

Joshua Horton was a resident of Watergate Street in Chester, and was said to have been arrested in 1695 having been accused of forging coins. Found guilty of the offence, he was held at the infamous Northgate gaol prior to sentencing but somehow managed to escape the precincts. Having secured himself a fast horse, Horton then rode back to his home city of London and disappeared from justice. The city's two sheriffs, who were responsible for the gaol's security, were later fined for allowing the prisoner to escape.

In common with today, the theft of personal property was often viewed far more seriously than personal physical attacks and consequently attracted much more severe penalties from the courts. The severity of the law was perhaps best reflected in the case of Sarah Jones who was tried and found guilty of stealing 28 yards of chintz in the city and was executed for her crime in 1778. Also that of two local men, Joseph Booth and William Elliot, who were tried and convicted of shoplifting in the city in 1791 and were executed shortly afterwards.

John Oakes was tried and convicted of 'coining' in 1784 and later executed in the city. Thomas Hyde was tried and convicted of horse stealing and subsequently hung in 1786. Henry Parsland was recorded at Chester's spring assizes in 1833 as having been tried and convicted of stealing a sheep at Bugsworth in Cheshire. He was sentenced to death for his crime and was later executed in the city at the county gaol on City Walls Road. James Mason was tried and found guilty of attempting to procure a miscarriage and paid for it with his life in 1834.

Home invasions or burglary were considered to be such a serious crime during the 18th century that many of those that committed such an act often paid for it with their lives. One of the most notable cases in Chester was that of John Clare who was tried and convicted of burglary in 1801. Clare did not believe that he would be found guilty of the offence, but on hearing that he was to hang for his crime immediately hatched a plot to escape the executioner. As the cart carried him and his two equally guilty companions to their inevitable fate, Clare leapt from the cart and attempted to swim the width of the River Dee and gain his freedom. Unfortunately for him the weight of the shackles he carried on his arms and legs dragged him down and he was drowned.

As his condemned companions waited the two city sheriffs were forced to summon a boat and drag the river bed to recover the dead felon's body. Having done so, they were then obliged to resume their duties in respect of all three guilty men and Clare's lifeless corpse was 'executed' along with the other two condemned men. These two men were Samuel Thompson who had been tried and convicted of counterfeiting alongside John Morgan.

William Ellis was found guilty of burglary in 1778 and was executed at Chester. In 1783 Resolution Heap was tried and convicted of burglary and suffered a similar fate. Edward Holt was executed in 1786 and James Buckley, along with his brother Thomas, was executed in the same year for the same offence. Alexander Morton was tried and convicted of burglary and executed in 1800. James Renshaw was tried and convicted, along with two brothers, Simeon and William Betson, of burglary in 1813. All three men were thought to have been executed at Chester's new county gaol, which stood on the site of the later Queen's School.

Abraham Rostern was tried and convicted for burglary and was executed in 1818 along with John and Isaac Moor, who had both been tried and convicted of a similar offence in the same year. Twelve months later John Johnson, along with Samuel Hooley, was convicted of the same crime and suffered a similar fate. Ralph Ellis was tried and convicted for burglary in 1820 and was subsequently hung on the gallows, as was Thomas Miller the same year. John Lair was tried and convicted for burglary in 1829 and paid with his life.

George Hunt was recorded at Chester's spring assizes in 1833 as having been tried and convicted of a burglary at Brinnington in Cheshire. Hunt was sentenced to death for his crime and was executed in the city at the county gaol. Tried along with Hunt was another man, Thomas Palfreyman, but he was acquitted of the crime and walked free from court. The same year George Webb was tried and convicted of a burglary at Rudheath in Cheshire. He too was sentenced to death.

Although burglary was and remains a predominantly masculine crime, then as now women often imitated their male counterparts. A Cheshire woman, Kitty Murphy, was recorded at Chester's spring assizes in 1833 as having been tried and convicted of a burglary at Stockport and was later sentenced to death.

The protection of the law and its enforcement officers became a priority for the Crown and the courts and remained so through to the 20th century, with the murder or attempted murder of a law officer regarded with the utmost seriousness and this was often reflected in the sentences handed down by judges. Thomas Mate was tried and convicted for killing a constable in Chester in 1789; Mate used his last speech on the gallows to accuse his long-suffering wife of being unfaithful to him. He was 64 years old and after denouncing his poor spouse in public was executed shortly afterwards.

One Peter Martin, who was also known as Joseph Lowton, was tried and convicted of firing at an excise vessel in 1798 and was executed at Chester shortly afterwards. William Proudlove along with his co-defendant George Glover, were tried and convicted of shooting at an excise man in 1809. Both men were subsequently executed on Chester's gallows. Even those that were appointed to positions of authority were protected by the law and any attack upon them was viewed in the most serious light. Joseph Henshall was tried and found guilty of firing at gamekeepers in 1829 and was later executed.

Not surprisingly, with wrongdoers being hung for common theft, shoplifting and burglary, those tried and convicted of wounding could expect little sympathy from the courts. Where a felony had been committed it was little wonder that extreme sentencing was employed. John Carr was tried and found guilty of felonious shooting in 1834 and was hung for it. In the same year Thomas Riley was tried and convicted of felonious cutting and lost his life on the gallows, as did William Naylor who was also tried and found guilty of felonious shooting.

In common with the state's defence of property, the protection of the nation's money supply was of the highest importance and those found guilty of counterfeiting or forgery were deemed to have committed a crime that was equal to murder. Mary Lloyd was tried and convicted of forgery in 1800 and was executed for her crimes in the same year. Thomas Bosworth, along with William Hollingworth, was also tried and convicted of forgery and subsequently executed in the city. Aaron Gee too was tried and convicted, along with Thomas Gibson, with passing forged bank notes: both men were executed at Chester in 1801.

One of the most surprising and unusual criminals involved with this particular crime was Joseph Allen; reported to have been a farmer from Crowton in Cheshire, he was tried and convicted of passing forged banknotes in 1817 and was subsequently executed at Chester gaol by the County Executioner Samuel Burrows. Prior to his being accused of the crime, Allen was said to have been a man of exemplary character and had been able to gain credit from suppliers on the strength of his name alone. He was the father of seven young children and also supported his mother and father on the family's farm in the county. Joseph seems to have been tempted to enter into the illegal enterprise with his brother, Samuel, and a man called Jelley, who presumably overcame his usual good sense and inevitably put him on the road to ruin. The court records suggest that the three men were not very good at forging bank notes and that they not only used the wrong colour inks but the wrong sort of paper as well. Nonetheless, the men managed to pass a couple of hundred pounds worth of forgeries before they were caught by the authorities and that was enough to see them hang.

Jelley though was thought to have managed to evade the authorities and Samuel was sentenced to 14 years' transportation. Joseph argued that he did not know the notes were forged, but his excuses were dismissed by the court and they passed the death sentence on him. Prior to his execution, he was said to have been transported through the city's streets on an open cart as a deterrent to anyone else that might be tempted to repeat the offence. Having been 'displayed' before the citizenry, Joseph was then taken to the city gaol in City Walls Road and executed.

Another crime which attracted the most severe retribution from the authorities was the deliberate or wilful destruction of property, especially that perpetrated by arsonists. William Rickington was tried and convicted of committing arson at the rectory at Coddington and was hung in 1820. Another man, William Wilson, was tried and convicted of arson and was executed at the city gaol in 1814. Samuel Cumberledge too was tried and found guilty of committing arson in Cheshire and was executed in 1832.

As today, sex crimes were regarded with the greatest horror and outrage. James Yarwood was tried and convicted, along with two other men, William Wilkinson and William Burgess, of rape in 1813 and were executed for their crime. William Tongue was tried and convicted for rape and executed in 1822. In 1823 John Kragon was tried and convicted of rape and was subsequently executed in the city. Joseph Woodhouse was another local man found guilty of the crime and was executed at Chester in 1829.

Before the arrival of the railways and their ability to transport large quantities of passengers and freight throughout England at speed, virtually all traffic used the well-established and extensive road network that ran the length and breadth of the country. Included within this were the mail coaches which carried important correspondence from town to town and city to city, as well as the valuables and assets of the burgeoning well-to-do classes. For those with an eye for easy pickings these treasure transports were an inviting target for criminals who dared to take the risk, given that these coaches often travelled lonely roads in the middle of the night when few people were around to either witness the offence or to defend the transport.

These attacks on the nation's communications were thought so significantly serious that those found guilty of the crime could expect to receive the most severe sentence. In 1791 William Lowndes was tried and convicted of mail robbery at Chester and was executed in the city. His lifeless body was later displayed on the gibbet at Helsby Hill as a stark warning to those that might be tempted to repeat his actions.

James Price was tried and convicted, along with Thomas Brown, of robbing the Warrington mail coach in 1796. Both men were executed at Boughton in Chester and their corpses later hung on the gibbet at Trafford Green immediately afterwards. Both men's bodies were said to have remained there for over 25 years, until they were finally removed in 1820. As they were taken down Price's skull was found to contain a robin's nest.

Another man, Joseph Walker, was tried and convicted for highway robbery on the Manchester to Northwich road in 1819 and was subsequently executed. One Samuel Healey was tried and convicted of highway robbery in 1821 and received the same punishment. Two men, George Groom and Thomas Brierly, were tried and convicted of highway robbery in the county and were executed in 1822. Edward Clarke was tried and convicted for highway robbery in 1823 and John Proudlove was convicted of the same offence in 1829. Both of these individuals were executed on the gallows shortly after their conviction.

Inevitably the most notorious criminals were those that had committed the ultimate crime, that of taking another life. One of the earliest murders recorded in the county was that which involved a group of Irish workmen that were passing through the city in the mid-18th century. John Connolly along with an accomplice, John Morgan, was recorded to have been tried and hanged for murder in 1750. Said to have been one of four workmen who were travelling to Parkgate to take a ship back to Ireland, along the way three of the group attacked and killed the fourth man, presumably to relieve him of his money. Having murdered their unfortunate companion, they robbed him of his earnings, stripped the body and then disposed of it by throwing it in a nearby ditch. However, instead of continuing their journey with any great haste, the three remaining men then appear to have spent a great deal of time in a local inn, during which time the body was discovered and reported to the authorities. Almost inevitably, the three surviving workmen were soon identified and apprehended before they had a chance to escape.

While they were being held at Chester gaol, one of the men was said to have decided to save himself and agreed to give evidence against his two companions. Having been convicted of the crime, Connolly and his co-defendant, Morgan, were sentenced to be hung at the Chester gallows on 22 September 1750. Immediately after their deaths, Connolly and Morgan's bodies were then said to have been taken back to the scene of their crime at Saughall and hung up in chains on a gibbet, a stark reminder to any other potential wrongdoers. Close to Saughall Heath and along the city's Parkgate Road, the modern-day 'Gibbet Mill' is thought to mark the spot where the two men's bodies were exhibited.

A notable and perhaps surprising killer in the county was Mary Heald, a Quaker from Knutsford who was tried and convicted of poisoning her husband, Samuel, with arsenic. She was sentenced to be burnt at the stake in 1762, but having taken pity on her the public executioner was said to have strangled her first before finally committing her body to the flames.

Samuel Thorley was tried and hanged for the murder of Anne Smith around 1777, with witnesses claiming that Thorley had first dismembered his unfortunate victim and then eaten part of the body. A Cheshire woman, Elizabeth Wood, was tried and convicted of poisoning James Simister at Bredbury in 1784 and was executed some time later. Peter Steers was tried and convicted of poisoning his wife and was executed at Chester in 1786.

In 1790 John Dean was reported to have been tried and convicted of murdering his pregnant wife and was executed in the same year. Another man, John Thornhill, was tried and convicted of murdering Sarah Malone in the county and was executed in 1798. John Done was tried and convicted for the murder of Betty Eckersley in 1810 and subsequently paid for his actions with his life. John Lomas was tried and convicted, along with his lover Edith Morrey, of murdering her husband in 1812. Lomas was executed at Chester in the same year, with his accomplice facing a similar fate the following year having first given birth.

Jacob McGhinne was recorded as having been tried and convicted of murder in the county in 1820 and was executed at the county gaol in the city. Samuel Fallows was tried and convicted of murdering his sweetheart in 1823 and was hung on the gallows later that same year. Joseph Dale was tried and convicted for the murder of a Mr Wood in 1824 and he too paid for it with his life.

Bartholomew Murray was tried and convicted for the murders of Joseph and Mary Cook of Over Peover and was executed in 1841. James Ratcliffe was tried and found guilty of murdering his wife and died on the gallows in 1842. Mary Gallup was tried and convicted of poisoning her father and was executed in 1844. William Bates was tried and convicted for the murder of William Wyatt in 1848 and was executed in the city in the same year.

Perhaps one of the most disturbing and sensational crimes of the mid-19th century, however, was that which involved William Jackson, a local upholsterer, who lived in the Handbridge area of Chester just outside of the city. Sometime around 1855 his young son and daughter were both reported to have gone missing, after having recently visited their father at his lodgings. A local search was undertaken and the children's bodies were soon discovered in a local orchard, both having been murdered. Jackson was arrested shortly afterwards and charged with the killing of his children. In the following year he was tried and convicted of the murders and was executed at Chester in 1856.

Samuel Griffiths was said to have been tried and convicted of murder at Chester in 1866 and is recorded as being the last ever person to be publicly executed at the city's county gaol.

Chapter 15

Builders, Breweries and Brand New Businesses

The accession of the teenage Victoria to the English throne in 1837 marked the start of a truly remarkable period in what had already been a long and colourful history for this country. During the next 64 years of her reign Britain and her people would see both the industrial and military might of the country at the height of her powers and the nation emerge as the world's leading political, military and economic superpower.

Throughout Britain the new changes in working practices and the progression towards greater industrialization through modern machine-based production methods allowed the country to outperform its foreign competitors, both in terms of quantity and unit cost. The advent of the steam engine and the steam turbine, allied to the developments in railway and ship-building designs, all helped to push forward the pace of change within the country and generate even greater wealth for those who were brave enough to embrace these exciting new opportunities.

Unlike its more northerly neighbours, Chester no longer had a major industrial port to trade from or a totally reliable watercourse where new mills could be located. It had no natural resources of its own, unlike the coal towns that had continued to spring up throughout Wales, and so was compelled to try and find a new purpose for itself and the people that lived within its city limits. The construction of the new canal networks, although initially limited, had helped to bring new business to Chester, but certainly not at the levels experienced by the likes of Liverpool and Manchester. The coming of the railways in the 1840s did make an important contribution to the wealth of the city, both in terms of the employment created by the new rail companies themselves and the increased business opportunities that were generated by the growing numbers of tourists that chose to visit the city for its retail shopping and historic attractions.

The commercial centre of Chester continued to remain within the historic precincts of the former Roman fortress, alongside the main shopping streets which met at the junction of the city's High Cross. Despite the development of new industrial sites in Hoole and Saltney which added to its growing prosperity, the retail core of Chester which was principally owned by the most influential citizens of the city led the way in terms of future planning and development. The city's corporation, along with a few of Chester's largest landowners, seemed to have shared a common view of Chester's future and were keen that large-scale commercial expansion outside of the city's historic walls should not undermine their own property holdings or indeed their influence in the city itself. This is perhaps best illustrated by the later construction of the Chester General Railway Station in around 1848 and the subsequent development of the City Road area in the 1860s. This new road was the main route into Chester for those travelling by rail and under normal circumstances would have been extensively developed along its full length through to the centre of the city. Instead, only the end closest to the station itself was commercially developed with a number of large hotels sited there and little else. One of these hotels, The Queen's Railway Hotel, which had been built in 1860 was reported to have been completely burned down in the following year and was rebuilt by 1862 as the Queen Hotel, which remains in the city today. This eastern flank of the city has been one of the areas hardest hit by the modern ring road that was built during the 1960s and by subsequent traffic systems which were designed to help filter vehicles into and around Chester.

Designed by local architect Thomas Mainwaring Penson, the first Queen's Railway Hotel was burned down within a year and had to be rebuilt, opening once again in 1862.

This was a separate entrance for the horses and carriages which would have been the main form of transport at the time.

Thomas Brassey was the contractor for Chester's General Station which was officially opened in August 1848.

Between 1848 and 1890 three separate railway stations were opened on the outskirts of the city, including the main general station which was located in the Newtown area. A second was constructed at the northern end of Upper Northgate Street and the final one was located on Liverpool Road, just outside of the city centre. The railways were thought to have first arrived in Chester with the opening of the Chester to Birkenhead line in 1838, followed by a Chester to Crewe line and the Chester to Holyhead service, which initially terminated at Bangor in North Wales. These new and emerging rail services offered a large number of economic benefits both to the city and its inhabitants, not least of which were the employment opportunities being offered by these new transport companies. The new heavy industries that were establishing their businesses in Birkenhead and later at Shotton needed a local workforce and the growing rail network was able to provide a reliable transport system for their labour force. By 1870 Chester was a central hub for much of the regional railway network, helping to enhance the city's position as a major regional centre. By the middle of the 19th century a large number of Chester's male workforce was either employed directly by the railways themselves or by service companies that supplied these same new transport companies.

The growing ranks of workers who lived in Chester needed new homes and this provided valuable new opportunities for the city's local builders and private landlords alike. The northern suburb of Newtown was one area used to build this much-needed accommodation and by 1870 the area was covered extensively by hundreds of small terraced workers' houses. These properties were owned in the main by private landlords or by the local builders who had constructed them. If there was a drawback to the area it was the presence of the nearby sawmills, tanneries, chemical works and engineering companies that were located around the Brook Street area and produced increasing levels of intrusive noises and smells that were related to their trades. Also close by were the cattle markets that had been built by 1889 at Gorse Stacks in the hope that Chester's livestock fairs might compete with the existing regional centre at Beeston. The market lacked really good transport links however and was always destined to struggle. The construction of the Newtown high-rise flats and the city's ring road saw the sheds finally demolished in the early 1960s. Today the site of the cattle market lies beneath the dual carriageways that encircle the city and the vast expanse of car parking that covers much of the Gorse Stacks area.

Beyond them and along the banks of the Shropshire Union Canal lay the expanding lead works which had located to the city in around 1800. Initially the works had been producing white and red leads for the paint industries, but by 1820 a rolling mill and other plant had been introduced to manufacture lead pipes which were then shipped to the wider region. Later in the 19th century the company was said to have installed its own gas works to run its furnaces and a dedicated rail siding was constructed to transport its products throughout the whole of the country. The city's lead works was probably one of the few success stories that ever came out of Chester's unsuccessful 'industrial' past, but in recent years it too has finally had to succumb to the unremitting modernization of the city and was replaced by several blocks of uniform modern apartments

On both sides of the canal and towards the city itself there were thought to be a number of mills operating during much of the 19th century that handled many of the cereal crops that were being

Cocoa House, located in Brook Street, Chester.

A number of animal feed mills were located alongside the new canal system.

brought into Chester. By the beginning of the 20th century however, many of those that were still in business had changed to handling animal feed only, but within a few years had themselves ceased to trade or were simply used as warehouses. The Milton Street Steam Mill has been converted to a hotel in recent years but still retains its chimney, which continues to dominate this part of the city's skyline.

Close to the Steam Mill the two banks of the canal had been joined by around 1814 following the construction of the compact Union Bridge which still remains in existence today.

On the northern bank of the canal, around Egerton Street, were the premises for one of the city's main brass and iron foundries lying to the east and a large engineering company that occupied a

Built by local builder and businessman Thomas Lunt to link Bold Square and Egerton Street in 1814.

greater part of the western side of the street. Scattered in between these two great enterprises were numbers of small terraced houses which had been built by the owner of the foundry for the benefit of his workers. By 1910, however, the foundry was gone and the site was used for the construction of the present-day Egerton Street School which is now a private playschool. Around the area generally, many of the old terraces were said to have finally been demolished during the 1960s and replaced by rows of concrete maisonettes and multi-storey flats.

To the north of this area lay the railway wagon repair yards which handled much of the maintenance and repair work required by the massive steam engines and freight wagons that transported goods throughout the region. These substantial yards were thought to have reached their zenith at the end of the 19th century but even as late as 1911 were still fairly extensive. A couple of the enormous engine sheds were still in place until the 21st century, but very much in a reduced state of repair as much of their former home had been given over to a relatively

The modern walkway in the foreground was built to link the Mill Hotel with its health club on the south bank of the canal.

Egerton Street School, one of many built by local businessmen and benefactors during the late 19th century.

new post office sorting office. Sadly, within the past couple of years these remaining sheds have finally been demolished to make way for even more private housing in the area. Across the main railway line stands the Hoole district of Chester and it was here in 1877 that a city hospital was founded for local people. It later became a dedicated geriatric hospital, but was finally closed in around 1994 and eventually demolished, only to be replaced by private living accommodations.

Just outside the northern limits of the city, in an area known locally as the Bache, a new hospital for the mentally ill was officially opened in 1829. It was called the Chester Lunatic Asylum, which today would seem to be inappropriate. In 1855 it was renamed as the Cheshire Lunatic Asylum and in 1921, after taking on the responsibility for the county, it was renamed again as the County Mental Hospital. By 1959 it was known as the Deva Hospital and finally in 1965 became the West Cheshire Hospital. It is said that Edward Langtry, the estranged husband of the 'Jersey Lily' Lily Langtry, the mistress of the king, spent his final days confined within the hospital having been found bruised and confused at Crewe's main railway station. Following his untimely death Langtry was buried at the Overleigh Cemetery in Handbridge amid much public interest, with crowds gathering to see if the infamous actress would attend the service for her estranged husband. They were to be disappointed however, as Lily was said to have sent flowers but not actually attended the sad event in person.

Above left: The Bluecoat statue is a representation of one of the school's pupils John Coppack *c*.1850.

Left: Founded by Nicholas Stratford to combat vice and debauchery within the city, built *c*.1717.

About a mile from the hospital is probably the last of Chester's early mills to have remained in operation until modern times. Lying on Mill Lane in Upton it was constructed in 1775 and was thought to have been a true windmill equipped with sails to drive the milling stones. It was purchased in 1839 by a William Carter and was busy supplying local bakers through to the late 1940s, but by that time was no longer driven by the wind but by a motor. Along the main Parkgate Road, which was thought to mark the path of an earlier Roman road to the Wirral Peninsula, Chester College was constructed in 1840 to educate the sons and daughters of the city's wealthy inhabitants. Back towards the city's northern gate, the Bluecoat School, which had been originally founded by Bishop Nicholas Stafford to combat vice within Chester, was restored and the figure of one of its pupils was erected above the central arch. The rows of almshouses at the rear of the building were said to have been rebuilt at the same time and offered housing to the very poorest of the city's inhabitants.

To the east of Chester in modern-day Boughton the construction of workers' terraced housing for the employees of the canal and railway companies was well underway by the 1870s. This part of the city was a favourite area for large numbers of Irish migrants that had come to Chester during the potato famine in the 1840s, seeking a better life for themselves and their families. It was perhaps appropriate that in 1873 a new Roman Catholic church was founded in the city close to Boughton and dedicated to St Werburgh. It has been said that the parish priest would regularly run from door to door on a Sunday morning calling for all his Catholic parishioners to get out of bed and come to

Bluecoat Alms Houses.

The 19th-century RC Church dedicated to the city's first and foremost saint, Werburga. It was established to meet the spiritual needs of the growing Irish Catholic community who settled in Chester during the mid-19th century.

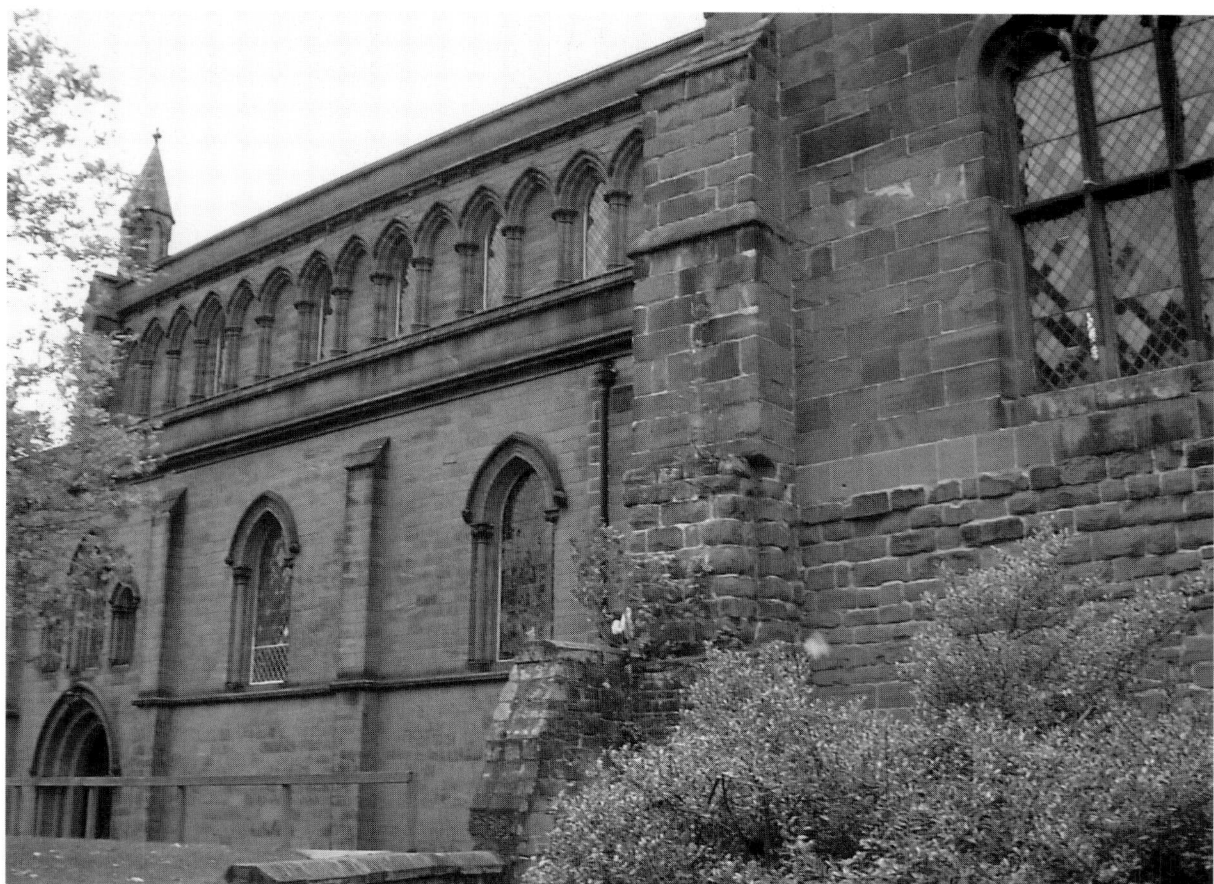

The open fields near St John's Church were gifted to the city by Richard, Marquis of Westminster.

church, so it seems lucky that he was on the doorstep, so to speak. A little further east again was the site of the city's gallows and stake where those who had been found guilty of heinous crimes were executed. By the 1880s this area, too, was crowded with lines of terraced housing for the city's workers, but its brutal past was publicly acknowledged in 1893 with the unveiling of a monument to George Marsh who had been burned at the stake in the middle of the 16th century.

Beyond the precincts of the ancient St John's Church lay open land which was primarily owned by the Grosvenor family. The area was said to have been originally made up of fields, with the largest marked as Billy Hobby's Field, according to the 1833 plan of the city. Richard, the second Duke of Westminster, was reported to have paid for the design and layout of a recreational park by the landscape designer Edward Kemp, a former pupil of Joseph Paxton, the architect of the Crystal Palace. This 20-acre complex was gifted to the city in around 1867 by the duke who wrote to the council: 'I am desirous of placing it (the park) in the hands of the Corporation as a gift on my part to the citizens of Chester, hoping that it may afford health and recreation to them and their families for many years to come'.

Grosvenor Park continues to be regarded by many experts as one of the finest and most complete examples of Victorian parks in the whole of the United Kingdom. Although many changes have taken place since its foundation, much of the design and features laid out by Kemp have remained intact. Many of the buildings in the park were thought to have been designed by John Douglas, a leading Victorian architect, including the Grosvenor Park Lodge, the boundary wall and gateways and the canopy to Billy Hobby's well. In the south-western

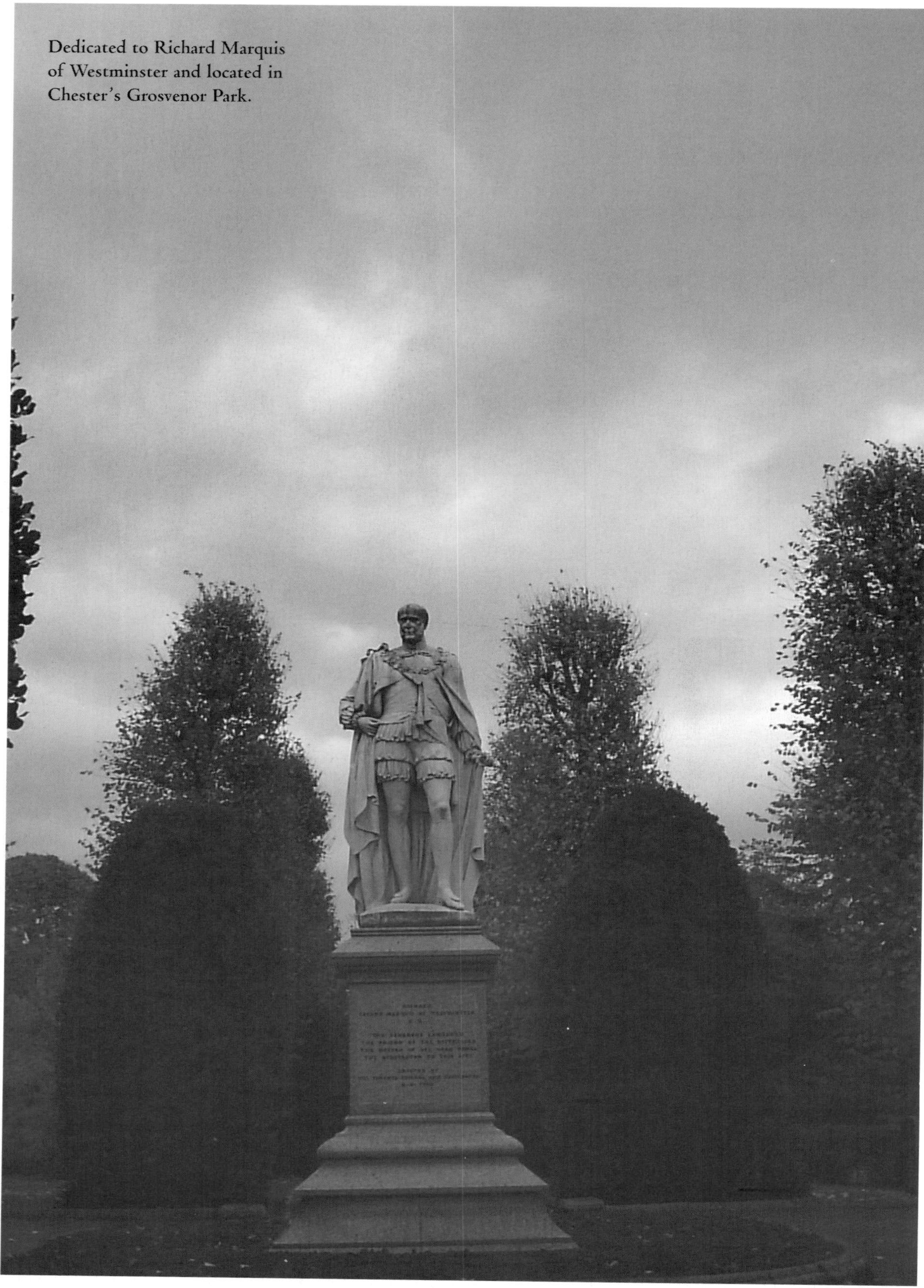

Dedicated to Richard Marquis of Westminster and located in Chester's Grosvenor Park.

A 1911 hotel frontage that was generally attributed to renowned Chester architect T.M. Lockwood.

corner of the park complex single arches from the long-disappeared St Bridget's Church and Benedictine nunnery stand with the city's ancient Ship Gate and were said to have been erected in 1897. Across the new Grosvenor Park Road, which was built in the 1870s and directly opposite the park complex, the city's public baths were built in 1901, offering the local residents an opportunity to both bathe and relax within the complex. In the 1960s the facilities were predominantly used as swimming baths by the general public and local schoolchildren. At that time the building was thought to have been divided into two separate sections, the Pacific and the Atlantic baths, but the complex later became a private swimming club. The

Chester's ancient Ship Gate.

An ancient archway from St Bridget's Church in Chester.

church of St John's, which lay along the western flank of the new park and was thought to have stood there for well over 1,000 years, suffered a disastrous collapse of its western tower on Good Friday 1881 and stands today as no more than a sad reminder of the city's glorious and historic past.

On the southern bank of the river the new suburb of Queens Park was designed and laid out by James Harrison in around 1852. It was connected to the city and the new park complex by a suspension bridge constructed by James Dredge of Bath. The bridge that spans the river today is a replacement and was reported to have been built in 1923. This particular area of Chester always was and still remains a fairly exclusive part of the city, made up of elegantly detached houses that stand within their own well-kept grounds. The Groves which ran along the river bank below Queens Park were heavily landscaped and improved during the late 1880s as a tourist attraction where visitors and local people could sit and enjoy the riverside environment. Times and tastes have obviously changed though and in the past few years the area seems to have suffered a fair degree of neglect and today appears extremely untidy and unattractive. Close to the Queens Park area the piece of land known as Edgar's Field was donated by the Duke of Westminster to the people of Chester as a second recreational park in 1892. Said to be the site from where the Mercian king was rowed into the city by a number of subordinate monarchs, its much earlier history was confirmed through the later discovery of a heavily weathered Roman shrine cut into the local sandstone nearly 2,000 years before.

Further west of Handbridge, along the river adjoining the new Grosvenor Bridge before it crossed the Dee into the city, the new Overleigh Cemetery was opened in 1850. The final resting place for some of the city's leading citizens, today it is an extremely peaceful and well cared for place with a large number of the attendant headstones testifying to its age.

This period bore witness to three major conflagrations at the ancient Dee mills which finally led to their demolition in 1913. The first fire occurred on the 22 January 1847 and was reported to have completely destroyed one mill and caused some damage to a number of the others that stood alongside. The second fire proved to be even more costly, both in terms of time and money, and caused potential owners and investors to seriously question

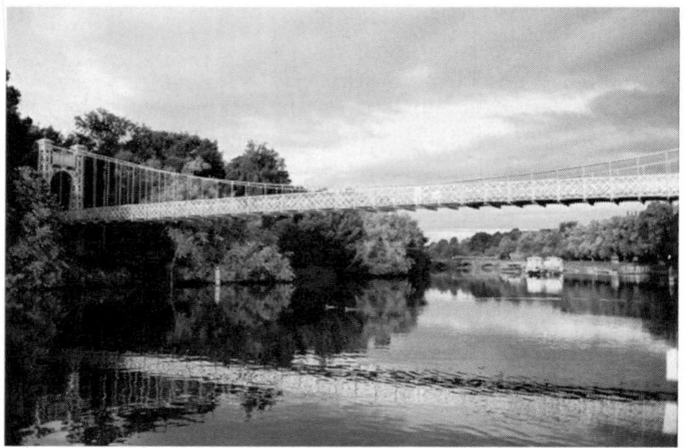

The bridge was designed to link the affluent Queens Park suburb of Chester with the city itself.

Stapleton Cotton, Viscount Combermere.

the economic viability of the industry. The third blaze, said to have occurred in 1895, was thought to have been so severe and caused so much damage that there was little if any prospect of their being reinstated as a commercial enterprise. The fate of the mills had already been sealed, however, by the changes that were occurring in the wider world. Cheaper grain and the introduction of more modern production methods had all conspired to replace out of date systems, and despite efforts on the part of some mill owners to resist progress the end result was almost inevitable. The last of the millers on the Dee was already in the process of relocating his businesses to the developing industrial site at Ellesmere Port and the fires simply represented the final nail in the Chester mills coffin. By 1895 an industry that was thought to have existed in the city for well over 800 years was at an end. In 1913 the mill buildings were finally removed and a hydroelectric power station was later constructed on the site under the supervision of Sydney Britton, the city's municipal engineer.

Chester's extensive new castle complex was thought to have been fairly complete by the time Victoria had ascended to the throne and it was the areas outside of the castle that were then the subject of new developments. By 1884 the gaol that had been built by Thomas Harrison had been closed, along with the relatively new prison that had been constructed on City Walls Road. The site of this second prison was later used as the location for the Queen's School which was constructed in 1882. In 1857 a new militia building was built outside the castle precincts on the site of the earlier mediaeval Benedictine nunnery. Constructed to house the families of the troops who were garrisoned at the castle, the militia building was later demolished to make way for the Cheshire police headquarters which was built in the early 1960s and has always been regarded as a bit of a local eyesore.

Standing between the police headquarters and the gateway to Chester Castle is a bronze statue of the mounted Stapleton Cotton, Viscount Combermere, which was erected in 1865. The second son of Robert Cotton of Combermere Abbey in Cheshire, Stapleton began his military career at 16 years of age, serving as a second lieutenant with the Welsh Fusiliers. He later purchased a captaincy with the sixth Dragoon Guards and served in Flanders during the campaigns of the Duke of York. Still in his early 20s he was said to have been a comrade of King George III and served with the Light Dragoons at Cape Colony in 1796. Three years later he was involved with the storming of Seringapatam and following the death of his brother became heir to the baronetcy and returned home to England.

Cotton then undertook further military service while helping to suppress a rebellion in Ireland and by 1805 was thought to have achieved the lofty rank of major general. In 1808 he was said to be campaigning in Portugal and was promoted once again while serving under Wellington to the rank of commander. He was cited for his actions during the Battle of Salamanca in 1812 and was wounded shortly after the conflict. Within two years he was reported to have been raised to the peerage and by 1817 he had been appointed as Governor of Barbados. Between 1822 and 1825 he was thought to have been commanding British troops in Ireland, but actually ended his military career in India. His capture of the seemingly impregnable fortress at Bhurtporea was said to be so remarkable that he was created a viscount and by 1834 had been appointed as a privy councillor. In 1855 he was promoted to the rank of field marshal and 10 years later was reported to have died peacefully at his home at Clifton on 21 February 1865 aged 92 years old.

The castle at Chester, although not directly attacked, was thought to have been the target for an unsuccessful Republican plot which was said to have taken place around 1867. The Liverpool-based group reportedly planned to seize the castle complex with a force of up to 2,000 sympathisers who were said to be located within the north-west region. Under the command of experienced Irish-American officers that had all served during the American Civil War, 300 armed men were ordered to meet in Chester and seize the arms store of the city's local volunteer force. Using these weapons they were then supposed to overpower the small military garrison that held the castle's armoury and steal the thousands of rifles and rounds of ammunition that were stored there. The rest of the Republican force was ordered to isolate Chester from the rest of the country by cutting all communication links to the outside world, including the telegraph lines and railway links. The main body of the force was also ordered to hijack a train so that the stolen arms and munitions could be transported out of the city and then taken to Holyhead in North Wales and put on a boat to Ireland.

Unfortunately for the gang, one of the ringleaders in Liverpool was said to have betrayed the group, so that when the men arrived in Chester on the 11 February they found the authorities waiting for them. Their primary objective, the volunteer arms stores, had been removed and the local police, militia and regular troops from Manchester had been mobilised to deal with the threat. Although many of the Republican leaders were said to have escaped the city, they found it difficult to try and contact the remainder of their men which resulted in large numbers of their secondary force arriving in Chester, unaware that their plot had been foiled. Once they realised that the plan had been discovered many of these Republicans disposed of their arms and made their way out of the city as quickly as possible. By the following day some 500 troops from London had arrived in Chester to secure the city, but the emergency was over and the Republicans had already dispersed.

Later, in around 1872, the castle complex was thought to have been used as a training centre for new military recruits and although its role as a strategically important position had diminished, Chester would later become the headquarters for Western Command in England and would remain a major administrative and logistical centre for the armed forces. The Chester Tramways Company were said to have operated horse-drawn carriages from the castle to the city's railway stations from 1879 and later on extended these routes through to Saltney on the outskirts of Chester. In 1901 Castle Drive was constructed to link the Grosvenor Bridge with the Old Dee Bridge crossing and in the process provided an elegant and attractive journey along the banks of the river, bypassing the remains of the castle's mediaeval wall and the newly built county hall building.

In 1861 the Church of St Mary-on-the-hill had been restored by the architect James Harrison and four years later he would be responsible for the total rebuilding of Holy Trinity Church in Watergate Street. This building was later reported to have been deconsecrated and today stands as the city's guildhall. In 1868 the Custom's House, the historic home of Chester's port controller, was reported to have been rebuilt by Harrison at the western end of Watergate Street, next door to Holy Trinity Church. The building had once housed the administrative centre for the city's harbour and the port officers would check the ships' cargoes that were going in and out of Chester to determine the taxes due and arrange for the appropriate levies to be paid. Another of his projects in Watergate Street was

Originating from around 1652, God's Providence House was largely rebuilt by architect James Harrison in 1862.

thought to have been God's Providence House, which Harrison was said to have restored in 1862. The inscription on the front of the building was placed there by the chandler who owned the property and was a way of thanking God for sparing its occupants from an outbreak of plague.

To the west of the guildhall stood the then relatively new Linen Hall, which had been built to house the linen merchants and traders that had brought so much prosperity to Chester in the past. By 1830 however, the cloth trades in the city were thought to be in serious decline following the relocation of the Irish linen trade from Dublin to Belfast which had pre-existing links with the port of Liverpool. Chester had made much of its position as the main trading centre for the extremely popular Irish linen in England and the loss of this large-scale commercial business was a major blow to its economy. A number of the city's traditional trades were also beginning to see the effects of the new economic reality that was dawning around the region. Chester's established industries like leather dressing were beginning to disappear from the city and others like glove-making had chosen to relocate to other towns and cities. From 1814 to around 1830 the ship-building industries located on the banks of the newly cut river channel were thought to have been extremely small-scale and very specialized, comprising mainly of inshore craft or flat-bottomed boats that could operate in shallow water. In 1869 the last of the city's ship building companies was in the hands of a Liverpool-based enterprise and following their successful launch of a series of iron-hulled river boats from the Dee yard they finally ended an industry that had existed in the city for hundreds of years.

As these 'historic' trades and industries inevitably disappeared from Chester they were in part replaced by the new and emerging businesses that were exploiting the latest technologies of the age. By 1870 there were said to have been at least 10 or 12 engineering and foundry companies operating in and around the city who were helping to meet the growing need for hydraulic and mechanical engineering schemes, which were a feature of the Victorian period. Rather typically though, only a small number of these businesses seem to have had the foresight to locate themselves in areas which offered them the opportunity to expand and further develop their transport links in the coming years.

By the 1850s the population of the city was thought to have increased dramatically as a direct result of the new employment opportunities that

The Dublin Packet marks the connection between England and Ireland and Chester's place as a staging point for those travelling to Eire.

were being offered by the large numbers of retail, transport and industrial companies establishing themselves in Chester. These increasing levels were added to by the arrival of significant numbers of Irish migrants who were escaping the famine in Ireland and had come to the city in the hope of making a new life for themselves. Prior to the construction of later, decent, low-cost housing by the local authorities, the provision of accommodation was very much in the hands of a small number of private landlords within the city who were able to monopolize and exploit the marketplace to their own advantage. Because of the high demand created by a growing population, unscrupulous landowners and builders were able to build poor-quality, high-density housing on vacant plots around the city and pack in as many tenants as possible. As the quality of life within the city diminished, its wealthier residents were reported to have moved out to the suburbs and their former homes were simply bought up to be converted into even more low-quality accommodation. The areas around Crook Street, Princess Street and Commonhall Street in Chester were all reported to have been crammed with slum housing and that remained the case through to the 20th century, when new social housing became the responsibility of the local council. Levels of criminality and wrongdoing were thought to be greater in these parts of the city and Chester was said to have housed a large number of fences, thieves and brothels within these poorer sections. The only area of the city that managed to escape such building was the north-east section of Chester and only then because the lands there were generally owned by the cathedral authorities and were not readily available to these unscrupulous landlords and builders.

For the corporation, and for those that owned businesses within Chester, this sudden explosion of poor-quality housing and general criminality around the city was of great concern as it impacted directly on the value of their own properties and made the city's streets unattractive to both visitor and customer alike. During the 1840s a series of new ordinances and regulations were said to have been drafted to address these concerns, the most important of which was the 1845 Improvement Act which prohibited any further building of these 'courts' as they were commonly known. The act also set down the required standards for businesses within the city and ensured that features which might spoil the city's attractiveness were removed from the streets. During an outbreak of cholera in 1848 the city's proactive attitude in trying to rid the city of these slums was no doubt a major factor in reducing the number of deaths that actually occurred within Chester. By 1854 the sewage system had finally been completed throughout the city and it was a matter of some regret that incompetence on the part of some council employees had prevented the system from being completed earlier. In 1872 the new Public Health Act finally gave local authorities the power to remove slum housing which might present a potential health risk to the local population. These Chester 'courts' were systematically cleared by the corporation and their sites later used for new commercial enterprises, schools and churches.

Perhaps not surprisingly, as the population and visitor numbers grew there was an appropriate increase in the number of public houses and hotels that served these new markets. By 1840 there were said to be well over 200 pubs around the city and these were themselves serviced by around 15 local breweries. A number of these establishments would eventually disappear as the retail centre was further developed or because of natural disasters occurring within the city. The destruction of the Exchange Building by fire in 1862 was the most notable, given that it had stood since 1695 and was said to have been the heart of both local government and commercial enterprise. A competition to find its replacement was won by W.H. Lynn of Belfast, whose new civic building was said to have been inspired by the mediaeval Cloth Hall at Ypres in Belgium. His 13th-century Gothic-style design with clock tower and sloping roofs is particularly unique as it only has three clock faces. The western side is blank because supposedly Chester will not give the Welsh the time of day. The new town hall was finally finished in 1869 and Edward, the Prince of Wales and future Edward VII, officially opened it that year. Two notable inns that were sacrificed for this new civic building were said to have been the White Lion Hotel, which was thought to be the city's main coaching inn, and the Saracen's Head, which had an extensive and popular history in the centre of Chester.

The market hall that sat alongside the new town hall had itself only been constructed in 1863 and was built to house the city's market traders, including the greengrocers and butchers who in past times had hawked their wares on the market's public square. A truly magnificent building, with a soaring roof that echoed to the noise of its many vendors, the hall would finally fall victim to the 1960s building revolution which saw elegant buildings replaced by uniform units of concrete and glass. The associated underground parking bays of the later Forum shopping centre required the wholesale 'scouring' of the natural bedrock in this area of the city and finally saw an end to much of the historic archaeology that lay below the surface. The only positive thing that was said to have come out of the scheme was that Chester's archaeology department was able to examine, record and map the history of the site before it was once again covered over.

The middle decades of the 19th century witnessed a spate of new buildings and redevelopments throughout the city. In 1854 Dee House just outside of the south-east sector of the walls was converted to an Ursuline convent which would later devote itself to educating the daughters of the city's upper classes. The building itself has become enmeshed in controversy over the past 60 or 70 years because of its position in relation to the historic Roman amphitheatre. Dee House itself is a listed building and therefore protected by statute, but unfortunately the house and part of its lands sit directly above the southern section of the amphitheatre which has recently been excavated at its northern end and is now treated as a major tourist attraction by the city authorities. It is to their credit that Chester's ring road system which was built in the 1960s was diverted around the site and so conserved this ancient monument. In June 1929 a workman who was carrying out some work at the Ursuline Convent School came across a Roman coin that was buried in the cellar of the building and because he was so intrigued showed the find to a local archaeologist. Further investigations of the site uncovered large sections of heavy sandstone walls which were said to be nearly eight feet thick and dating from around the first century BC. Four decades later the site was finally cleared to expose the ancient structures that lay below ground and in 1972 the site was officially opened for the general public to view.

Close to Chester's cathedral, the city's Theatre Royal was redeveloped as a new music hall in 1855 and was itself sited on the old foundations of the 13th-century St Nicholas's Chapel that had formerly stood there. Today the building is employed as a retail unit by a high street chain. A short distance away, the eastern side of St Werburgh Street leading to Eastgate Street was said to have been designed and developed by the renowned local architect John Douglas in the 1880s. The former Linen Hall, workshops and warehouses that had previously stood in the area were swept away and replaced by the half-timbered shops and offices that remain in the city today. Douglas was also responsible for the redesigning and reconstruction of the former 'Shoemakers Row' which stood on the western side of lower Northgate Street in 1899. In the cathedral building itself extensive renovations were reported to have been undertaken by Sir

Designed by John Douglas, these buildings were built between 1870 and 1903. The conical turrets are typical of the architect.

George Gilbert Scott and in the ancient lady chapel, in around 1868, his work uncovered evidence of a Roman floor, a drain and traces of a road running diagonally under the south-eastern buttress of the cathedral. Scott also discovered that many parts of the former abbey had no foundations to speak of and that the whole area needed serious underpinning. Some 40 years later Scott's grandson was reported to have undertaken yet more remedial work within the cathedral and helped to restore both its historic refectory and cloisters.

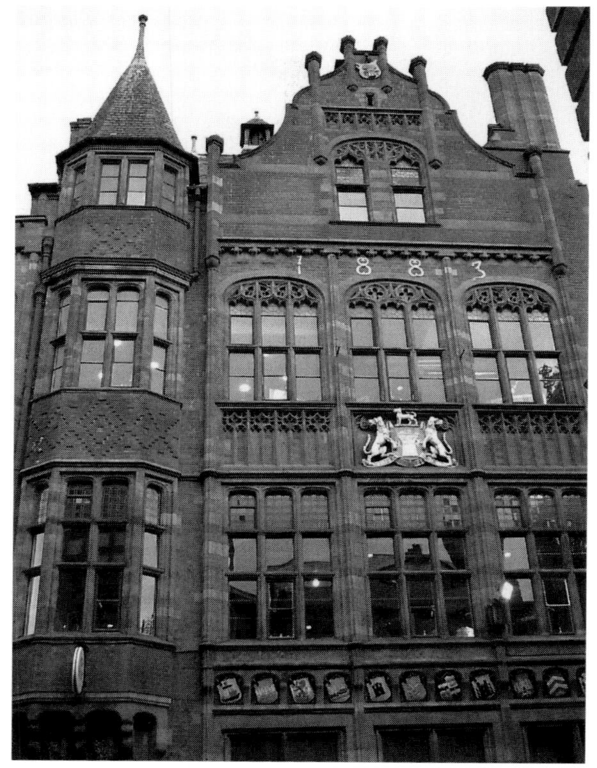

Designed by John Douglas, this building was first used as the Grosvenor Club, before housing the N & S Wales Bank. It has since served as the location for several high street banks, as it does today. It was built between 1881–83.

Shoemakers Row in Northgate Street.

In Eastgate Street the new Grosvenor Hotel was reported to have been built in 1863 on the site of the former Royal and White Talbot Hotels and was constructed in response to the continued growth of the tourist trade within the city. Large parts of the area lying on the southern side of the main thoroughfare were owned by the Grosvenor family who would be so influential in the planning and implementation of many of the future developments within Chester. The city's East Gate which had been largely financed by the Grosvenors and which stood only yards from their new city-centre hotel was further embellished in 1897 by the addition of the world-famous clock that exists today. Built to celebrate Victoria's 60th anniversary, it is said that the clock was not officially started until her birthday on the 27 May had arrived. Another building within the city that bears the Grosvenor name is the museum which was built in 1885. The building houses many of the historic artefacts that have been found in the numerous archaeological excavations that have taken place in and around Chester.

A fountain in the form of a dolphin was reported to have been donated to the city by a former lord mayor of Chester and was said to have been sited at the southern end of Bridge Street around 1860. A little over 100 years later however, it was removed and presumably disposed of to make way for the Chester ring road which was constructed in the early 1960s. The nearby Pepper Street or Newgate Street area had already seen enormous changes, even before this new ring road cut through the area, and in 1864 the old Albion Hotel and its extensive gardens had been demolished to make way for terraced workers' housing, some of which continue to exist today. The Volunteer's Drill Hall, a home for the city's irregular artillery and rifle forces, was thought to have been built around the same time, but unlike much of the area did not immediately fall victim to the later ring road scheme. Many of the workers' terraced houses which lay adjacent to the proposed route were simply demolished, as were those that lay on the opposite side of the street, close to the remains of the Roman bathhouses.

The local architect T.M. Lockwood was thought to be responsible for the development of the city's High Cross area, including the eastern side of Bridge

Chester's cathedral has been refurbished by a number of noted architects including Sir George Gilbert Scott.

Erected on the site of former hotels The White Talbot and The Golden Talbot, The Grosvenor Hotel has been credited to architect T.M. Penson.

Street and down along Eastgate Street. Lockwood also undertook the improvement of the western side of Bridge Street, including its junction with Watergate Street. The mix of stone, brick and timbers in his buildings helped to create the unique Chester 'look' which has long since become synonymous with the city itself. A later project at St Michael's Row in Bridge Street which was undertaken by Lockwood in 1910 was so different to this earlier work that there was general uproar among the corporation and the business community. Such was the controversy that the landowner, the Duke of Westminster, ordered Lockwood to demolish the buildings and to reconstruct them in the accepted half-timbered style which was then completed by 1914. One of the oldest inns in Chester was said to have been demolished to make way for the new shopfronts, elevated rows and St Michael's Arcade in Bridge Street. The Feathers Hotel was thought to have been well over 200 years old and was one of the most popular coaching inns in Chester at the time of its demolition.

These costly and extensive redevelopments tended to make the resulting properties expensive to rent, which then impacted directly on the large numbers of smaller businesses that had previously occupied the sites. Many of them were subsequently forced to relocate to less expensive areas of the city including Watergate and Lower Bridge Streets, neither of which had been substantially improved in the earlier decades. The south end of Lower Bridge Street was reported to be markedly rundown and as such attracted little passing trade for the businesses that existed there. Even through to the late 1960s many of these premises were known to be in an extremely poor condition or were simply left vacant and boarded up.

The Chester Cottage Improvement Company was founded in 1892 and sought to build low-cost, high-quality residential housing in the city for local workers. In 1901 the Love Street cottages were said to have been designed and constructed by John Douglas. These small terraced properties are still in the city today and are located along Love Street and the Grosvenor Park Road. Seven years later and just around the corner from these initial buildings the same architect was responsible for the construction of the Bath Street houses, which are built of sandstone and topped with conical roof turrets. Towards the eastern end of Foregate Street, another of Douglas's projects was reported to be Parker's Building, a series of workers' apartments that were built on the site of a former city brewery owned by the Sellars family; they remain occupied through to the present day. The second half of the 19th century also saw the relocation of the city's workhouse from its site close to the Roodee to a new location in Hoole Lane on the other side of Chester. The old workhouse premises were then said to have been rented out by the corporation to local businesses to be used as workshops and warehousing space.

The Volunteers Drill Hall occupied the site of two of Chester's worst housing 'courts' and was built in 1869.

These frontages overlook St Michael's Row, which was designed by architect W. Lockwood, son of T.M. Lockwood. This whole street terrace and the elevated rows sit atop the western flank of the now substantially destroyed Roman bathhouse.

Away from the city itself, the outer suburb of Saltney was by the 1840s beginning to develop a small-scale industrial capacity that attracted both work and prosperity to the wider area. In around 1847 the Woods Anchor and Chain Company was said to have established itself there, drawn by the presence of the new canal system and a railway link which could carry materials and products in and out of their business premises. Within a few years more new firms were relocating themselves in Saltney including three coal oil companies, an ammonia plant and a bone manure factory. By 1847 a locomotive and carriage repair works, owned by the Chester and Shrewsbury Railway Company, had also sited their workshops there.

The wider area was thought to have been helped by the approval in 1911 of smallholding plots around the Lache area of Chester, which encouraged the development of small-scale rural activities and greatly added to the general diversity of the suburb itself. All around the city the main roads leading in and out of Chester were being occupied by people that could afford to live out in the suburbs. Curzon Park and the immediate area around it became the exclusive preserve of the well-to-do and generally remains so through to the present day.

As with the much vaunted 'New Cut' river scheme and the regional canal systems, Chester only seemed to derive short-term and marginal benefits from the industries that chose to locate their businesses in the city. It seems to have often been the case that a number of these enterprises were sited in Chester simply as a result of the city's improved quality of life, rather than for any obvious commercial consideration, which would inevitably lead to many of these new businesses failing at some point in time. In the years following Queen Victoria's death in 1901, many of these new transient industries had come and gone and the city of Chester was once again forced to fall back on the retail and tourist industries that had become such a fundamental part of its economy.

Designed by local architect T.M. Lockwood.

Chapter 16
A Modern City with a Disappearing Past

By the start of the 20th century much of the benefit brought by the industry located within Saltney was slowly beginning to wane, especially following the closure of the economically important coal oil companies. This recession in trade was only slightly offset by a modest revival in the ship building trades, but as elsewhere in the city this was only in the production of small inshore and coastal crafts. At the Groves on the river there was a small leisure craft industry, but that was thought to have only survived up until 1906 when it was finally tendered out to other outside builders. Canal barges and boats were also thought to have been built at Tower Wharf until around 1913 but the decreased demand for such craft, brought about in part by the new rail and road transport, saw an end to the trade altogether by the first few years of the 1900s.

This new economic realism was not just confined to the Saltney area, as many other local businesses in the city were known to be falling prey to the modern demands made on industry at the beginning of a new age. Their failure to fully adapt or to plan properly for future growth found a large number of Chester's fledgling companies going out of business or having to relocate away from the city altogether. By about 1910 only one brewery was reported to be operating in the city, the rest having been amalgamated into larger chains or having simply found that they could not compete and choosing to shut their doors forever. The shoemaking industry which had previously engaged a large number of self-employed outworkers changed to become a machine-based business that did not require lots of individual employees. The only shoe factory that had

The site of a former shoemaking factory built along the southern bank of canal during the 18/19th century.

established itself in Chester was said to have been located along City Road, but was never that successful and finally closed its doors in around 1906. The outworkers that had worked within these industries constantly had to adapt quickly and women craftworkers in Chester were said to have been particularly adept at swapping from one trade to another. Traditional crafts were declining as machines slowly replaced the human element in the process and by 1910 a large number of women were thought to have been employed in peripheral industries like tobacco and snuff making.

By the outbreak of World War One the city of Chester was generally regarded as no more than a medium-sized market town that was located in the north west of England. Three hundred years earlier it had held the status of a major economic and military centre that was vitally important not only to the north-west region but of national importance as well. However, its position in both the region and the country had been completely eclipsed by the two new northern industrial powerhouses of Liverpool and Manchester, both of which had been beneficiaries of the Industrial Revolution and Britain's increasingly important role in the global marketplace.

In the 100 years or so after 1830 the city of Chester was known to have expanded well beyond its historical limits, so much so that the outer townships of Newton, Upton and Hoole eventually became part of the greater Chester conurbation. The almost inevitable development and modernisation of the city centre for purely retail and tourist activities led to the widespread abandonment of this central core by many of its residents, either by choice or simply because of the cost. Up until the 1940s and through the early 1950s however, certain areas of the city were still full of low-cost, high-density housing, notably some of the large former private residences which lay along the eastern side of modern-day Nicholas Street. Migrants arriving in Chester during the early 1950s were still generally compelled to accept individual bed-sitting rooms with their communal facilities within these older tenement buildings. In the areas adjoining Commonhall Street and Crook Street more low-cost, poor-quality housing was known to have existed and would continue to stand through to the late 1950s when the new council estates of Newton, Hoole and Blacon began to be constructed. These earlier privately owned terraced properties offered extremely basic accommodation to some of the city's poorest inhabitants and were typically two-up two-down buildings that had their mains water supplied by a single standpipe which was located in the street outside.

The levels of poverty experienced by these residents ran completely counter to the rather overt prosperity of the business community whose shop premises fronted the worst of Chester's slum areas. By 1915 well over two dozen of the country's leading retailers were said to have had stores within the city centre and were added to by a number of the newly emerging banks and building societies that were beginning to spread throughout the country. The annual race meetings held at the Roodee were becoming an integral part of Chester's local economy, with tens of thousands of people flocking to the city every year to watch the horses and to spend their money in the local hotels, restaurants and public houses.

Around the same time a number of new medium-sized business ventures were beginning to establish themselves on the outskirts of the city. Several hundred people were thought to have been employed in the new market garden, nursery and seed production industries that had sited themselves around the Upton and Sealand Road areas of the city. The newly established Williams' Brothers Windows manufacturing factory was founded in around 1911 and was soon operating in new spacious premises on Liverpool Road in Chester. Their finished products were later supplied throughout the country and the firm remained a major employer in the city through to the 1960s. It was only later that changes in production methods, materials and fashions generally brought about a decline in the company's fortunes and resulted in the closure of the plant in the 1990s.

The growing rail and road networks, allied to the new developments in motorised transport and the founding of local and regional coach companies, helped to expand Chester's outlying housing estates and suburban communities. In the early years of the 20th century regular bus services were being run to Ellesmere Port and Birkenhead and the towns and villages that ran along the route. These services however, were a double-edged sword simply because they allowed business to flow both ways and retail centres like Chester could now lose trade to the likes of the competing Ellesmere Port and Wrexham markets.

For those people that worked in the city's many shops and stores, the need to live close to their jobs was finally removed by the arrival of these regular transport links. The new 'professional' classes that worked in the centre of Chester could now buy or rent homes in the outlying areas, confident that they could easily commute to the city every day. As a result new middle-class suburbs began to grow up on the fringes of the city and well beyond the areas that were now filled with rows and rows of low-cost terraced workers' housing. The main routes in and out of the city along Hoole Road, Liverpool Road, Saughall Road and Wrexham Road slowly but surely began to be filled with these elegant and expensive properties, further extending the boundaries of the city limits.

From the outbreak of World War One through to its conclusion four years later there were difficult times for the city, as there were for the rest of the country generally. The conflict, not surprisingly, caused a dramatic reduction in Chester's tourism industry due in part by the absence of many of the country's young men who left to undertake their military service with the army, navy and the emerging air force. The negative effects on the city's economy caused by the conflict were marginally offset by the influx of military and irregular forces as Chester once again resumed its place as an administrative and logistical centre for the country's armed forces. The Roodee was once again extensively used throughout the period as a storage, exercise and parade area for many of the units that were garrisoned in and around the city, a role that it would fulfil once again in World War Two. Chester's long association with a permanent military garrison was known to have stretched back nearly 2,000 years to the first legionary fortress of the Romans, and was only finally ended in the late 20th century following the restructuring and amalgamation of a number of British infantry units by successive national governments.

It has been suggested that many of the buildings and much of the land that ultimately became military sites in and around Chester were those that had first belonged to the religious orders of the city and had reverted to the Crown following the dissolution of those houses in the mid-16th century. Western Command, the administrative and logistical army headquarters, was known to have been primarily based in the Upton area of Chester, much of which had been owned by St Werburgh's Abbey in mediaeval times. The later Saigton army camp which was constructed at the beginning of the 1940s to the east of Chester was also said to be located on part of the former abbey's thousand acres of parkland, which the monks had first created in the 11th century. The city's long and extensive association with the military is still recognized today at the castle complex with the St Mary de Castro Chapel being dedicated to the Cheshire regiment. The history of the regiment is also displayed in a museum located at the castle housed within the inner bailey.

In 1938 the present Newgate was constructed to replace the ancient Wolfe Gate which still stands adjacent to its later replacement. Built to the design of Sir Walter Tapper and finished after his death under the control of his son Michael, the Newgate is said to be built of concrete and faced with Runcorn stone. This later gate was built to span the newly

The Newgate replaced the much earlier Wolfe Gate and was designed by architect Sir Walter Tapper.

widened roadway that had once run through the mediaeval Wolfe Gate, which was itself known to have existed well before the reign of Edward VI in 1547. It has been speculated that the original Wolfe Gate can trace its own foundation to the time of the Saxon King Wulfhere, who ruled the kingdom of Mercia in the seventh century.

The city's economic fortunes during World War Two generally mirrored those of the first as Chester was again utilised as a logistical and administrative centre by the armed forces. The new military bases at Saigton, Blacon and the Dale and the thousands of recruits that passed through them over the period were an additional boost for the local economy and the numerous shopkeepers and pub landlords that came to rely on their trade. Even after hostilities had ended in 1945 Chester still benefited from the presence of the local garrison at Saigton and that would continue through to the 1980s when the country's armed forces were restructured in the light of new technologies and the prevailing political climate. The Blacon camp was thought to have finally disappeared in the early 1950s, elements of the Dale camp in Upton were sold off in the 1990s and the Saigton camp currently stands idle and empty, but is thought to have been sold off to a property developer in order to construct even more private housing.

The late 1940s and the 1950s saw the whole country in recovery mode following the five years of war that had reduced Britain to an international hardship case. Mercifully the city had escaped air attacks which might easily have destroyed the historic heart of Chester. The utter destruction wrought on the likes of Coventry and Dresden must have made local people realise just how lucky the city had been. At the latter end of the 1950s the country was slowly beginning to recover from rationing and the enforced shortages that everyone had endured. As civic confidence and finances improved Chester began what now could be regarded as the very best and worst of the city's modern development. The construction of new civic housing in Blacon and Newton which finally did away with much of the city's slum housing was a great stride forward for those that had been forced to live in such squalid accommodation and was good news for Chester's reputation generally. These massive projects, which saw the building of thousands of good-quality council houses and the creation of new suburban communities continued throughout the period, brought new work and opportunities for both local businesses and for the city's resident workforce.

Developments within the heart of Chester itself were less socially conscious however, and seem to have been driven more by architectural fashion and the economic needs of a small number of local investors and landowners that were determined to modernise, regardless of any archaeological consideration or local objections. The Chester ring road system, built during the 1960s and 1970s, led to the total destruction of Egerton House in

A relatively modern archway cut through the city's northern wall.

Northgate Street and caused the city's ancient walls to be breached between Morgan's Mount and Pemberton's Parlour on the north-western flank of Chester. This unwarranted gap was created to carry the new ring road's two carriageways from the end of Northgate Street southward to Chester's castle complex and in the process brought about the destruction of many buildings which lay on the east side of both Princess Street and Nicholas Street. Although much of this area contained housing and buildings that were generally in poor condition, the great track of concrete, tarmac and traffic signals were a poor substitute for the streets and buildings that had previously stood there. At its most southerly junction with the castle, the new ring road was then detoured around a traffic roundabout which had been the site of the city's relocated St Bridget's Church and which was once again demolished for the sake of modernisation. The new road then either led out of Chester over the Grosvenor Bridge or went back through the city via Grosvenor Street, which then carried the traffic across the city to its eastern limits.

Just past the point which is marked today by Chester's Heritage Centre stands the Grosvenor Shopping Precinct, the grim concrete monolith which is typical of the function-over-form style of architecture that was a predominant feature of the 1960s. Under construction around the same time as the city's inner ring road project, the building of the Grosvenor precinct is known to be responsible for causing an even greater amount of archaeological damage to the city's historic fabric. The ruins of the former fortress's ancient legionary bathhouses were thought to have resisted all efforts to remove them for nearly 2,000 years and represented one of the greatest archaeological treasures from the Roman occupation of Chester. That particular fact did not appear to impress the building contractors however. With little time allowed for historians to fully investigate the site and its numerous antiquities, these ancient artefacts were simply bulldozed into oblivion and lost forever. What appeared to make this act of civic vandalism even worse was the apparent indifference of a section of the city's residents who simply allowed their irreplaceable heritage to be wiped out, never to be seen again.

Such apparent public and civic indifference to the vitally historic nature of the city seems to have been fairly typical of the period and is perhaps indicative of a much wider malaise that was affecting both Chester and its citizens. Personal memories and published accounts from the period all recollect the elevated shopping rows, the walls and many other areas of the city being in a state of some disrepair or just being generally uncared for. It appears that the preservation of our country's historic architecture

The platform marking the site of a royalist gun battery during the civil war siege of the city during the mid-17th century.

Located in the city's market square, this sculpture reflects the changing face of our 2,000-year-old city.

was not a major priority for most local authorities during the early part of the 20th century and it was only in later years that national statutes were enacted to fully protect our earlier heritage.

Had the inner ring road continued along its planned route, then a second equally important Roman treasure would have been lost forever. The amphitheatre at Chester had been known about for decades, so when it was proposed that the new road should just simply run through such a vitally historic site there was uproar throughout the country. Fortunately for the people of Chester the local authorities were persuaded by the clamour for the site to be protected and the new ring road was eventually diverted around this ancient monument. Even today the very presence of this historically valuable asset continues to vex and agitate the minds of those that are supposed to be responsible for the preservation of our city's heritage. Currently the local authorities are seeking suggestions as to how this archaeological treasure might be best managed, having already discounted the options of covering it over again or fully excavating the amphitheatre at the expense of the much later Dee House, which is itself a listed building.

Once again, at another pivotal moment in its history, Chester's archaeological past was ill-served by a series of short-sighted and badly conceived ideas that seem to cause more problems than they actually solved. The ill-fitting and unsightly buildings which have been regularly constructed in the city during the second half of the 20th century are generally poor replacements for those that they took the place of. Not only that, but their very construction has also led to the city centre being inundated with increasing levels of both pedestrians and motor vehicles that it was never designed for in the first place, or was ever likely to cope with in the future.

The former police headquarters building, which had until recently stood outside the Chester castle complex, replaced the much earlier militia building which had stood since the middle of the 19th century. At the town hall the modern Forum shopping centre replaced the much older and more elegantly atmospheric market hall, which had once housed the city's traders and merchants stalls. Aside from the increased revenues that these new shopping malls brought to their owners, they also attracted an increasing number of people from the wider region. Visitors flocked to these new cathedrals of consumerism from as far away as North Wales, mid-Wales and from all over the north-west region. During the 1960s, 70s and 80s Chester's main shopping streets were often packed to bursting and the roads which ran in and out of the city were typically jammed solid with car traffic.

Escalating business rates and the lack of space for new developments within Chester centre has led to the growth of new out-of-town retail parks. The city's former football ground and greyhound racing stadium, both of which were located in the Sealand area, were subsequently demolished to make way for the new Greyhound Retail Park. All of this land had originally been recovered from the sea following the canalisation of the River Dee in the middle of the 18th century. The building of new retail parks at Sealand, Broughton and Boughton which are all outside of the city centre have helped to reduce the numbers of cars and pedestrians coming into the middle of Chester.

Despite this, the city's inner ring road continues to suffer from terminal traffic gridlock on a regular basis and Chester's buildings, both old and new, continue to be subjected to the high levels of pollutants emitted by increasing levels of modern road traffic. There are a number of reasons for this continued situation, including the ongoing urbanisation of the wider area in general and the seemingly limitless construction of both office space and residential buildings close to and within the city centre.

This 'modernisation' of Chester is not a recent phenomenon but has been steadily going on since the late 1960s. As with many other towns and cities in England, the growth of the service sector and tourism industry in and around Chester was matched by a developing retail trade catering entirely for the needs of the consumer. Public transport systems have grown up to carry customers to these new retail stores, specifically local bus services that ferry passengers in and out of the city centre wreaking untold environmental damage to the ancient fabric of its historic buildings.

Up until the late 1960s and early 1970s the market square area of Chester acted as a bus terminus for services operating in and out of the

Dating from the 14th century, a bridge in one form or another has existed on this site for 2,000 years.

city. Hundreds of bus journeys were made every day, carrying people to and from the newly built housing estates in Blacon, Newton, Hoole and Saltney. Lines of uniform bus shelters ran from one end of the market square to the other, each one filled with scores of shoppers, schoolchildren and shop workers making their way in and out of the city centre. It was only when the old Victorian market hall was replaced by the new Forum shopping centre in the late 1960s and early 1970s that these bus shelters were finally removed from public view and only then to a site at the rear of the town hall, which only served to resite the problem and not actually solve it.

Chester's inherent traffic problems have their roots in the city's geographical location, its lack of a third bridge across the River Dee and the ever-increasing levels of road transport. Despite the construction of two separate road systems which were built to specifically address these particular issues, the problem of traffic congestion in and around the city remains with us to this very day. Given the city's previous history as both a military base and a logistical centre, Chester was always regarded and treated as the gateway to North Wales. Prior to the canalisation of the River Dee and the reclamation of lands along Sealand Road, the only bridge crossing was the Old Dee Bridge, which had existed in one form or another since Roman times. This single link between England and Wales was then finally added to by the later Grosvenor Bridge which was officially opened by the then Princess Victoria in 1833. Neither of these structures had been designed or built to handle the volume of modern-day traffic that uses them and as a result both are both completely unsuitable and highly inefficient.

Historically Chester lies at the centre of two significant trading routes – from the north of England through to the whole of Wales which lies to the south and from the eastern counties of England through to the North Wales coastline which lies to the west. Before the widespread use of motorised transport the majority of road traffic going in and out of the city consisted of horse-drawn carriages, carts and electric trams which carried people rather than freight. The commercial transport of goods, livestock and fuels was largely undertaken by the new canal and railway systems which ran throughout the region and helped to minimise the environmental cost to the city's historic fabric.

As the 20th century progressed however, these transport links began to decline and were themselves replaced by the predecessors of our modern-day motor vehicles. Cars, buses and lorries began to carry people and freight to the growing number of businesses in and around the immediate area as well as shipping goods from one part of the country to another. Acting as a regional traffic hub for vehicles crossing from one part of the country to another, Chester and its historic bridges were slowly but surely inundated by these new road transports and subjected to the kinds of loads and speeds never imagined by their builders.

The construction of the outer ring road system on the outskirts of Chester during the 1960s helped to alleviate many of these problems initially by redirecting much of the Wales-bound traffic away from the city centre. The inner ring road system which was built around the same time and designed to circumnavigate the centre of Chester has proved to be less successful. In the 40 years since it was first built the growth in personal car ownership has risen dramatically and has been accompanied by a corresponding rise in the numbers of larger commercial vehicles. In recent years these numbers have been added to by a growing level of residential traffic caused by the increasing numbers of high volume hotels and residential accommodation that have sited themselves in and around the city centre.

Chester's plight is not untypical. This modern lifestyle is often at complete odds with both the layout and purpose of our historic towns and cities which were originally constructed to service a smaller and much more rural population. In rare

Chester's Visitor Centre caters for the growing number of tourists.

The façade belongs to the now defunct Westminster Coach and Motor Works and is one of the market square's landmark features.

instances, the growth of such places is carefully managed and an equal balance is struck between modernisation and preservation. This allows for the appreciation and protection of our archaeological heritage, without the need to deprive residents of the modern conveniences that enhance their lives.

Sadly for Chester this does not appear to have been the approach that has been taken by successive generations of local councillors who have been charged with its administration and the protection of its archaeological treasures. Instead, a rabid unwillingness to commit ideas, imagination and, perhaps more importantly, public money seems to have been the main characteristic of their individual tenures. Where projects were undertaken it was only the ready availability of funds from central government that has seen them brought to fruition.

For the visitor to Chester, the city must appear to be a real amalgam of ideas, styles and periods of time. The world-famous Eastgate clock and the elevated shopping rows are two of the most immediate and unique features of this historic city, which only good fortune and physical location have helped to promote and preserve. The city's ancient cathedral only survives today because of the churches' land ownership and their prevention of widespread development of its religious precincts. The only exception to modernity in the cathedral's precincts is the bell tower which lies in the south-east corner of the site, close to the Cheshire Regiment memorial gardens. Built in 1974 to the design of George Pace and faced with Bethesda slate, the tower represented the first free-standing bell tower built for a cathedral since the 15th century. Its bells are said to be named after a number of saints that have all been venerated in Chester.

On the western side of Chester's market square,

Chester relies extensively on its reputation as a major tourism centre.

Chester's Eastgate and clock in background. The gateway was designed by a Mr Hayden and the world-famous clock by John Douglas.

only the city's Gothic town hall provides any real evidence of its true historic past. The remaining buildings, the Forum Shopping Centre and the public library, both of which make up a large part of this western flank, are of modern construction and appear to be at odds with their earlier civic counterpart. The art deco cinema, the Odeon, which is located at the north end of the square also seems out of place and is itself currently under threat of being replaced by a modern nightclub.

At the rear of the town hall is where much of the modern ugliness of Chester can be found. The city's main bus station and taxi ranks are sited here, along with the bulk of the new market hall, its underground parking system and the derelict St Martin's health centre, all of which are an eyesore on the very fabric of an ancient township like Chester. There are plans for the large-scale redevelopment of this north-west section of the city, which it is hoped will be far more suitable for and sympathetic to the historic nature of the city, but only time will tell.

In recent years the city council has sought to reduce the number of vehicles entering the city's main streets by introducing widespread traffic restrictions and pedestrian-only areas. Both of these measures have helped to reduce the environmental damage caused to the city centre in earlier years and to make Chester a much more pleasant place to be.

The great shame for Chester is that the city is continually sold on the basis of its long and colourful history, beginning with its legionary builders and continuing right through to the present day. Sadly, in today's modern city we would be hard-pressed to clearly identify what and where this heritage is within Chester, given the level of modern developments that have subsequently surrounded

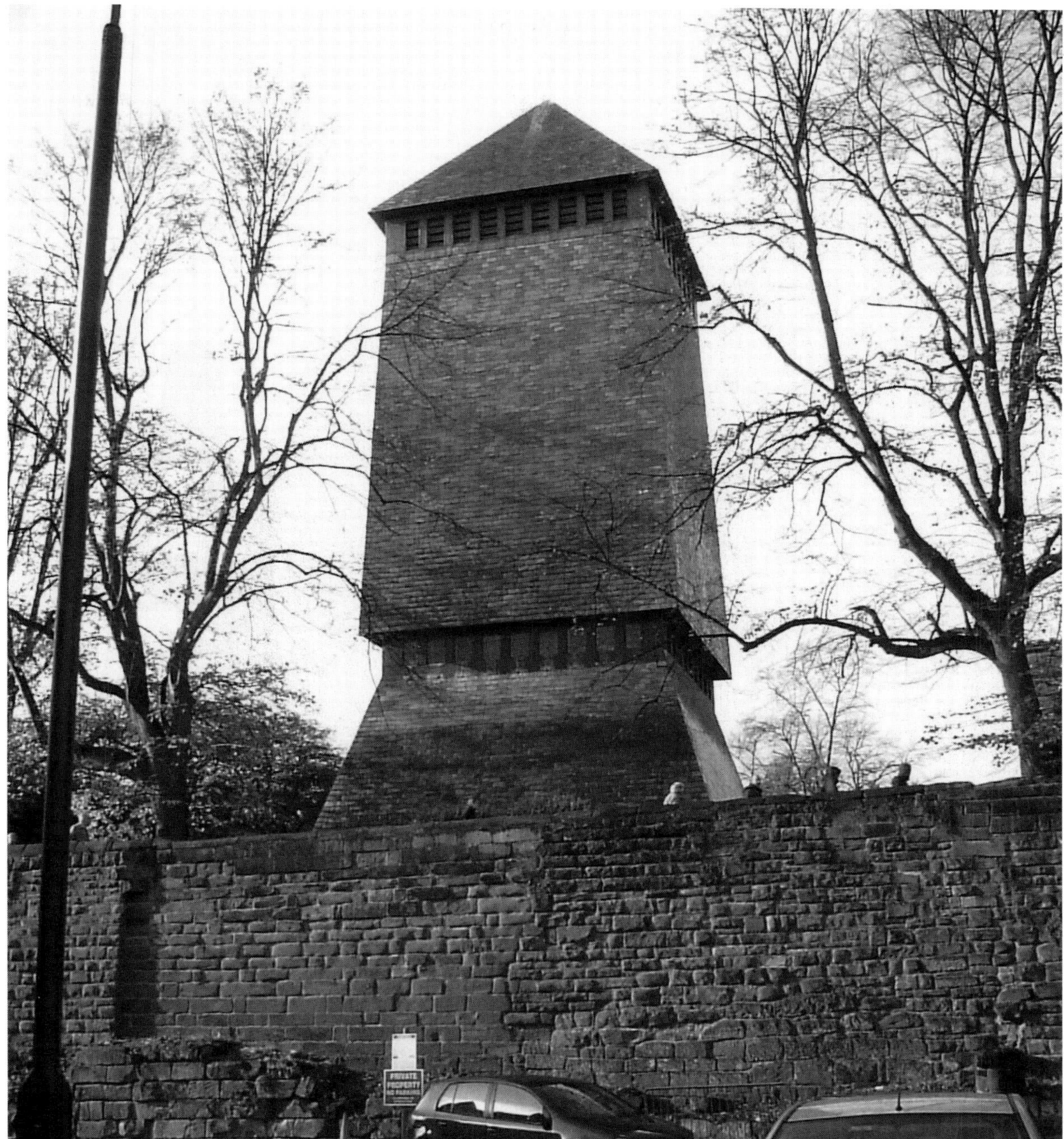

Designed by George Pace, the bell tower was raised in 1974 and is faced with Bethesda slate.

them. Nowadays we even have the situation where the city's historic walls are at risk once again, simply because local government cannot seem to prioritise or clearly identify which of Chester's few remaining artefacts should be preserved for posterity.

Much of what Chester was in the past remains hidden beneath its much later buildings or has been lost forever through accidental or deliberate destruction. Given the history of the past 40 years or so, it is questionable whether or not the next four decades are likely to be any better for the city's so far extensive and turbulent existence.

INDEX